Adobe Illustrator 2025
Handbook for Beginners

A Complete Guide to Master the Art of Digital Design with the Latest Tools and Techniques

Rhett Lysander

TABLE OF CONTENTS

CHAPTER 1

INTRODUCTION TO ADOBE ILLUSTRATOR 2025

Overview of Adobe Illustrator

If you need a logo, icon, or artwork that can be resized without sacrificing quality, Adobe Illustrator is the program for you. Its foundation in vector graphics makes it a favorite among designers as it allows them to create visuals that maintain clarity regardless of their size. You can easily create clean, expert-looking artwork with Illustrator thanks to its precise drawing tools for shapes and lines. For instance, the Pen tool is ideal for making delicate curves and lines, which are necessary for intricate designs. You can easily work on certain sections of your design without affecting other sections since the program organizes your work using layers. Illustrator provides tools for making patterns, using color gradients, adding shading for depth, and creating bespoke text designs. You can simply transfer files between Illustrator and other Adobe tools like Photoshop, which is another useful function. Its dependability in producing clean, scalable graphics makes it a popular choice for many tasks, including branding, digital illustrations, and web design.

Key Features of Adobe Illustrator 2025

Align, arrange, and move objects on a path

With **Objects on Path**, you can align and connect objects to paths, whether they're straight or curved. You can shuffle them, modify their spacing, rotate them, change their attachment points, and move them down the path without losing alignment after you attach them. The linked objects will automatically reorganize themselves if you make changes to the path or add or delete objects.

Trace images with more accuracy and control

By using the updated **Image Trace** feature, you can make precise traces with curves that are a near match to the original image. Make sure you don't accidentally trace white on transparent backgrounds while using **Color** mode by using the **Transparency** option. With the **Gradients** option, you can detect and trace linear gradients in either Color or Grayscale mode according to the strength you choose. Once you've traced the gradients, you can simply use the **Gradient** tool to tweak them. The trace output is more editable with fewer anchor points and the **Auto Grouping** feature that organizes paths into sensible groupings. To make things even easier to modify, the **Shapes** option item lets you trace common shapes like squares, rectangles, and circles as live shapes.

1

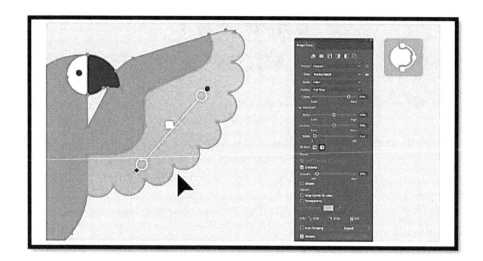

Create vector art in 3D with Project Neo (Beta)

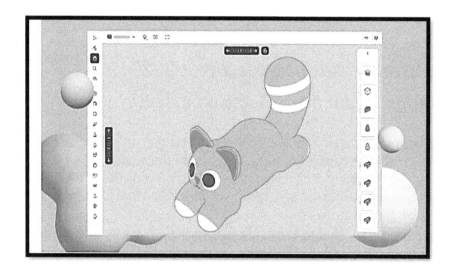

Experience improved mockup quality for planar surfaces

Vector graphics fit well on flat surfaces when you make mockups.

Adjust density strength for pattern creation

You can choose the density level of the patterns you'll make using **Text to Pattern**. You can now access Text to Pattern from the **Swatches** panel, too. The **Color & Tone** can also be reset.

Add shape fills with more control

For more freedom of expression, you can now toggle the prompt ideas in **Generative Shape Fill** on or off. For a clean slate, you can also reset **Style Reference, Effects**, and **Color** and **Tone** individually or simultaneously.

Create vector graphics with more control

For more freedom of expression, you can now toggle the prompt ideas in **Text to Vector Graphic** on or off. Bounding boxes may now fit the artwork neatly as no background layer is created when you make subjects and icons. For a clean slate, you can also reset **Style Reference, Effects,** and **Color and Tone** individually or simultaneously. Both the Generative Shape Fill and the Text-to-Vector Graphic Reset functions operate autonomously.

Access and explore tools and tasks directly on the canvas

The Contextual Task Bar helps you access the most frequently used next actions for the selected object and tool. The **Contextual Task Bar** provides some editing options, such as **Simplify** and **Smooth**, when you use the **Direct Selection** tool ▶ to choose a path. The **Contextual Task Bar** makes it easy to reorganize associated objects while working with **Objects on Path**, without sacrificing alignment. In addition, the **Contextual Task Bar** is visually identical to the heritage task bars of the **Smooth** , **Free Transform** , and **Dimension** tools . Using the **Contextual Task**

Bar, making mockups is a breeze when dealing with both images and vector objects. It facilitates speedy access to related tasks after it is generated.

Manage East Asian text layouts

East Asian language text layouts can be seen, examined, and updated with ease using **Reflow Viewer**. Illustrator alerts you if there may have been modifications to the text arrangement when you access a project made in an older version. The original layout is still available, or you can opt to update it.

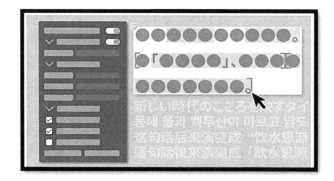

Scale artwork with artboard

To keep the dimensions and layout consistent across various surfaces when designing for things like hoardings, publications, and posters, you may have to resize the artwork and artboard.

Create stunning gradients from the Swatches panel

Use the **Swatches** panel to create your gradients by dragging and dropping colors or groups of colors. With these gradients, you can give vector objects more depth or create a dramatic lighting or shadow effect in your artwork.

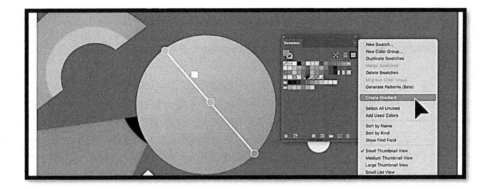

Cut objects evenly using the Knife tool with smart guides

The **Knife Tool** can be snapped to any objects you wish to chop into equal sizes by positioning it in line with the smart guides.

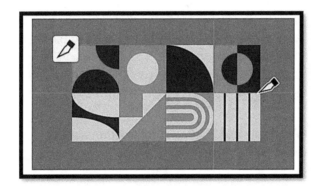

Experience faster performance

With connected image rendering, you can expect performance that is up to five times quicker.

System Requirements and Compatibility

The following are required on your computer to run Adobe Illustrator 2025:
Windows:
- **Operating System**: Windows 10 (64-bit) version 1903 or later.
- **Processor**: Intel®, AMD, or ARM processor with 64-bit support.
- **RAM**: At least 8 GB; however, 16 GB or more is recommended for optimal performance.
- **Hard Disk Space**: 4 GB of available space; additional space is required for installation.
- **Graphics Card**: To enhance performance with the GPU Performance feature, your system must have a minimum of 1 GB of VRAM (4 GB recommended) and support OpenGL version 4.0 or greater.

macOS:
- **Operating System**: macOS Monterey (version 12) and later, including macOS Ventura (version 13).
- **Processor**: Multicore Intel® processor with 64-bit support or Apple silicon processor.
- **RAM**: At least 8 GB; more is recommended for better performance.
- **Hard Disk Space**: 4 GB of available space; additional space is required for installation.
- **Graphics Card**: For GPU Performance, a minimum of 1 GB of VRAM (4 GB recommended) is required, along with support for OpenGL version 4.0 or greater.

These are the bare minimums that must be met. It is advised to use higher specs for best performance, particularly when dealing with complicated designs or huge files.

Installation and Setup Guide

To install and set up Adobe Illustrator 2025, just follow these steps:
- **Visit Adobe's website**: Go to the official Adobe website and navigate to the Illustrator section.
- **Sign In or get a Subscription**: If you don't already have one, go ahead and get a subscription or sign in with your Adobe account.
- **Download the Installer**: Click on the download link for Illustrator 2025 and save the installer file to your computer.
- **Run the Installer**: Open the installer file and follow the on-screen instructions to install Illustrator 2025 on your computer.
- **Open Illustrator**: After the installation is finished, you can access Illustrator from the start menu or app folder.

CHAPTER 2

NAVIGATING THE ILLUSTRATOR INTERFACE

Understanding the Toolbar, Panels, and Workspaces

Panels, bars, and windows are among the elements you use to create and edit your files and documents. Any configuration of these elements is referred to as a workspace. You can effortlessly switch between applications in Creative Cloud since their workspaces are visually similar. Illustrator has some predefined workspaces that you can use as it is or create your own to suit your needs.

Creating a New File in Adobe Illustrator

Open Adobe Illustrator and you'll be greeted with the welcome screen.

In the center, you can view the current open files and a list of commonly used file sizes from which to choose. A new file can be created on the right, or an existing one can be opened. Let's click **New File**. Pressing this button will take you to a new screen where you can configure your file. Along the top, you'll see templates for popular file sizes, and in the middle, you'll see any recent file sizes you've worked with.

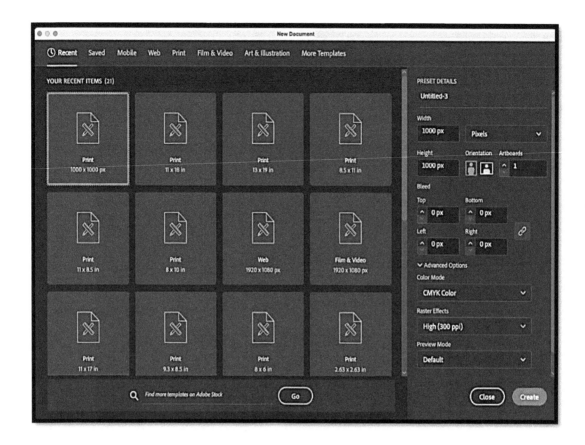

One can choose their preferred unit of measurement on the right. I usually begin with a **1000px x 1000px** page, even though this is vector software; I've become used to working with pixels. If you want, you can also pick from some different units including inches and centimeters. While making SVG files, I usually keep in mind that printer's use the **CMYK color mode**, whereas displays use the RGB mode. This is because the color of the cut file is irrelevant; for instance, you can utilize a purple file on yellow paper. However, in addition to SVG files, I also provide bitmap image formats like PNG and JPEG. Plus, I'd prefer the colors to be as accurate as possible as they will probably be printed. You can switch to RGB from the color option on the left if you're solely designing for screens since your colors will often be more brilliant. Press the **Create** button.

Adobe Illustrator Workspace Overview

Your workspace is now visible to you! I understand that the whole screen is daunting. (Whenever I get into Photoshop, I am completely overwhelmed and have no idea what anything is.)

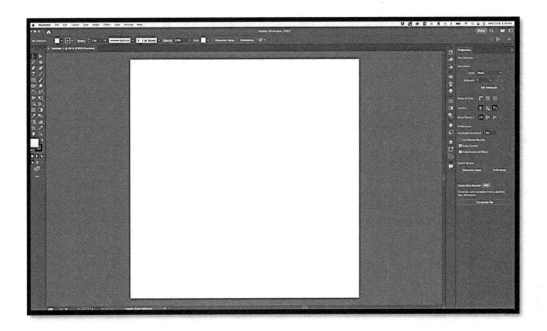

I can attempt to be on the same page even if my workspaces are somewhat different. A symbol resembling a screen with a right sidebar may be seen in the top right corner. Click on that and select **Essentials Classic**.

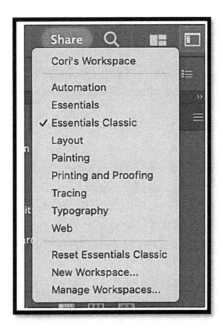

At this point, my screen should be more similar to yours. You shouldn't be concerned if the Properties panel isn't visible on the left. In a few moments, I will have it added.

Keep in mind that you can completely modify your workplace. Among other things, you can rearrange and add tools, as well as open and shut panels. You can also save your workspace by selecting New Workspace from the same dropdown menu if you find a configuration you like. Then you may be certain that everything will be according to your liking. **Let's examine the workspace components, which I've color-coded for your convenience.**

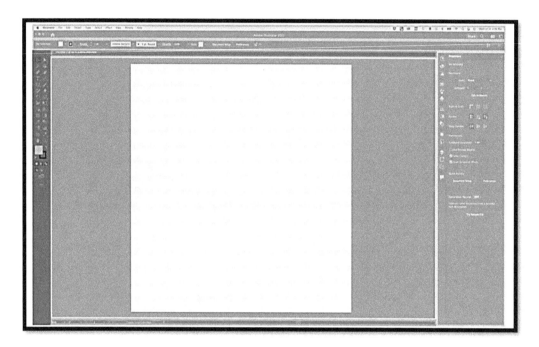

(**Note:** if your toolbars and menus vanish and you can only see your artboard in the center, it's likely because you've pressed the tab key. Press the tab key again, and everything should be back.)

The Menu Bar (Light Pink)

You can see the Menu Bar up top on your screen. The fact that it has the menus for most of the tools you see on the workspace makes this a very potent section. You should be able to locate what you're looking for in one of these menus: **File, Edit, Object, and Type, Select, Effect, Window, View,** and **Help** if you can't find it anywhere else in your workspace. I will make extensive use of the tools available in these menus as I go through this Illustrator series.

The Control Panel (Light Blue)

The Control Panel can be found under the menu bar. What this implies is that the Control Panel is contextual, meaning it adapts to your current art board selections. For instance, when you have text chosen, you'll be presented with choices for fonts, size, and spacing. A set of tools for aligning and scaling shapes will appear when you pick a shape. I also use the color dropdowns at the upper left to deal with colors in Illustrator here. These colors will serve as your fill and stroke. The color within your shape is called fill, and the color outside it is called stroke. However, there are several additional areas where colors may be used; hence, if you find a more suitable method, go ahead and use it.

Document Tabs (Dark Pink)

This is where you can access each of the open documents; you can have many windows open at once. They function similarly to tabs in a web browser.

Artboard (Yellow)

The wonder begins here! The artboard is where all of your design work will take place. The white portion represents the page size that you chose earlier; for example, a 1000px by 1000px square was my choice. Consider it analogous to a blank canvas or sheet of paper. You can utilize the empty area to temporarily remove distractions, but you will want all of your final artwork to stay on the artboard. Additionally, your workspace can accommodate many artboards. If you'd like, you can increase the number of artboards on the New File screen. Presentations and other multi-page documents benefit from this.

Toolbar (Dark Blue)

The toolbar rests on the left side of the screen. A brief video describing the tool's use and its keyboard shortcut will appear when you hover over it. You can access related tools by clicking the little arrow in the tool's lower right corner. Although there are many tools available, I will just go over the ones that you should be familiar with immediately. **As the series progresses, I will discuss them in further depth:**

- **Select (V)**: This is your "home base" tool. You can use this tool to do a lot of cool stuff with the objects on your screen, including resize, rotate, and move them around. The shortcut key to return to this tool is V, so get accustomed to using it.
- **Direct Select (A)**: To choose a specific area of an object, you can use the Direct Select (A) tool.
- **Pen (P)**: This powerful tool will let you draw your images. It's not easy to pick up, but once you do, the possibilities are endless.
- **Text (T)**: Use the text tool (T) to enter text.
- **Line Segment (\)**: A line can be drawn with the Line Segment tool (\).
- **Rectangle (M)**: This tool draws a rectangle. To draw a square with certain dimensions, hold down shift. To access more shapes, such as ellipses, polygons, and stars, click the little triangle that sits next to the rectangle tool.
- **Color**: You can also alter your colors using the two-colored boxes located at the bottom of the toolbar.

You can find a lot more tools in this area, but for now, try out the ones listed to see what they're capable of.

Panels (Green)

More complex operations reside in the Panels. Instead of merely drawing a rectangle, you can utilize the tools in this area to modify the shape by merging it with other shapes, for instance. Be kind to yourself since this part can become a bit complicated. It will inform you what an icon on the panel is when you hover over it with the mouse. If you are unable to locate a certain panel in the left-hand panels, you can access all of them by selecting Windows from the drop-down menu in the Menu bar. After that, you can just move the panel you want to use to the panel toolbar. **You can find the following panels interesting to experiment with:**

- **Properties**: If you can't see the symbol resembling three little sliders, it represents the Properties panel, which is comparable to the Control Panel but more powerful. To access it, go to the menu and choose **Window > Properties**. Like the last panel, this one is contextual and adapts to your choices. Because I find this panel very useful, I often move it to the panel's right side and then open it by clicking the two little arrows on the bar's top. I like using it for applying various procedures to objects; however, you can always reduce it by clicking the slider symbol if it's taking up too much of your screen. With a rectangle chosen on the artboard, for instance, I can access the following: basic sizing tools, the rectangle's fill, stroke, and opacity colors; align tools; and quick actions, such as the ability to create an offset.

- **Color / Color Guide / Swatches:** More panels to alter the colors of your art board's objects.
- **Pathfinder / Align / Transform:** Select **Window** > **Pathfinder**. These three interconnected tools will become available if you do this. We'll be dragging and dropping these tools into the left-hand panel toolbar from the top of the window as we'll be using them often.
  - **Pathfinder**: If you're acquainted with the Combine tools in Cricut Design Space, you'll recognize a lot of similarities between Pathfinder and them. It alters overlapping shapes. Unite, Minus Front, Exclude, and so on are all part of this. For a quick test of this tool's capabilities, try drawing two intersecting rectangles on the artboard and then modifying their properties.
  - **Align**: Applying one of the align tools to a single object on the artboard will align it with the rest of the artboard. For instance, using align left will move the object to the left side of the artboard. Aligning all the objects you have chosen by their left edges is what "align left" does when you have several objects selected; otherwise, they will be arranged to each other. To test out the various alignment possibilities, try drawing many rectangles on the artboard and see what occurs.
  - **Transform**: Basic resizing options are available in Transform, and more contextual tools may be available depending on your selection.
- **Layers**: As I go into creating SVG files, this panel becomes more significant. This panel will let you know whether you've done everything right so that it can be imported into your cutting design program.
- **Glyphs**: You'll have to go to **Window** > **Type** > **Glyphs** as this panel isn't standard. Every letter in a font is called a glyph, and some fonts even contain alternative glyphs that you can use instead.

Status Bar (Teal)

To be honest, I seldom use this bar, although it could be useful for seeing the current artboard zoom level.

Moving Around the Artboard

When you want to zoom in or out of your artboard, press **CRTL+/CTRL**-on a PC or **CMD+/CMD**-on a Mac. This works instead of utilizing the dropdown in the status bar. Compared to using the menu or going to **View > Zoom In / Zoom Out**, this is a lot quicker. An additional option is to press and hold the spacebar, which will bring up a small hand that you can use to "grab" and drag the art board. You can navigate the artboard using an Apple Magic Mouse simply by dragging your finger over its surface. Oh my! All I covered was the fundamentals of the workspace and a handful of tools, and that was already a lot.

Exploring the New Contextual Task Bar Feature

You can access the most relevant next actions for the object or tool you've selected via the **Contextual Task Bar**, a floating bar on the canvas. It guarantees that the object you're working on maintains your primary attention. The **Contextual Task Bar** can be repositioned to your liking. From the "**More options**" menu, you can also choose to hide it, pin it, or restore its position. Go to **Window > Contextual Task Bar** to bring it back into view after hiding it. By using the contextual **Task bar**, you can quickly access frequently used activities and tools whenever you make a selection. You can often do simple tasks more quickly by using the choices in the task bar rather than opening the properties panel.

1. Pick out the artwork.

At this point, the **task bar** ought to appear either above or below the chosen artwork. You can do things like recolor the text, duplicate, lock and repeat in that bar.

2. To create an exact copy of an object, just click the "**Duplicate This Object**" button 🔲 on the **taskbar.**

Using the little gripper on the left side of the screen, you can move the taskbar. To reset the position, go to the **More Options** menu (🔳) on the right side of the **Task bar** and choose **Reset Bar Position**. **Window > Contextual Task Bar** is where you can disable the taskbar entirely if you want it hidden.

Customizing Your Workspace for Efficiency

The Starting Point

Upon starting Illustrator and navigating to a new document, a selection of tools and panels are shown in the workspace. If you go to **Window > Workspace** and play about with the settings, you can discover a lot more hidden features. In addition, the program window's title bar on the right side of the window displays the Switch Workspace control, which you can click to switch desktops. For a head start, choose the **Essentials workspace**.

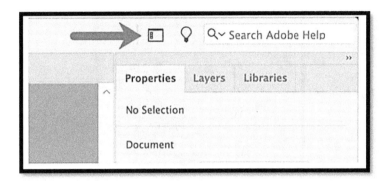

Changing User Interface Colors and Scaling

You can customize Illustrator's look before you set up your workspace by going to **Illustrator > Preferences > User Interface...** on a Mac or **Edit > Preferences > User Interface**... on Windows. Take your pick from the available options for scale, brightness, and more.

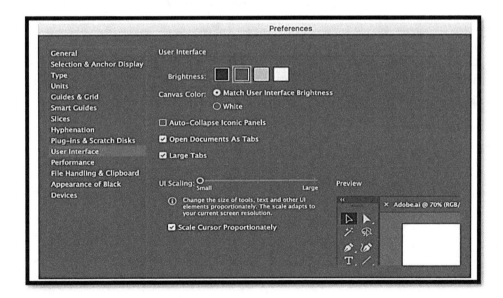

Moving and Arranging Panels

There are three tabbed panels on the right side of the screen: Properties, Layers, and Libraries.

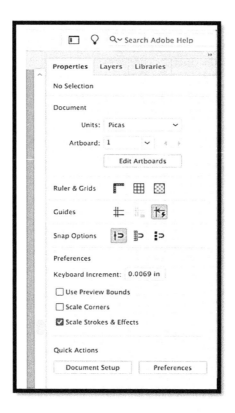

To move panels inside this docked zone, just drag their tabs. You can turn a docked tab into a floating panel by dragging it out of its dock. From the margins or the bottom, you can adjust the size of panels, and you can move them about by dragging their tab or title bar. To restore a panel's previous size, click the double chevron$^{(»)}$ in its upper right corner. To show or hide additional panel features, use the double-arrow button located to the left of the panel's name.

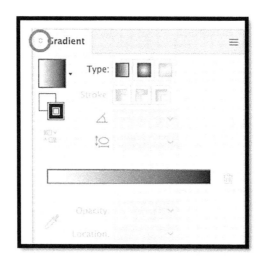

Contextual options can be found in the flyout menu located in the top right corner. Panels can snap together to form ideal neighboring arrangements when you pull them side by side. Gather many tabs from different panels into one by dragging them next to one other. For a vertical connection, just drag the title bar from one panel to the bottom of another.

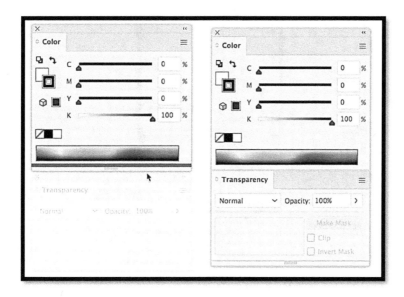

Panels can be docked by dragging them to the application window's margins. Find a plethora of extra panels under the Window menu.

Showing the Control Bar

To show the application's control bar across the top of the window, choose **Window** > **Control**. This handy bar adapts its tool-specific controls and settings to the current environment.

Arranging the Toolbar

The Essentials workspace displays a Basic toolbar down the left side of the window in one column. **Windows > Toolbars > Advanced** will bring up two extra columns of tools. The area just under a toolbar's title bar can be dragged to undock and relocate it. Alternating between single and double-column layouts is accomplished with the chevron (»).

Customizing the Toolbar

To access the **All-Tools Drawer**, click the three dots located at the bottom of the toolbar.

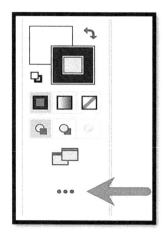

The current toolbar's tools are grayed out. To add or remove tools from the toolbar, just drag them to and from the drawer. To add several tools at once, press Shift and click on them. You can rearrange the tools on the toolbar by dragging them around while the drawer is open. To create a new toolbar with your desired layout, use the flyout menu located in the drawer's top right corner.

Saving Your Workspace Changes

After you've customized the workspace with the panels and tools to your desire, you can save your changes. Name your new workspace as you go to **Window > Workspace > New Workspace...** The current state of the workspace's panels and tools is preserved. At any moment, you can move between different workspaces. Illustrator keeps track of your workspace configuration changes as you drag and drop panels and tools as you work. You can restore a workspace to its last known state by going to **Window > Workspace > Reset (workspace name).**

Edit an artboard

The paper on your desk serves a purpose similar to that of an artboard in Illustrator. You have the freedom to create for several projects and output sizes simultaneously since artboards can be any size and your document can contain many artboards of different sizes. This will save you time. Navigate to **Window > Properties**. When no artboards are currently chosen for your project, click the **Edit Artboards** button. You can alter the artboard's dimensions by inputting new width and height values in the Properties panel's **Transform** section. To add more artboards, go to the toolbar and click the New Artboard button. You can manually adjust the size of an artboard by dragging its widgets or removing it using the Delete key after you've chosen it. To exit the Properties panel, either use the Esc key on your computer or select the **Exit** button at the panel's very top.

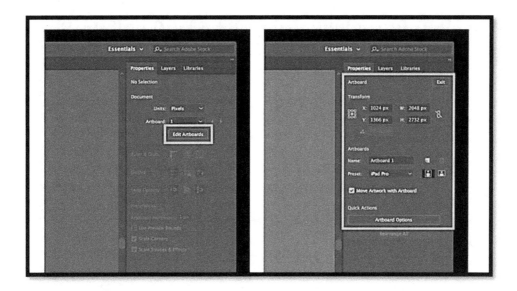

Edit the document

Regardless of the number of artboards in your project, it is as easy to make a global change. Look for the **Document Setup** button in the Properties panel's **Quick Actions** section and click on it. Before clicking **OK**, make sure the units and bleed settings are as you want them. Illustrator also has a **Preferences** button in the Properties tab that you can use to quickly access and change any setting in the application. (Any adjustments you make to the Preferences are saved when you close Illustrator.)

How to open Adobe Illustrator files with Illustrator

Method 1: Double-Click Method

1. **Launch Adobe Illustrator**: Simply double-click the Adobe Illustrator icon to launch the program.
2. **Access File Menu**: If you're already in Illustrator, you can go to the **File Menu** by selecting "**File**" from the main menu.
3. **Pick Open**: After clicking "**File**," a drop-down menu will show; choose "**Open**" from that menu. When you do this, a file browser window will pop up on your screen.

4. **Select Your .ai File**: Browse your computer's files for the Adobe Illustrator file you want to open. To open a file in Adobe Illustrator, find it in your computer's file system and look for an extension ending in .ai, such as **"myartwork.ai."** After you've selected the file, click the "**Open**" button in the folder browser.

Method 2: Drag and Drop Method

1. **Find Your .ai File**: On your computer, find the .ai file that you want to open in Adobe Illustrator. You can find it in a folder, on your desktop, or in the file explorer.
2. **Drag the File:** Click and hold the .ai file with your mouse or trackpad until it stops moving, and then drag it. While still holding the file, move it such that it lands on the Adobe

Illustrator icon. The Illustrator program will be highlighted when you drag the file over the Illustrator icon.

3. **Release to Open**: Once you've chosen the Illustrator app icon, you can open the file by dragging and dropping it onto the icon. Doing so will launch Adobe Illustrator and open the .ai file for you.

Method Three: The Right-Click Approach

1. **Locate Your .ai File**: Find the .ai file on your computer that you want to open.
2. **Right-Click on the File**: Using your mouse or trackpad, right-click on the .ai file. When you do this, a context menu will pop up.
3. **Choose "Open With"**: To access the "Open With" option, either click on it or move your mouse cursor over it in the context menu. There will be a list of suitable applications shown in the submenu.
4. **Select Adobe Illustrator**: From the drop-down option, choose "**Adobe Illustrator**." This will open the file in Adobe Illustrator without any intermediate steps.

Each of these three methods provides a foundational framework for gaining access to and opening your .ai files inside Adobe Illustrator. Here you have a range of choices to choose from, so you can tailor it to your preferred workflow.

Performance Improvements and Enhancements

Optimize Illustrator Settings

1. **Disable Animated Zoom:** Find the "Enable animated zoom" option and deselect it in **Edit > Preferences > Performance.** The responsiveness of scrolling and zooming can be enhanced in this way.
2. **Use Low-Resolution Proxy for Linked EPS:** Check "**Use low-resolution proxy for Linked EPS**" from the "**File Handling & Clipboard**" submenu in **Edit's preferences**. By doing so, you can lessen the strain on your computer when handling EPS files.
3. **Enable GPU Performance:** Navigate to **Edit > Preferences > Performance** and turn on GPU performance. Things like previewing and rendering will be accelerated using your graphics card.

Optimize Document and Workflow

1. **Simplify File Structure:** Avoid overly complex file structures and use nested layers effectively. Both the file size and performance can be improved in this way.
2. **Optimize Image Resolution:** Rasterize photos till their resolution is just right for your assignment. Images with high quality can slow down Illustrator.
3. **Use Smart Guides and Snap to Grid:** Make use of Smart Guides and Grids to precisely align objects and keep the layout neat. Your process can be made more efficient and less tweaky using this.

4. **Utilize Compound Paths:** Convert multiple paths into compound paths to reduce the number of objects and improve performance.
5. **Optimize Fonts:** To minimize font loading delays, optimize your fonts by using embedded or linked fonts. Make sure to change any fonts to outlines if needed.

Regular Maintenance and Updates

1. **Regularly Update Illustrator:** You get the latest performance improvements and bug fixes, be sure you keep your Adobe Illustrator program updated.
2. **Perform Regular Maintenance:** Clearing up unnecessary plugins, fonts, and preferences files is a great way to regularly maintain and make it run faster.
3. **Optimize Startup:** Look over your startup programs and remove any extraneous ones that might slow down Illustrator.

CHAPTER 3
DRAWING AND ILLUSTRATION TOOLS

The Basics of Drawing in Illustrator

Without a doubt, Adobe Illustrator is among the greatest vector programs available for drawing and making graphics. There are some straightforward tools and methods for learning how to draw with Adobe Illustrator, as you will see. There is a so-called steep learning curve that you may have to climb to master Illustrator. So that you don't get confused by all the technical terms and features in Illustrator, I've broken down these techniques into smaller stages in this section. No prior experience as an artist or graphic designer is required. Its user-friendly tools allow you to effortlessly master drawing any subject you can imagine. The nicest part is that you can simply click "undo" to return to an earlier version if you change your mind.

Main Drawing Tools in Adobe Illustrator

Adobe Illustrator comes with a set of fundamental drawing tools that you can use to start drawing anything. These are the ones:
1. *Pencil Tool (keyboard shortcut is N)*
2. *Paint Brush Tool (keyboard shortcut is B)*
3. *Pen Tool (keyboard shortcut is P)*
4. *Blob Brush Tool*
5. *Curvature Tool*

Most likely, these tools are hidden from view if you don't see them in your Toolbar. Locate the three dots at the very bottom of your Toolbar; clicking on them will add them to your Toolbar. A tooltip reading **"Edit Toolbar..."** will show when you hover over the three dots. When you click on it, a list of tools will appear.

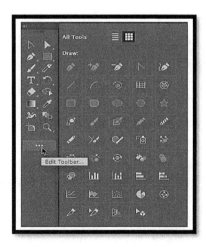

You can sort all the tools by their potential applications. For a complete list of drawing tools, go to the **Draw** section. Simply click and drag any tool you want to the Toolbar if you'd like to have quick access to it. By dragging it to the Edit Toolbar area, you can return the tool to the hidden view. Learning to draw lines is the next stage in becoming comfortable with these drawing tools.

How to Draw Lines in Illustrator

A common question people have about Illustrator is whether or not it can simulate hand-drawn objects like triangles and stars. Particularly when using a mouse rather than a tablet, I can imagine that there will be times of frustration. Learning to draw with Adobe Illustrator doesn't need any special talent, which is great news. Simply drawing lines can give you a lot of creative control in Illustrator, whether you're using a real pencil or one of the various tools available. One approach to learning Illustrator is to start by drawing lines; from there, you can learn to draw whatever you want, depending on your eventual artistic goals.

Does Illustrator Have a Line Tool?

How Do I Make Straight Lines in Illustrator?

Line Segment Tool

There is a tool called the Line Segment Tool that you can use if you just want to draw lines. You can access it by navigating to the Toolbar, finding the Rectangle Tool, and right-clicking on it. The Line Tool, represented by the diagonal line icon, will be visible. One alternative is to use the \ key on the keyboard, which will transform your cursor into a Line Tool equivalent.

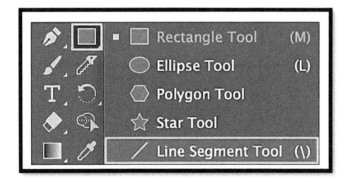

Once you've found the spot on your artboard that you like, click and let go of the cursor. The options for the Line Segment Tool will show up. Both the desired line length and the angle to be drawn against can be entered here. Once you're ready, hit enter or Return on your keyboard or click the OK button in the dialog window.

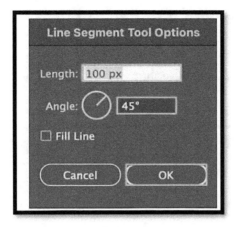

Quickly create lines at 0, 45, or 90 degrees by dragging the cursor over the artboard while holding down the Shift key. You can draw a straight line horizontally at 0, 180 degrees, vertically at 90 degrees, or diagonally at 45 degrees in angle relative to the horizontal line (constraint to 45 degrees).

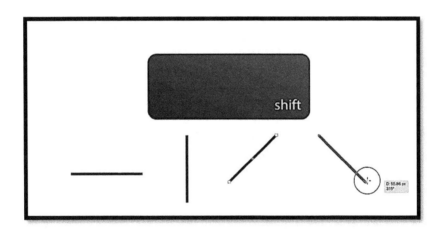

Without pressing Shift, you can also draw a straight line by dragging the mouse; however, it will not be limited to 45 degrees. Any angle from the point you began drawing the line will still allow you to make a straight line. Using this method, the dialog box for Line Segment Tool Options will not be shown. A line may be drawn quickly, however, without the need for an additional step.

Alternative Tools to Draw a Straight Line

To create a straight line, you can use the Line Segment Tool or any of the following: Pen, Paint Brush, Blob Brush, Curvature, or Pen Tool. There are many options, and they will all be effective.

Draw a Straight Line with a Pencil Tool

Pick up a pencil by navigating to the Toolbar or using the context menu that appears when you right-click the paintbrush icon. Another option is to use the N key to transform your cursor into a pencil tool.

Now you can create a straight line on your artboard by clicking and holding the Shift key while moving the mouse. Afterwards, release the Shift key. Like a real pencil and paper, all you have to do this time is click, hold, and move the cursor. Although your line may not be completely straight, you will no longer be limited in where you can move the cursor. You can use this method to create a freehand drawing.

Draw a Straight Line with Pen Tool

Unlike the Pencil and Paint Brush Tools, the Pen Tool does not mimic the feel of an actual pen or pencil when used. The Pen Tool in Adobe Photoshop is functionally identical, in case you're acquainted with that program. The steps for using the Pen Tool to create a straight line are as follows: Use the keyboard shortcut **P** or the toolbar's pen icon to bring up the pen. Release the mouse or trackpad after clicking once on the artboard; then, drag the pointer to a different region of the artboard and click again. As you drag the Pen Tool from one location to another after clicking, a line will appear at the tip of the tool. Every time you click one more to release it, a straight line is drawn and they are all linked.

After you click once to make an Anchor Point or path, release the mouse or trackpad. Then, while holding down the Shift key, drag the pointer to a different spot and click again to draw a straight line at a 0 or 45-degree angle.

Draw a Straight Line with Paint Brush Tool

To use the paintbrush tool, either press the **B** key on your keyboard or use the drop-down menu.

With the PaintBrush Tool, which is analogous to a real brush, you can create freehand drawings in Illustrator, much as with the Pencil Tool. Lines can be drawn in any direction by clicking and dragging the mouse. If you press the Shift key and the Line Segment Tool, you can get the same result: a perfectly straight line. The line thickness will be thicker than when using the Pencil and Pen Tools by default.

Draw a Straight Line with the Blob Brush Tool

With the Blob Brush Tool, you can create straight lines much as with the Pencil and Pen Tools. However, there is a separate path line. Select the Paint Brush Tool from the toolbar, then right-click on the paintbrush icon with the rectangle around it. This will bring up the Blob Brush Tool. You can also use the keyboard shortcut **Shift + B**.

The next step is to click and drag the cursor on the artboard while holding down the Shift key. Lines made using the Pencil, Pen, and Paint Tools will have closed paths instead of open ones, resulting in a straight line.

When you use the Blob Brush Tool to create a line, its thickness will fluctuate depending on how big or little you make it. The single-lined paths that have been opened have not been widened just yet. These lines will remain the same thickness regardless of how long you make them.

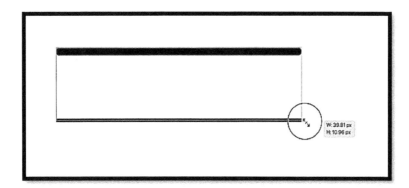

How to Draw a Curved Line on Illustrator in 3 Ways

Drawing curved lines, in addition to straight ones, can greatly enhance your ability to produce images that use curves. You are not alone if you find freehand drawing curves to be a challenge. You can utilize a variety of curved line tools in Illustrator.

1. **Draw a Curved Line with the Pen Tool**

With the Pen Tool, you can draw both straight and curved lines, but there are several approaches for each. Click once on the artboard after selecting the Pen Tool from the Toolbar. Next, go to a different area of the artboard by dragging the cursor. Click on the area you want and hold down the mouse button as you move the cursor. When you release the mouse button, a pair of straight lines joined by a sharp corner will be drawn. A straight line will begin to curve and handles will start to extend from the anchor point as you move the cursor. A more gradual curve can be achieved by extending the handle.

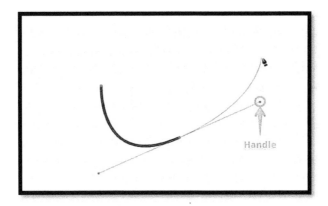

The angle of your curve will be increasingly acute as the handles are pulled closer to the anchor point, which in turn makes the pivot point sharper. To make a specific curve, just click once to establish an anchor point, and then drag the handle to the desired location. The curve drawing is now complete. To switch to the **Direct Selection Tool** and release the Pen Tool, press and hold the Command key on your keyboard. Then, on a blank area, click once with the cursor.

2. **Draw a Curved Line in Illustrator with the Curvature Tool**

Locate the symbol of a pen with a curved line emanating from its tip on the Toolbar. You may not be able to view it on the standard Toolbar since it is hidden. Locate the three dots on the Toolbar's base to add it there. You can edit the toolbar using that button. A menu with drop-down options will eventually show up. To add the Curvature Tool to the standard Toolbar, locate it in the drop-down menu and click and drag it. In this manner, the tool will be more convenient for you to utilize when time is of the essence.

The next step is to click once on the artboard, then release the cursor and go to a different area of the artboard. Reposition the cursor to a different area of the artboard, click and release, and then click again. In contrast with the Pen Tool's perfectly straight lines connecting the anchor points, the Curvature Tool will automatically bend them.

3. **Draw a Curved Line in Illustrator with the Ellipse Tool**

You can use the Ellipse Tool to create symmetrical curves. Drawing symmetrical shapes like circles or ovals is a good place to start, and you can then transform them into curving lines. Simply right-clicking the Rectangle Tool will bring up the Ellipse Tool. Afterward, either click the L key on your keyboard or choose the Ellipse Tool (the one that has the oval shape).

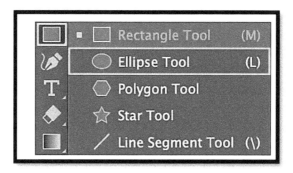

Then, on the artboard, click and drag in any direction starting from the point where you first clicked. The shape of the oval will change to a circle, fatter ovals, or flatter ovals if you continue to hold on to the cursor and move it about. Just let go of the cursor once you see that the oval curves satisfy your requirements. Holding down the Shift key while drawing will make your drawing seem like a circle. You can make an imperfect circle with a flawless drawing operation by holding down the Shift key.

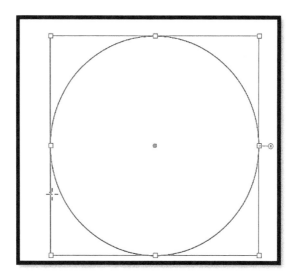

A curved line will be left after removing half of the circle. That can be accomplished by either pressing A or navigating to the Direct Selection Tool in the Toolbar. A solid arrow of white hue replaces the cursor. On the circle's path line, you'll see four anchor points; choose one. While the other three anchor points will remain white, the one you've chosen will become solid blue. Afterward, you can remove half of the circle by using the Delete key on your computer. This will leave you with a single symmetrical curved line. As part of your drawing process, you can use Illustrator tools like these to clip objects or erase paths. To make what you want out of your drawing, it's like using an eraser to get rid of the bits you don't want.

How to Make a Wavy Line in Illustrator with the Zig Zag Tool

Sometimes you just want to produce a fast sketch or wavy line in Illustrator to represent water or for aesthetic purposes. An easy way to start is to use one of the primary drawing tools—the Line Segment, Paint Brush, Pen, or Pencil—to create a straight line. To bring your line into focus, go to the Swatches Panel and choose a stroke color. Next, go to **Effect > Distort & Transform > Zig Zag...** to turn this line into a wavy one. In the Points area of the dialogue box that appears, choose Smooth and then click OK. Illustrator now gives you a wavy line.

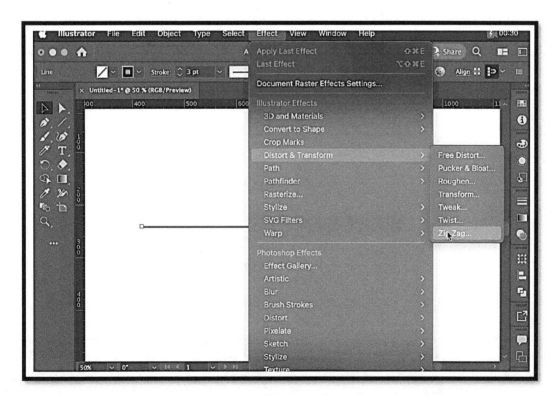

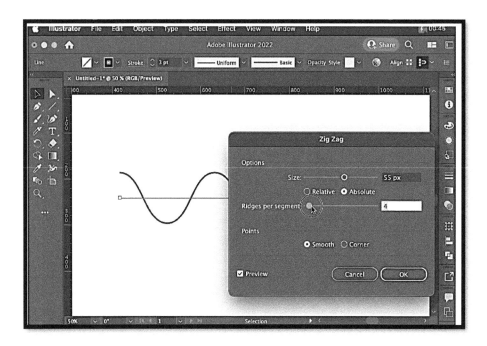

How to Smooth Lines in Illustrator

If you're using Illustrator's Pen or Pencil Tools to sketch or trace a picture, you can get an error message like this:

You see that the roughness of your lines and strokes is not producing the effect you were going for. You will need to figure out how to make them less angular in this instance. You could use the Pen Tool to do this, but the Smooth Tool is simpler and quicker. Get your drawing path chosen using the **Direct Selection Tool** first. The next step is to locate the Smooth Tool in the Toolbar. It has a pencil symbol that is divided into three parts. You can either hide it from visibility or move it to the **Advanced Toolbar** if you can't find it in the **Basic Toolbar**. Locate the three dots on the **Basic Toolbar's** bottom and click on it to open the **Advanced Toolbar**. A variety of tools will appear in the dropdown menu. When you get to the drop-down menu, look for the options menu with the checkbox symbol on the top right. Click on it. Next, go to the drop-down menu and choose **Advanced**. The Toolbar will begin to display some new tools.

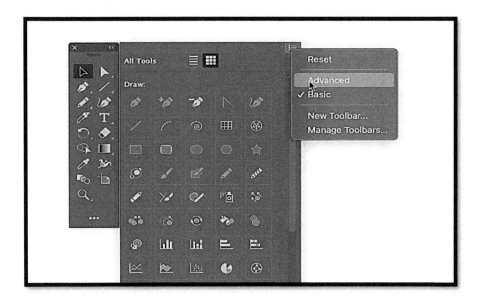

Select the **Shaper Tool** (it looks like a pen with a circle under) and then right-click to get the **Smooth Tool**. Next, from the submenu, choose the **Smooth Tool**. The next step is to smooth out the path by clicking and dragging the **Smooth tool's** cursor along it, making sure the Direct Selection Tool is still chosen.

How to Manually Trace Image in Illustrator in 3 Steps

You have achieved a remarkable feat! Having mastered the art of line drawing in Adobe Illustrator, you now possess all the necessary tools to emerge as a true Illustrator. After you've mastered the basics of Illustrator's tools, the next step is to trace a picture and start drawing. You can automatically trace an image into a vector file in Illustrator using a tool called **Image Trace.** However, you may need to utilize Illustrator's drawing tools to tweak your work since the results aren't always accurate. To become proficient with Illustrator's drawing tools, you will learn how to manually trace a picture here. By selecting a picture or graphic to trace from the internet, you can get started. Please be aware that this is OK provided that you do not assert ownership or market the work as your own. This is intended just for your use or practice. If you'd rather not use an existing picture from the internet, you can always draw something from scratch. The next step is to photograph your drawing and upload it to your computer so you can later rework or trace it. Both methods can teach you how to use Illustrator's drawing tools to create an object.

Follow these methods to trace a picture manually and sketch in Illustrator.

Step 1: Start a new document

I will be using this picture as our trace. It all started with a pen sketch on paper, followed by a photo snapped using a cell phone, and last, the image files were uploaded to the computer.

Afterward, launch Illustrator and create a new document by going to the File menu (top menu bar) and then selecting New from the dropdown menu. If you already have an Adobe Illustrator file, you can open that instead. Pick **Web** from the option bar of the New Document choice box after it opens. Select the page size and orientation that best suits your needs. The default settings for this example are landscape orientation and Common size (1366 × 768 px). To begin, click the **blue Create** button.

Step 2: Place or import the selected graphic that you'd like to trace

- Either hit **Shift + Command P** simultaneously on your keyboard or go to the top menu bar, choose File, and then choose Place from the dropdown menu.
- The dialogue box appears. You can choose the sketch or picture you want to trace.
- Next, locate the "**Options**" button at the dialog box's base and click on it.
- A pop-up menu will appear; in it, find the term "**Template**" and tick the checkbox.
- The picture you've chosen cannot be used as a template if the option to do so is greyed out and you are unable to check it.
- In terms of picture file formats, you can use everything from JPG and JPEG to PSD, PNG, TIFF, and PDF.
- After you've chosen a template, click the blue "**Place**" button.

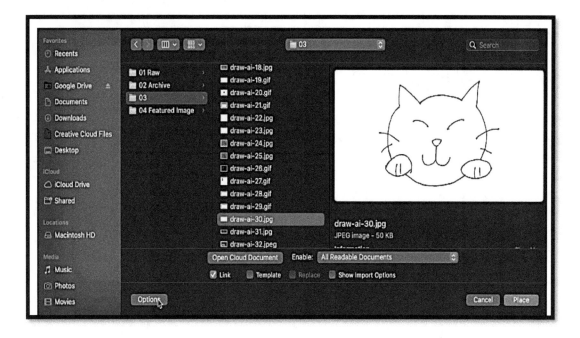

The picture or drawing is now on your blank artboard. The picture is blurry and unmovable, as you can see. You can immediately trace or repaint this picture since Illustrator has already done the job. Two layers will be shown when you open the Layers Panel. To save time and effort, use the initial layer as a sketch or trace surface. Then, you can easily separate the layers later. The other layer is a template layer; it's locked to prevent accidental movement while you trace. You can see your work when tracing since it is faded with lowered opacity to maybe approximately 50%.

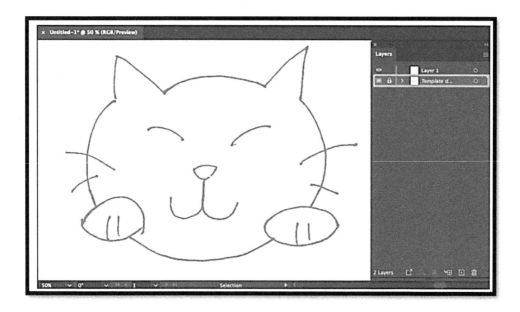

Step 3: Trace image

Here I will trace the outline of this adorable cat using the Curvature Tool. You can access the **Curvature Tool** via the Toolbar or by pressing Shift and the single quotation mark (`) simultaneously. To access the drawing's outline, click once at any point in the sketch. There will be the establishment of an anchor point. Next, go to the next point where the drawing takes a turn. At the point of the cat's ear, I will begin by clicking once. Once you've reached the ear's mid-curvature, click once. After you let go of the mouse and drag it to the curve's end, click once, and a tidy curve will appear around one ear.

- Click once for curve.
- Double-click to draw a straight line.

- Some paths may be filled with a solid color. The swatches' default settings could be to blame.

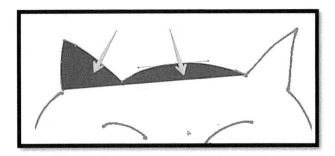

Put a dark color, say black, for the path's stroke after turning off the color fill. So you can trace your drawing precisely, you need a good view of it. Keep holding down the button if you accidentally press the incorrect area. Keep dragging the cursor, and the anchor point will follow suit. Continue dragging until the path accurately follows the picture. To create a curve, click once; to leave an anchor point and continue with another straight line, double-click. To make the path more in line with the sketch, just hit A on the keyboard. The **Direct Selection Tool** will become your cursor. The anchor points or path handles can now be adjusted for location and curvature by selecting them.

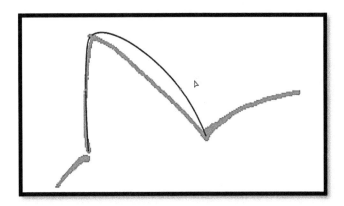

Retrace the remaining portion of the picture in the same way.

Paths, Anchor Points, and Handles

These components may seem daunting at first, but I assure you, they will become second nature. If you take the time to learn these fundamentals, you'll have the skills you need to edit and alter text, shapes, lines, and more in Adobe Illustrator. After a lengthy period of confusion, the design world became crystal clear to me when I learned about paths, anchor points, and handles. If I can impart these skills to you early on, I hope you'll have a firm grasp of Illustrator's capabilities later on.

1. **Paths**

Definition: Illustrator paths are the lines or curves that generate shapes or free-flowing lines by connecting a sequence of anchor points. You can think of a path as either **open** (like a line with two distinct endpoints) or **closed** (like a circle or other enclosed shape).

Types of Paths:

- **Straight Paths:** The creation of straight paths is accomplished by linking anchor points with straight lines.
- **Curved Paths:** These can be made by connecting points with curved lines and then adjusting them using handles.
- **Editing Paths:** With the ability to add or remove anchor points, as well as move points and manipulate handles, you can change the shape of paths.

2. **Anchor Points**

Definition: The defining points along a path are known as anchor points. They identify the beginning, the end, or any corner of a shape and serve as the "pins" that keep the path in place. There are always at least two anchor points along a path, and sometimes more for more complicated shapes.

Types of Anchor Points:

- **Corner Points:** These can connect straight paths and form acute angles. You can add handles to corner points if you need them, but by default, they don't have any.
- **Smooth Points:** Curved paths can be made with the use of smooth points. Coordinates on both sides of the point can be easily achieved with the smooth points' accompanying handles.

Adding and Removing Points: To insert additional points along a path, use the **Add Anchor Point Tool (+),** and to delete them, use the **Delete Anchor Point Tool (-).** With the **Convert Anchor Point Tool (Shift + C)**, you can turn corner points into smooth ones as well.

3. **Handles**

Definition: To precisely regulate the angle and radius of a curve, one must use handles, which are control points that radiate out from the path's anchor points. There are two ends to each handle; one attaches to the anchor point, while the other is free-floating so you can manipulate it to change the curvature.

How Handles Work: Handles regulate the **length** and **angle** of the curves on each side of an anchor point:

- **Angle:** The direction of the curve leaving or entering the anchor point is determined by the angle.
- **Length:** Handle length determines the radius of a curve; longer handles provide more noticeable curves.

Moving and Adjusting Handles: To adjust handles, use the **Direct Selection Tool (A)**. The symmetrical movement of the handles will produce equal curves, making them ideal for use as anchor points. With the ability to adjust each handle separately, you can convert corner points to smooth points and create bespoke curves on each side of the anchor.

Now, let's Work

Bounding Boxes

Let's open up the file we are to work with. Mine is 1000px x 1000px. Select the Ellipse tool (**L**) and draw a circle by clicking and dragging your mouse. A circle will be your proportional constraint if you drag while holding down the shift key.

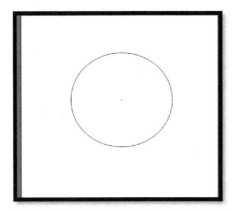

Make sure you have the **Select tool (V)** selected before moving on to paths, anchor points, and handles. The whole circle will be selected when you click on it. Additionally, a box will be shown around the circle. A Bounding Box is the name given to this. Enclosing your complete shape is this rectangle. To scale or rotate your shape, you can make use of the bounding box.

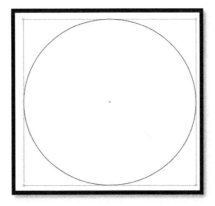

Paths, Anchor Points, and Handles

Choose the **Direct Selection tool (A)**. To choose only a region of a shape rather than the whole thing, use this arrow.

Paths

Place your cursor on the circle's outline to begin. Just look for the word "path" highlighted in pink.

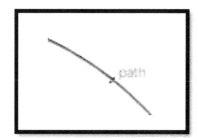

Simply said, a line in Illustrator is a path. Everybody knows about the three different kinds of paths:
1. **Open paths:** Open paths are lines that have two ends.
2. **Closed paths:** A closed shape with no endpoints, like our circle.
3. **Compound paths:** Two or more closed paths are called compound paths. The design of SVG files relies heavily on compound paths.

With the Direct Selection tool (**A**), click and hold on a path and drag it around a bit.

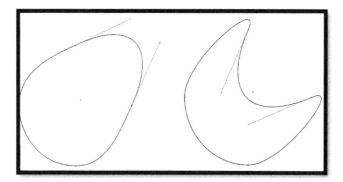

When you move the path, you can see how your circle warps. One technique to manipulate shapes is this. Additionally, you will see a few handles, which the lines are emanating from the edges of your shape. To restore your circle, use the undo button (**Control+Z on a PC or Command+Z on a Mac**).

Anchor Points and Handles

Since anchor points and handles are interdependent, I will address them both at once. Stay with me, even if this can be challenging!

Basic Anchor Points

Choose the Direct Selection tool (**A**). You ought to see a little square above the circle. The word "anchor" should appear when you hover over it. The little square there represents an anchor point. These could be referred to as points or nodes by other people.

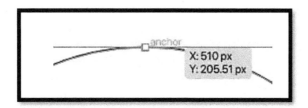

To move the top anchor point around a little, use the Direct Selection tool (A) and click and hold it. Just like up there, you can build similar shapes.

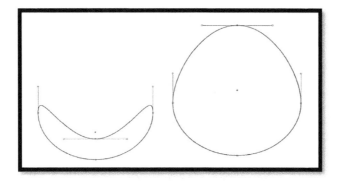

Basic Handles

The lines that branch out from the anchor points, each terminating in a circle, will become visible as you rotate the anchor point. As you rotate your anchor point, they shift and transform. You can see the handles there.

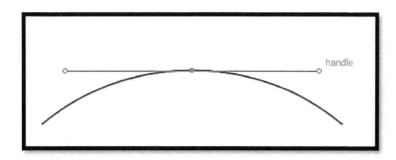

Handles regulate the path's curvature at each anchor point, which are points along the path.

Types of Anchor Points / Handles

You can classify anchor points and handles into three groups. Although they all originate from the same anchor point, they will be different based on their handles:

- o **Smooth**: A curved path, similar to our circle, is formed by these anchor points on both sides.
- o **Corner**: these anchor points form a right angle to one another, much like a square's corners.
- o **Combination**: In a combination, the anchor point has a straight side and a curved side.

Our circle is something to consider. At the very top, very bottom, very left, and very right of our circle are four anchor points. Each anchor point has a set of handles that are moved a predetermined distance away from it when you click on it using the Direct Selection tool (A). You can't see all of the anchor points at once in Illustrator because of how things are chosen, but they all have the same handles, thus the shape of the circle is created.

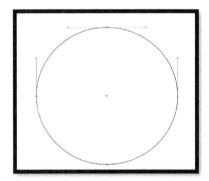

Select the **Anchor Point tool (Shift+C)**. Simply choose an anchor point by clicking on it. It changes the smooth anchor point into a corner anchor point and takes the handles off of it. Clicking on any of the four anchor points will result in a square with a 90-degree rotation. Currently, every one of the anchor points is a corner point.

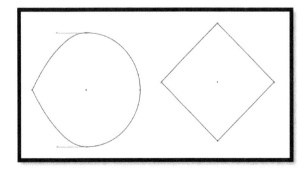

If the anchor points are still straight, you can attempt to turn them back into a circle by clicking and dragging them using the **Anchor Point tool (Shift+C).** Going from a corner anchor point to a curved anchor point isn't exactly easy (that's why the circle tool exists!), but you can see the process. You can modify the flow of each path using anchor points and handles to create incredible shapes and visuals.

Manipulating Adobe Illustrator Handles

Length

I can experiment with the handles some more now. Another circle, **L**, should be drawn. To use the Direct Selection tool (A), click on the top anchor point. Again, you'll see that the handles will pop out. **Pulling handles changes the length of the path.** To move the right handle to the right side of the artboard, click and hold down the shift key while you drag it. Doing so will maintain the handle's horizontal and straight position. Your path will lengthen and the arc will widen as you go.

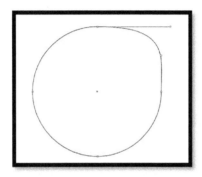

Hold down the shift key when you click the right anchor point and move the top anchor point nearer the top edge of your artboard. As it draws nearer to a corner, the arc will lengthen. After that, you can reduce the segment's length by pulling the two handles back toward the anchor points. One can see how the length of the path segment between the two anchor points is affected by both handles.

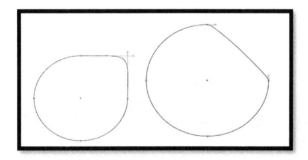

Curves

Rotating handles create curves. Start with your circle again (L) and choose the Direct Selection tool (A). Drag the handle to the right of the top anchor point in a circular motion above the anchor point by clicking and holding it. On each side of the anchor point, it forms a curve, as you can see. The now-top handle controls the portion of the curve above and to the right of the anchor point, while the bottom handle controls the portion of the curve below and to the left of the anchor point.

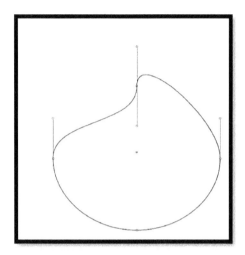

Try out different shapes by experimenting with the many ways the handles can be rotated around the circle.

Manipulating Individual Anchor Points

Frequently, you'll see that the handles on each side of the anchor point are in motion. With this, you can make curves that are easy on the eyes. However, picking both isn't always the best option. Clicking on a handle will pick only half of it if you hold down the Option key (Mac) or Alt key (PC) at the same time.

Adding or Removing Anchor Points

While you're hovering over the path, you can add or remove anchor points by clicking the addition (+) or minus (-) buttons. Subsequently, you may insert or delete anchor points by clicking on the path. If you observe too many anchor points in a picture or can't get a curve to do what you want, this could be useful.

Homework

Would you want any homework? Changing the length of the handles and rotating them are two things you may play around with. Make note of the ways you can use these components to modify shapes. Explore the many shapes available by selecting the Rectangle tool from the left-hand toolbar and holding the mouse button down.

CHAPTER 4
WORKING WITH SHAPES

Shape Tools

You can rapidly create generic rectangles, ellipses, stars, and polygons with the help of the Shape Tools, a modest set of tools that includes the Rectangle Tool, the Ellipse Tool, the Star Tool, and the Polygon Tool, respectively.

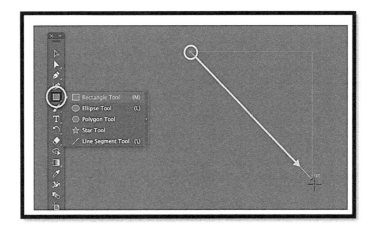

Presently, I will be using my project file. With your file, you can follow along. To begin, move your view of the artboard to the bottom left box titled "**Shapes with Pathfinder**," then create a new layer with the same name, "Shapes with Pathfinder."

Some things to know: Working with drawing modes

You can find Illustrator's three drawing modes—**Draw Normal, Draw Behind, and Draw Inside**—at the very bottom of the toolbar. To design shapes, you can utilize any of many drawing modes.

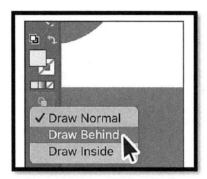

- **Draw Normal mode:** When starting a new project, draw many shapes in Normal mode and stack them.
- **Draw Behind mode:** Using the Draw Behind mode, you can draw behind all the objects on the given layer if no artwork is selected. The new object is drawn just underneath the selected work of art.
- **Draw Inside mode**: In the Draw Inside mode, you can effortlessly create a clipping mask of the selected object by inserting live text and other elements, drawing or positioning photos inside them, and so forth.

Using Draw Inside mode

Using the drawing modes, you can insert, paste, or create content behind other content or inside a vector object.

Add content behind all other content

To add, paste, or move content behind other layer elements, uses the Draw Behind option located at the bottom of the Toolbar. Make a selection, then copy and paste or insert anything else into the page; everything you do will show up below whatever is on the layer you're presently selecting.

Add content directly behind selected content.

Once you've picked some material and turned on Draw Behind mode, you can move, copy, or insert more stuff behind it.

Add content inside the vector shape

You can place content within the chosen shape by using the **Draw Within** option from the Toolbar's bottom. After that, the text, paste, or other input will appear within the selected form, essentially hiding it.

Edit content inside the shape

Isolation mode can be activated by clicking the shape twice. Subsequently, the remaining text might be edited or expanded upon. To exit isolation mode, use the Escape key. Select Draw Normal from the Toolbar's bottom menu to get back to your other tasks.

Rectangle Tool

Select the **Rectangle Tool (M)** from the menu on the left. If you can't see the square symbol, try looking beneath the circle, shape, star, or line icon of one of the other tools. If that's the case, you can get the **Rectangle Tool** 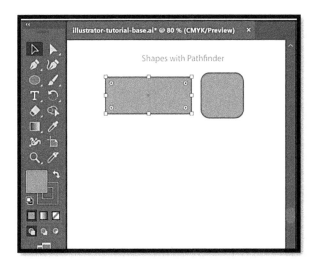 by right-clicking the shape and selecting it from the menu that appears. From the Swatches menu on the right, you can choose your preferred fill and stroke colors. You can do this by using the Stroke swatch, which is located adjacent to the Fill swatch, after clicking on a color swatch underneath it. The Fill swatch is located in the top left corner of the panel. When you're satisfied with the hues, go to the "**Shapes with Pathfinder**" section and use the mouse to create a square. After you're satisfied with the shape, release the click. Next to the first rectangle, place a second rectangle; to make it square, press and hold Shift as you click and drag. Holding down Shift makes shapes have uniformly sized sides. Take note of the little dots around the indicated area. These are called "**corner widgets.**" To change their position, click on one of the square's corners and drag it slightly toward the center of the shape.

You can also change the size of shapes by clicking and dragging on any of the square points on the box those shapes are in. You can rotate the shape, as shown by its curved appearance, by dragging the mouse pointer next to those square points.

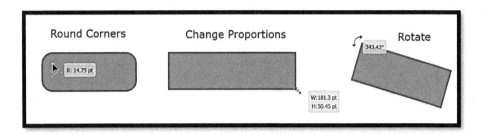

The Ellipse Tool

Among the tools available, choose the Ellipse Tool (L) and choose it. After removing the shapes, you can alter their colors by pressing **Ctrl + Shift + A (or Command +Shift + A on a Mac).** Next, choose the new hues that you'd want to use. In the absence of their removal, the colors of the squares can substitute for your own. Click and drag the Ellipse Tool on the artboard underneath the squares to create an ellipse. A little circle will connect to the right-hand selection box when you use this tool to create an ellipse. By dragging and dropping this circle around the oval, you can choose the angle from which the circle will be cut off. At any point within the circle, release your mouse. Make a new circle next to the first one while holding down the Shift key. Holding down Shift will make a perfect square with the Rectangle Tool, and this will make a perfect circle.

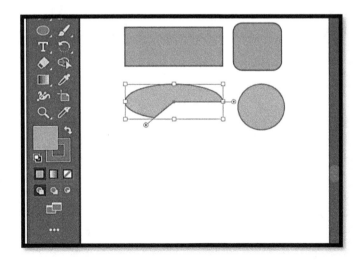

The Polygon Tool

To get the Polygon Tool 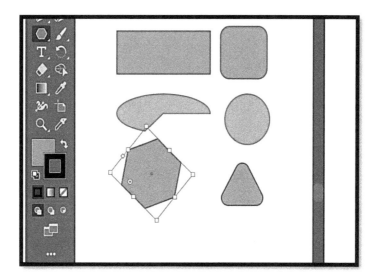, press the Rectangle tool. Before you start making shapes, you can choose new colors if you like. Unlike other shape tools, you can adjust the number of points on the rectangle as you go along. The Polygon Tool, when clicked and dragged under the ellipses, will accomplish the trick. Keep your mouse button down as you press and hold the up and down arrow keys. When you press up, the polygon will grow by one point. **For example**: if you have a heptagon, pushing up will make it an octagon. A single point will be subtracted from the polygon as you press down. Release your click when you're satisfied with the number of points on your rectangle. Holding down Shift, make a second polygon with three points (a triangle) next to the first.

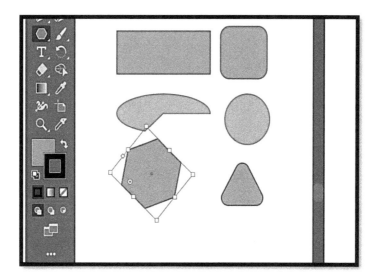

Star Tool

Pick out the **Star Tool**. It can be found by clicking on the Rectangle tool. A new **Fill and Stroke** color can be selected. Simply click and drag the shapes below to create a star. You can control the size of the star by holding down Shift, much as with the Polygon Tool. To add or remove points, hit the up or down keys on your computer. The stars' arms can be extended or contracted as you draw them. You can find the Star Tool on the artboard right next to the first star. You can move it there by clicking and dragging it. Next, move the star's position relative to the center by holding down **Ctrl (or Command on a Mac)**. Holding down or releasing **Ctrl (Command on Mac)** while placing the star can bring about varied effects. Once you're satisfied with the star's shape, release the click.

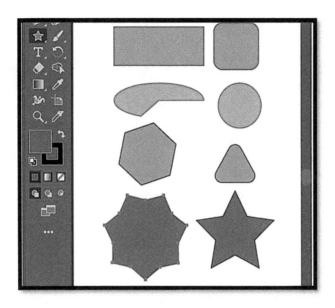

Line Segment Tool

Pick up the Line Segment Tool. Because they aren't designed to display Fill, line parts cannot have a fill color applied to them. Only the stroke color can be selected for lines drawn with this tool. Use the artboard's click-and-drag functionality to position the line segment underneath the stars. Following that, release your mouse. Hold down Shift and click to insert a second line segment next to the first. Holding down Shift while clicking, for instance, will only cause the line to bend at 45° angles. Simply dragging the cursor around the artboard will reveal this. Once the line portion is at the angle you choose, you can release your mouse.

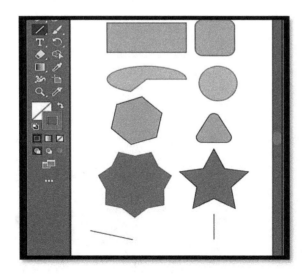

How to Combine Shapes

You can combine shapes in two primary methods. The shapes will need to be arranged such that some of them intersect before you can proceed. Across the tops of the squares, you can click and drag the **Selection Tool (V)** located on the left side of the screen. Here you can see the shapes you selected with the colorful border box applied to them. Use the same tool to click and drag the squares until some of them are beneath the ellipses. To choose the shapes, just click and drag the Selection Tool over them. Rearrange the shapes so that some of them sit above the ellipses. After placing the line segments above the stars, repeat the process. The next step is to rearrange the stars so that they partially cover the polygons. The shapes should contact slightly for them to fit together.

Arrangement of objects

Knowing the layout of the artboard's components helps join existing shapes. Be sure to see that the ellipses appear below the polygons and that the squares you initially created appear below the ellipses as well. This is because, when you make items, the computer will automatically arrange them in their steps in reverse. If you construct a triangle with a bottom, a top, and a central section, the rectangle will be at the rear, the star at the front, and the circle in the center. The first image depicts the objects' arrangement in the program, while the second one displays the identical objects' three-dimensional arrangement.

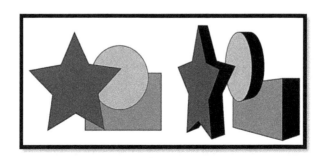

Arranging your objects is something you can do. Hold down the mouse button on top of the rectangles and click again. Then, drag your cursor across the tops of the rectangles to pick them. When something is chosen, right-click and choose "**Arrange**." Click on **Bring to Front** to move the rectangles to the front of the group, where they will sit on top of the ellipses and other shapes.

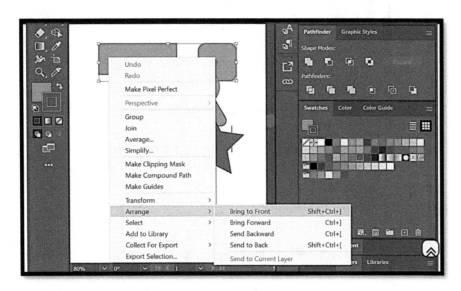

There are also the options of Bring Forward, Send Backward, and Send Back. Pushing the shapes one step to the front with Bring Forward, one step to the back with Send Backward, or to the back with Send Back will move them.

The Pathfinder Panel

The ability to merge and remove shapes is a common use case for Pathfinder. To get even more precise results, you can use the set buttons to perform things like cross shapes, divide shapes, leave out shapes, and more. By hovering the cursor over each button in the Pathfinder panel to the right, you can see their names. Among these buttons are **Minus Back, Intersect, Unite, Minus Front, Exclude, Divide, Trim, Merge, Crop, and Outline**. Depending on the arrangement of two or more things determines the functionality of each button. Specifically, the outcomes are dependent on the relative positions and amounts of contact between the various shapes. o choose all of the overlapping shapes, use the Selection Tool (V) and drag it over the canvas. Select Unite from the row to your left of the top row on the Pathfinder screen. All of your pieces were merged into a single shape and assigned the fill and stroke colors of the adjacent squares, as you can see. Also, you won't find any protruding line pieces anymore. Wait for your shapes to return to their original colors and lines, and then press **Ctrl + Z (or Command + Z on a Mac)** to undo your previous action. While the objects are still chosen, go to the Pathfinder panel's top row and click on **Exclude**. Now that you've cut off all of the overlapping shapes, your objects are the same color as the rectangles.

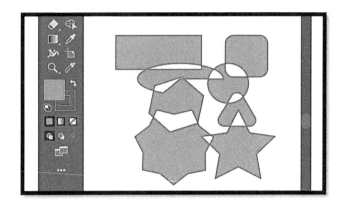

The consequences of pressing each Pathfinder button on a configuration of three overlapping circles, as well as the disassembled shapes, are shown in the tabbed box below.

The ShapeBuilder Tool ( )

The Shapebuilder Tool follows the Pathfinder's functionality in that you can merge and delete shapes. By manually joining shapes instead of utilizing a predefined set of buttons, the Shapebuilder Tool can also generate more complex shapes. Find the "**Shapes with Shapebuilder**" box in the artboard's bottom right corner and position your perspective of the board above it. After that, create a new layer and give it the same name.

New shapes will now have to be added. Check that the Swatches box only shows stroke colors and not fill colors ("**None**" color swatch). In the **Ellipse Tool** (**L**) located on the screen's left side, draw five circles of about the same size. Create a two-by-two grid with four of them using the Selection Tool (V). Arrange the circles such that two are adjacent and two are directly below each other. Make sure that two of the other circles on the edges contact each of the four circles. Center the last circle on top of the other four.

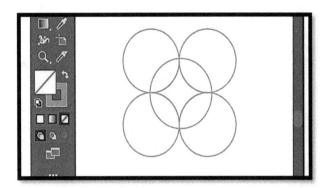

Create a long, narrow rectangle that begins in the center of the rings and extends downward and away from them using the Rectangle Tool (M). Making three little ellipses using the Ellipse Tool (L) is the last step. Afterward, drag them with the Selection Tool (V) until they contact the square's edges and are underneath the larger circles. The current shape should resemble a flower, complete with a stem, three leaves, and four petals.

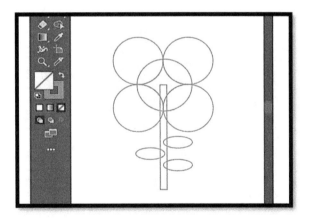

Utilize the **Selection Tool (V)** to select all the shapes, and then utilize the **Shapebuilder Tool** (**Shift + M)** located on the left side of the screen. Moving the mouse over the shapes will demonstrate how the tool recognizes the lines and points out potential shapes. By combining them using the tool, these highlighted areas form new shapes. The center circle of the flower can be highlighted by clicking and dragging the mouse around its shapes. Release the click afterward. Doing so will combine all of the indicated shapes into a single new shape. If you see any points that remain within the central circle, please enlarge them. Applying this technique will assist you in connecting their shapes to the circle. If you commit an error, you can always undo your previous action.

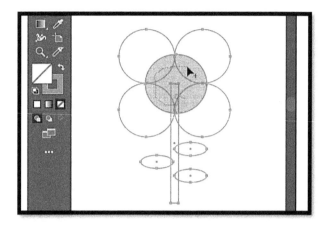

You may have noticed that the Shapebuilder Tool's mouse has a little plus symbol (+) next to it. To unite shapes, the tool has to display the plus symbol. When designed to delete shapes, the pointer will be accompanied by a little **minus symbol (-).** When you click on a single shape or drag over many shapes with the hold-down **Alt (or Option on a Mac)** key, you can remove them from the Shapebuilder Tool. Press and hold the **Alt key (or Option on a Mac)** while clicking on a leaf of the flower to activate this property. The segment of the circle that landed on the rectangle needs to remain.

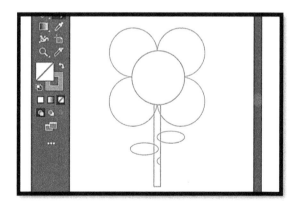

Connect the flower stem and petal ends with the Shapebuilder Tool. The last step is to attach the stem, two leaves, and the remaining third leaf. Popping in for a closer look can help you piece together a few shapes. After you're done, it should resemble a flower with four petals, a stem, and two leaves—though yours may turn out somewhat differently.

Editing shapes

Editing with Direct Selection Tool (▶)

You can use a range of tools to change the shape, size, and color of current lines. **The Direct Selection Tool, Shapebuilder Tool, and Width Tool** 🖋 are the primary tools you will need to change the shapes and lines you have already constructed. You can use the Direct Selection Tool to pick out specific line segments and base points. Contrast this with the Selection Tool, which allows you to select and reposition whole objects. To return to the spot where you tested the Pen Tool, look up in the upper left corner of the artboard. Then, at the very top of the left toolbar, you should see the Direct Selection Tool (A). If you believe anything has to be modified in your path or anchor point locations, you can quickly do it using the Direct Selection Tool. Pick out a point on either curve of your flag that you want to change. As an alternative to dragging an anchor point, you can just click on it. You can see the handles of the selected center point in this. To ensure that the anchor point you choose remains underlined, you may have to toggle the borders of your points on and off. If so, you can enable the feature by going to the program's main menu, picking View, and then clicking on Show Edges. You can delete points by clicking on a blank area on the artboard if you accidentally click on them. To change the curve's shape, click and drag the handles until you're happy with it.

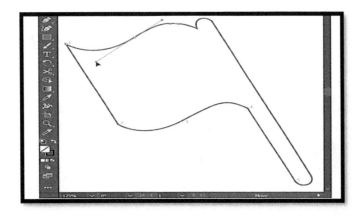

You can also use the Direct Selection Tool to reposition path segments and anchor points without removing them from the overall path. As an example, you can change the flagpole's width by moving the path from one side to the other. Select the path that encircles the flagpole on the right to proceed. Here you can choose any road section by clicking and dragging it, or by holding down Shift while clicking on each one. Drag the line segment around once you've selected the appropriate route or path. Maintaining its connection to the object's rest, you can reposition the line portion. It may be necessary to deselect and pick the correct path once again if the flag is a whole shift.

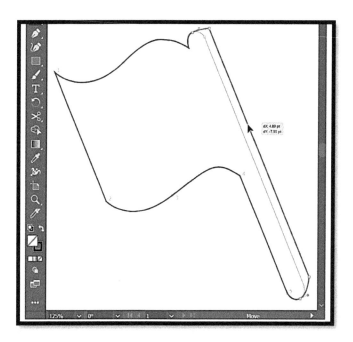

The line segment should be returned to its initial position along the flagpole's template lines.

Editing with Curvature and Pen Tools

It may have been challenging to get a nice curve shape at the ends of the flagpole when you traced the template lines with the Pen Tool . If that's the case, the Curvature Tool can repair it.

From the left-hand toolbar, choose the **Curvature Tool** (Shift + '). All of the points that denote bends on the path are seen here. Drag the point at the very top of the flagpole's curvature slightly higher with your mouse to make it smoother. You can see that the Curvature Tool automatically smooths out curves when there are just two points on each side, as shown in the next image.

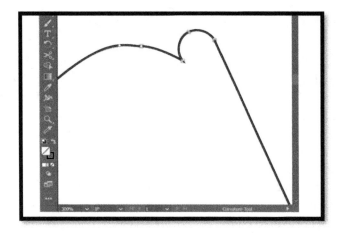

Here, you may discover that the Curvature Tool is of little use or even makes the curve seem worse if you use more anchor points instead. This can be fixed by removing a few support points from the top of the pole. Press the **Delete** key after clicking the section you want to remove. Absolutely! If you find the handles on the anchor points to be too small to view, you can always zoom in. You can also insert additional points by clicking once on the line using the **Curvature Tool.** New points will be automatically curled as you add them. As you move the point, the corresponding line segments will likewise be bent. To make the pieced-together line straight, you can double-click on the point to transform it into a sharp edge. **Use the Curvature Tool to tweak the flag's final base points and lines until you're satisfied with the result. Bear in mind that:**

- By clicking on anchor points and then using the **Delete** key, you can erase points.
- Click once on existing paths to get points.
- Double-click on the endpoints of bent lines to make them straight, and vice versa.

After you're done, it should align with the template lines better than before.

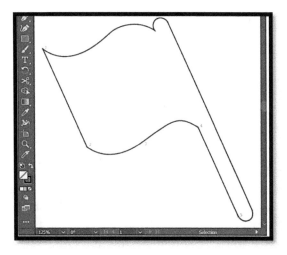

Coloring with the Shapebuilder Tool

Yes, you can alter the line's fill and stroke color as you draw it, but this becomes tedious fast when working on more complicated designs. If you want to get things done faster, you can color existing pieces using the **Shapebuilder Tool**. You should return your focus to the flower you created in the lower right corner of the artboard. The next step is to choose the whole blossom using the Selection Tool (V). Pressing Shift and M on the left side of the screen will bring up the **Shapebuilder Tool**. You can use this tool to choose several patches of color without really affecting the color of the object you're working with. The tool does not alter the stroke color, therefore there's no need to choose one. I can adjust the fill color, however. After clicking once in the flower's center, choose a yellow fill color from the Swatches box. Clicking and dragging over other shapes will cause the tool to unite the indicated shapes. Fill in the middle of the flower first. After that, choose a shade of green for the fill by using the Swatches box. Touch the stem or leaves to finish. Changing the fill color and clicking on individual flower buds is the final stage. Your finished flower should be like the one in the picture below.

How to Use the Width Tool (🖉)

After you've sketched the flower, you can alter the stroke color and width. Press the V key again to choose a new stroke color after you've selected the flower. Keep the Shapebuilder Tool closed if you'd want to make an immediate alteration to the stroke color of the flower. Typically, to alter the breadth of a path's stroke, you can adjust the Stroke Weight, which can be found on the control bar next to "Stroke" towards the programs top.

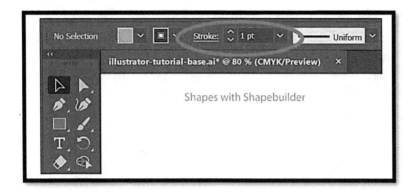

Mouse over this box to access the arrow buttons, input a number, or scroll the wheel; from there, you can adjust the lines' width as well. Alternatively, you may choose the "**Variable Width Profile**" option that is next to the "**Stroke Weight**" box. You can adjust the stroke thickness as you go along the path. When you first set the **Variable Width Profile** to "**Uniform**," all of the lines will be the same width. Make sure you still have your flower chosen. To adjust the flower's stroke width, choose the Stroke Weight box and use the up button until "**3pt**" appears. The difference should be obvious to you.

To create an image where the stroke weight isn't uniform, you can adjust the width of path components by dragging their points with the Width Tool. Examine the left-hand side of the screen for the Width Tool (Shift + W). Press and hold the path to position your width point on the tip of a flower petal. After that, you need to slightly remove the point off the path. A preview of the revised stroke shape will be shown in Illustrator. When you're satisfied with the preview's shape, you can release the button to make the modifications permanent.

It is expected that you can see the three points linked to the custom width, namely:
- The width point on the path that sets the custom width's location.
- The other two points (on either side of the width point) specify the shape of the new width.

If you're not satisfied with the current placement of the width point, you can drag it along the line to a different spot. By repositioning one of the other points, you can alter the thickness of an existing width point as well. Use the Width Tool to stroke the tips of the remaining flowers until they resemble the first petal. Make sure that the depth of your lines is consistent, just as in the figure below.

New Objects on Path Tool

If you want to align or reorganize objects along a straight or curved path, you can do so with ease with the **Objects on Path** tool.

Attach and align objects to a path

1. To begin selecting objects, go to the toolbar, find the **Selection tool** ◥, and click on it.

2. From the toolbar, choose the **Objects on Path tool** ⬚.

If you can't find the **Objects on Path** ⬚ tool in the toolbar, select **Edit Toolbar** ••• and then select it from the **Modify** section.

3. Choose the Path. The **Objects on Path** group is formed when objects connect and align with the path.

Please check that the path has enough support. As you move the cursor over a supported path, it will get highlighted and the **Objects on Path** tool icon will appear.

Note:

- The path can be open or closed, curved or straight-line.
- The path can be of one of the objects you've chosen.
- Almost all object types can be attached, except for graphs.

- Once objects are attached, the path remains visible, unlike the **Type on a Path** tool ⤸

- You can also access the **Objects on Path** ⬚ tool from **Object > Objects on Path > Attach**, and from the right-click menu when you select two or more objects.

Default arrangement of objects on a path

- **Order:** The objects' placement on the canvas dictates their path order. The objects are selected in a left-to-right fashion, column by column. Objects are selected inside each column in descending order. Beginning at its beginning point, they are then laid out along the path. For simple shapes made using tools like the **Rectangle** and **Star** tools, the starting point is already set.
- **Attachment point:** Regardless of the stroke weight, the attachment point—the exact center of each object—attaches to the path's shape.
- **Distribution and spacing:** Object 1 connects to the starting point of the path on both open and closed paths, while object 2 attaches to the ending point of the path on an open path; this is the distribution and spacing information. The distance between each object's connection points determines how far apart they are placed.
- **Alignment of each object relative to the path:** Attaching objects either vertically or horizontally to the path, objects round off their initial rotation angle, and ensuring that each object is aligned relative to the path. Consequently, the net rotation is shown as zero in the Properties panel's Objects on Path Options section.

Change the default attachment point and rotation

1. Select the **Objects on Path** tool from the toolbar by double-clicking it.

2. To modify the attachment point, choose one of the nine **Pivot** points in the **Objects on Path Tool Options** box.
3. Select **Save** after making any necessary adjustments to the rotation angle using the **Rotate** option.

Only objects that you want to attach to a path in the future will be affected by the updated settings. Nothing has changed with the ones who are already attached.

Any time you want, you can go back to the defaults:

1. Double-click the **Objects on Path** tool in the toolbar.
2. Pick **Reset**, and after that, hit **Save**.

Rearrange objects after attaching to a path

You can rotate, modify the distance between attachment points, and move objects along paths after you've attached them to them. You can't modify individual objects; these modifications affect the whole group. In addition to rearranging the objects on the path, you can also remove them and add new ones.

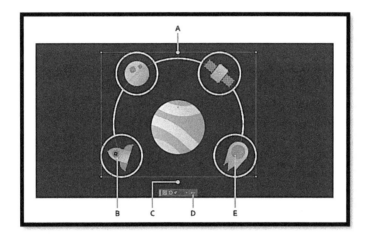

A. The Space widget **B.** The Move All widget **C.** The Rotate All widget **D.** The Contextual Task Bar **E.** The Select/Move widget

Rotate the objects

1. On the canvas, locate and choose the **Objects on Path** group.

2. To rotate the objects, use the **Rotate All** widget. At the point of attachment, the objects rotate.

When using the **Rotate All** widget, use the **Shift** key to rotate the objects in 15-degree increments.

3. If you want to get the angle just right, you can achieve that by using the **Rotate** option in the **Properties** panel's **Objects on Path Options** section.

An object's tilt relative to an imaginary line perpendicular to the path at the attachment point is shown by the rotation angle in the Properties panel.

Change the attachment point of the objects

1. On the canvas, locate and choose the **Objects on Path** group.
2. To modify the objects' attachment point, go to the **Properties** panel and find the **Objects on Path Options** section. From there, choose one of the nine **Pivot** points.

A change in the attachment point causes the objects to spin, but the angle of rotation stays the same. **Rotate All** widget and **Rotate** dropdown are the only ways to modify the rotation angle.

Change the spacing and distribution of the objects

1. On the canvas, locate and choose the **Objects on Path group**.
2. You may change the distribution and spacing of the objects by using the **Space** widget on the enclosing box:
   o **Space widget alone:** By using the space widget alone, all objects in the path may travel in any direction from the first object, which stays anchored.
   o **Space widget with Option (macOS) or Alt (Windows):** No objects are anchored. Objects move toward or away from the path's center from either end.

You can choose exact numbers by adjusting the spacing and seeing the measurement next to the widget.

Move all objects along the path.

1. On the canvas, locate and choose the **Objects on Path** group.
2. To move all objects along the path, use the **Move All** widget on the initial object.

Only if the object distribution is less than the path's length can you utilize **Move All** on an open path.

Shuffle the objects

1. On the canvas, locate and choose the **Objects on Path** group.
2. Press and hold the object's attachment point to transfer it to a new location. The **Select/Move** widget is located there.
3. Letting go of the widget will cause it to move to the other object whose location the one you picked will replace. All objects in its immediate vicinity move up or down the path when the chosen object becomes attached to it.

Rearranging the objects on the path in the **Layers** panel's **Objects on Path** group will not affect their order.

Detach an object from the path

1. On the canvas, locate and choose the **Objects on Path** group.
2. Select the object's attachment point by hovering over it and then using the **Move or Select** widget. At that point, the widget will become solid blue.
3. Remove the detached object from the group by selecting **Detach** in the **Properties** panel's **Objects on Path Options** section.

Using the **Select/Move** widget, you can only detach one object at a time. Hold down the Shift key and drag the selected objects out of the **Objects on Path** group in the **Layers** panel to detach them all at once.

Auto-rearrangement of objects after detaching an object

You detach an object from the path when:

- Detachable objects' subsequent movements are sequential and upward, but they do not always follow a path. The second object ascends the path to replace the first if it becomes disconnected.
- If you haven't modified the default spacing or distribution, those settings will be preserved, but the spacing will be altered. It is guaranteed that the starting and ending points of an open path will always be filled with objects so long as there are two of them.
- The new spacing will be preserved, but the distribution will be adjusted if you have changed the default spacing or distribution.

Attach more objects to the path.

Drag the objects to the **Objects on Path** group in the **Layers** panel. They will be attached to the canvas at the end of the path automatically. **Take the following steps while in isolation mode to attach objects to the path:**

1. Copy the objects that you want to attach.
2. To activate isolation mode, double-click the **Objects on Path** group on the canvas. After that, you can paste. As soon as the path reaches its end, the objects will automatically attach to it.

Note: The objects you create in isolation mode will be attached to the end of the path the moment you make them.

Create a copy of an attached object

1. Find the object in the **Objects on Path** group in the **Layers** panel and pick it.
2. Press **Option** (macOS) or **Alt** (Windows) and drag the object on the canvas to make a copy. At the very end of the path, the copy will be attached automatically.

Note: Only while operating in isolation mode will a copy made with **Ctrl/Cmd + C or Ctrl/Cmd + V** immediately attach to the path.

Expand the Objects on Path Group

To make the Objects on Path group into a normal group, use Expand:
1. On the canvas, locate and choose the **Objects on Path** group.
2. Click on **Object > Objects on Path > Expand**.

Working with the Knife Tool

By cutting through pre-existing shapes and text, the knife tool facilitates the creation of one's unique look. **You can activate the knife tool by going to the sidebar and click-holding the Eraser tool to select the knife tool and then draw through a selected object to cut.**

Key Takeaways

- For more organic shapes, you can cut in freeform mode with the Knife Tool by holding down the Alt (Windows) or Option (Mac) key.
- With an object chosen, you can use Illustrator's knife tool.
- The Knife Tool can be used to cut through groupings of objects, and it will split the group into individual shapes.
- For cleaner cuts without sharp edges or undesired parts, try using the "**Path Eraser**" tool.

Note: The images were captured using the Windows version of Adobe Illustrator CC. The Mac version and others can look different.

How to Cut Shapes with the Knife Tool in Illustrator

Using Illustrator's knife tool, you can quickly and simply cut off shapes. You should be interested in seeing this put into action.

Step 1: The first and most important step is to make a shape. You can make any shape you can imagine by clicking the shape tool. I'll make a circle using the Ellipse tool.

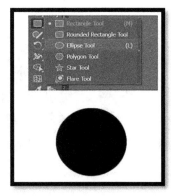

Step 2: Make the knife tool active. Go to the sidebar and select the Knife tool under the Eraser Tool.

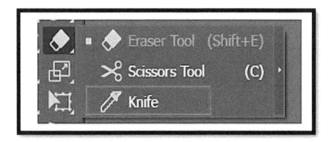

Step 3: Cut the shape. Cut by drawing through the shape. To cut your shape, you can draw a freehand or straight path.

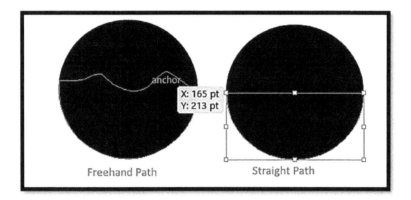

Freehand Path   Straight Path

Step 4: Modify the shape after selecting it. The shape can be repositioned, parts can be removed, colors can be changed, or any other edits can be made. I want to get a white-and-black appearance; therefore, I will separate the shapes to expose the white artboard.

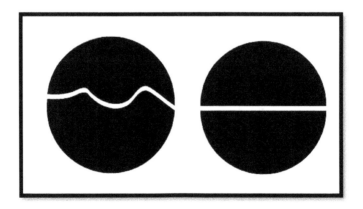

How to Cut Text with the Knife Tool in Illustrator

To make your special designs out of text, try using the knife tool to cut it. To fit your design demands, you can play around with the colors, spacing, and even distort the look of the text. **Let's use the knife tool to cut the example text that's below.**

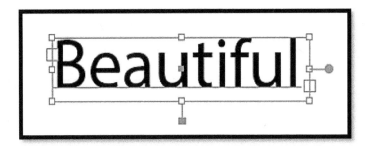

Step 1: First, create your text. In the absence of a text, you can generate new text with the **Type Tool**. To access the Type Tool, either go to the toolbar or press **T** on your keyboard.

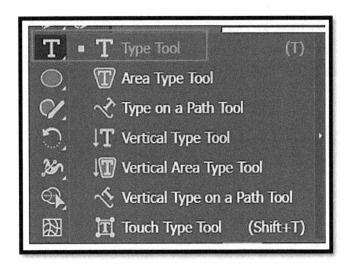

Step 2: The second step is to outline the text. Use the keyboard shortcut **Shift + Ctrl + O (for Windows) and Shift + Command + O (for Mac)** or go to the overhead menu and select **Object > Expand**.

Note that to make live text editable, you must first construct a text outline. When you outline text, it becomes a separate shape that you can alter just like any other shape.

Step 3: Ungrouping text is the third step. Ungroup text can be achieved by right-clicking on the enlarged or highlighted text and selecting that option.

Note: Illustrator automatically groups text when you outline it. To edit each letter separately, ungroup the text.

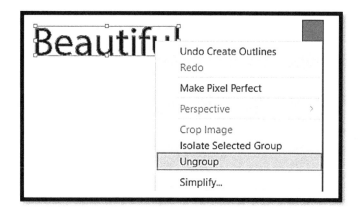

Step 4: Make a straight or freeform cut across the text with the knife. Choose the path you want to cut and then make the necessary adjustments.

After deciding on the cut path, I colored the top yellow while leaving the bottom black. Edits can be made to meet your specific design requirements. For instance, you can shift them laterally or create a gap between the chopped paths. What you want to accomplish is the determining factor.

I'm done! You have recently mastered the art of cutting text and shapes using the knife tool.

FAQs

Using the Knife Tool in Illustrator is a breeze, and the results are stunning. On the other hand, you can have some further inquiries about Illustrator's knife tool.

What's the Difference between the Knife and the Pathfinder Tool in Illustrator?

How they divide shapes or paths is where the Divide effect in Adobe Illustrator's Pathfinder tool differs significantly from the Knife Tool. For more precision in deciding where and how to make cuts, try using the Knife Tool, a freeform cutting tool that is used manually. But the Pathfinder tool's Divide effect automatically splits shapes at their intersections with pinpoint accuracy.

Why is the Knife tool not working in Illustrator?

You may not be able to use the knife tool for a few different reasons. When attempting to cut a raster image, the knife tool may not be the best choice. To transform a raster image into a vector format, you need to trace and enlarge the image before you can use the knife tool to cut it. How you apply the knife to an object is another reason why the knife tool in Illustrator doesn't function. The knife tool will not be visible if you cut into the object. If you want to use the knife tool, you have to cut through the object from the outside, on both sides.

What's the Knife tool shortcut in Illustrator?

To access the knife tool in Illustrator, you can only see it on the toolbar; there is no shortcut.

How do you use the Knife tool in Illustrator on an image?

Converting a picture to a vector format is the first step in using the knife tool.

The Scissors tool

A helpful tool in Adobe Illustrator is the Scissors Tool, which allows designers to cut paths or components along a line or at a specific point. For precision cutting and dividing up images or designs, this function is a lifesaver. With the Scissors Tool, users can precisely modify and alter their artwork. You can cut paths and shapes with superb precision and control with the Scissors Tool, a digital tool in Illustrator. The cut will simply need to be marked where it will start and terminate, unlike with actual scissors. With this tool, you can divide any shape or object in half, open closed paths, delete paths, and cut shapes in two. You can acquire anything you want in digital format using this adaptable tool.

Using the Scissors Tool in Illustrator

Two options lead to the Scissors Tool.
- You can either utilize the shortcut or look for it in the toolbar on the left.

You can access this versatile tool for cutting and editing in both ways.

To rapidly use the Scissors Tool in Adobe Illustrator, you can utilize a helpful shortcut. Your tool will launch when you hit the "C" key. Alternatively, you can access the tool via the program's menu by following these instructions.

- To access the Scissors Tool, hold down the Eraser Tool located in the center of the tool panel on the left side of your screen.
- Use the **Eraser Tool** to locate it, and then select it.

Cut Simple Objects with the Scissors Tool in Illustrator

The Scissors Tool is used for cutting out objects in Illustrator. The procedure is straightforward, albeit it may be more challenging with more complex objects. Select the path you want to divide after using the Scissors Tool. With this tool, you can effortlessly cut and alter your patterns.

- Select the **path point** on the object where you want to split it.
- Pick the **reference point(s)** or **paths** that appear after breaking an object.
- By using Illustrator's Scissors Tool, you can easily cut objects.

Cutting Text with the Scissors Tool in Illustrator

There is a catch when using the Scissors tool to trim text in Illustrator - it only works for anchor points and paths. It will be immediately apparent that it does not function when applied to live text. Fortunately, outlining the text first is an easy way to solve this issue. After you've done that, cutting text in Illustrator with the Scissors Tool is almost the same as cutting objects. **To cut text using the Scissors Tool in Illustrator, follow these steps:**

1. Before you can cut the text in Illustrator using the Scissors Tool, you need to ensure the text is drawn. This can be done by selecting **Create Outlines** from the Type menu, or by using the keyboard shortcut **Command+Shift+O** on a Mac or **Control+Shift+O** on a PC.

The text will be transformed into anchor points that can be edited using the Scissors Tool after it has been drawn.

2. Either the "**C**" key or the side menu window can be used to access this tool.
3. Select the point where you want to cut the text. The text has been outlined and reference points have been added, so remember that you can click on any portion of it. You may have a closer look at the central points by zooming in.

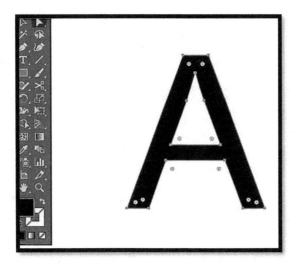

4. To begin, draw a line over the desired text area. Next, to break the text entirely, ensure that there are many anchor points along the line. A clean cut requires the addition of at least four pinpoints.
5. The Scissors Tool in Illustrator simplifies text cutting.

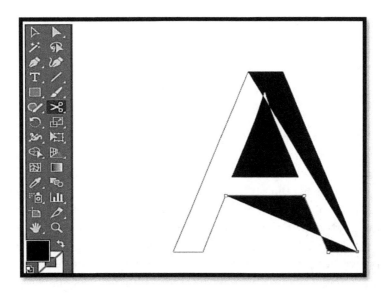

6. Remember that clicking on the fill portion of a letter will not activate the Scissors Tool in Illustrator if you want to cut text from that document. Select the text by clicking on its fixed points or path.
7. A line may appear between the four cutting points of a letter when using Illustrator's Scissors Tool to cut text. To remove this line, use the **Direct Selection Tool**.
8. Pick the **Direct Selection Tool** from the menu to get things started. Just click on the line you want to cut.
9. After selecting an area, you can erase it by using the **Delete** key on your keyboard. Pick the tool you want to use and then click on the points to cut. Furthermore, by rearranging the central points, you can alter the appearance.

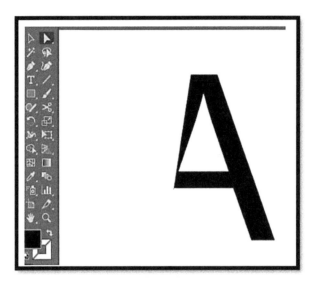

Remember that the clipped text ends will appear as open paths and not connected when you use this tool. Press **Command+Y** on a Mac or **Control+Y** on a PC to get to the outline view, where you can see these paths.

Using the Eraser tool ( )

When you use the Eraser Tool to cut, it can perform extra tricks. Drag it over any shape, like the Knife, and it will slice through it (unlocked shapes excepted). After cutting, it will conceal the paths of the shapes it formed, much like the knife. The third advantage is that you may pick individual shapes to cut out while leaving the others in their original groups if you simply need to remove a portion of a shape. It's similar to how the knife operates. The Eraser tool, in contrast to the Knife tool, will erase any portion of a shape when dragged over it. The two tools vary mostly in this respect. The size of the brush-like Eraser Tool can be adjusted. After being covered by the circle, the erased shapes will remain in the region around the edge of the brush. Once a stroke was produced around the initial shape, it would carry over to the chunks made on either side of the erased line. To use the **Eraser Tool**, choose it from the menu. Now, drag the Eraser tool over the shape, whether it is chosen or not. If you use the Eraser Tool, you will create two objects within the expansive area where the tool was moved.

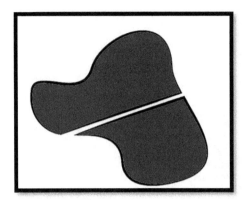

You can also alter the size and shape of the Eraser Tool—or at least make it rounder—by double-clicking the tool button in the ToolBar. Additional options will be shown to you. Simply as with other brushes, you can adjust the Eraser's brush head to your liking by adjusting its size, angle, and roundness. A window listing the options will pop up. To some extent, this is analogous to adjusting the brush's parameters.

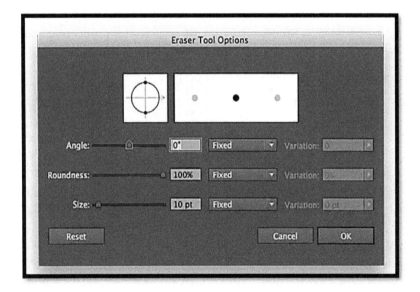

Erasing in a straight line

1. **Select the Eraser Tool (Shift + E):**
   - Locate the Eraser Tool in the toolbar or press **Shift + E** to activate it.

2. **Adjust Eraser Options:**
   - Double-click the Eraser Tool icon to adjust its settings like size, shape, and behavior.
3. **Hold Shift for Straight Line:**
   - Click and drag the Eraser Tool while holding down the Shift key to erase in a straight line.
4. **Erasing in a Straight Path:**
   - You can drag the eraser tool along the path or line you want to delete in a straight line.

Smart Guides

With Adobe Illustrator's Smart Guides, you can position and align objects with pinpoint accuracy. You may see them as dotted lines that show up whenever you move one object close to another or a guide. You can use Smart Guides to center objects horizontally, vertically, or at an angle. Additionally, they can be used to uniformly distribute or space objects.

How to Enable Smart Guides

Get Smart Guides enabled by following these steps:
   - **Open the View menu.**
   - **Select Smart Guides.**

Alternatively, you can use the Ctrl+U keyboard shortcut. When you activate Smart Guides, dotted lines will show up whenever you move an object close to another object or a guide. By following these lines, you will be able to align and place objects with accuracy.

Using Smart Guides

Objects can be aligned vertically, horizontally, or at a precise angle using Smart Guides. Additionally, they can be used to uniformly spread-out objects or disperse them. You can vertically align objects by dragging them to the vertical guide. By dragging an object until it attaches to the horizontal guide, you can horizontally align objects. You can line up objects at a certain angle by dragging them until they attach to the angled guide. If you want to spread out your objects equally, you may do that by selecting them and then clicking the corresponding buttons on the toolbar. After selecting the objects you want to space equally, go to the toolbar and click the **Space Evenly** button. To **align and position objects** precisely, Smart Guides can be a useful tool. With their assistance, you can save time while improving the quality and accuracy of your ideas. To accurately position and align objects in Adobe Illustrator, you can make use of the Smart Guides tool. You can save time and effort with them, and they are straightforward to use. Try out Smart Guides if you're seeking a method to enhance your Illustrator precision and accuracy.

Enhanced Image Trace Feature

You can transform raster images saved in formats like JPEG, PNG, and PSD into professional-grade vector artwork by using **Image Trace**.

Trace an image quickly with limited tracing options

Even without the Image Trace panel's customization options, you can run Image Trace at different speeds and with different degrees of control:
- With the **Default** preset, you can quickly launch **Image Trace** by selecting the picture and then clicking the **Image Trace** button in the **Contextual Task Bar**.
- When you're ready to use a different tracing preset in **Image Trace**, just choose the image and go to the **Properties** panel. From there, choose **Image Trace**.

Any of these ways will still allow you to run **Image Trace**, and then you can use the **Image Trace** panel to make adjustments to the final product.

Release the trace

Release an image to discard its trace and restore it to its original state:
1. Choose the trace result.
2. Press **Release** after selecting **Object > Image Trace**.

Edit the trace result

You need to expand a trace result before you can modify it like any other vector object. No tracing settings can be changed once expanded:
1. Find the traced result on the canvas and click on it.
2. From the **Image Trace** panel, choose **Expand**. **Expand** converts the results into grouped customizable paths.
3. Edit the paths as needed:
   - To modify without ungrouping, double-click the result to enter isolation mode.
   - Choose **Ungroup** in the **Contextual Task Bar** to ungroup and edit.
4. If you need to eliminate extra anchor points, you can do so by selecting **Object > Path > Simplify.**
5. To color the paths, choose **Object > Live Paint > Make** once you've selected them. The paths are transformed into Live Paint groups.

Image Trace panel options

You can adjust the outcome using the basic and advanced tracing settings in the **Image Trace** window. You can only access these settings once you've chosen a picture.

Preset

For quick access to commonly used Image Trace workflows, utilize the icons located at the panel's top:

- **Auto-Color** : Creates a posterized image from a photo or artwork.
- **High Color** : Creates photorealistic artwork of high fidelity.
- **Low Color** : Creates simplified photorealistic artwork.
- **Grayscale** : Traces the artwork to gray shades.
- **Black and White** : Simplifies the image to black-and-white artwork.
- **Outline** : Simplifies the image to black outlines.

Check the **Preset** dropdown if you can't find a preset in the icon list.

View

Displays the traced picture or the original image, outline, or no outline at all. Choose **Press & hold to view source image** next to **View** to quickly compare the trace result with the source image.

Mode

Sets the color mode that will be used for the trace. Your traced artwork can be easily transformed into simple color or grayscale formats using the available choices.

- **Color:** When you choose **Color** as your **Mode**, the **Colors** slider or dropdown will display, depending on the **Palette** type you've chosen. You can adjust the number of colors used in a color trace by dragging the **Colors** slider, and you can choose the color group from the Colors selection.
- **Grayscale:** When you choose **Grayscale** as your **Mode**, the **Grays** slider will show up. In a grayscale trace result, it indicates the quantity of grayscale to be utilized.
- **Black and White:** To get a black-and-white trace, you may adjust the **Threshold** slider that displays when you choose **Black and White** as the **Mode**. White is applied to all pixels that are brighter than the value, while black is applied to all pixels that are darker than the value.

Palette

Sets the palette that will be used to create the color tracing from the original picture. This option is available only when you set the **Mode** to **Color**.

You can choose from the following:
- **Automatic:** Based on the input image, it automatically toggles between full tone and limited palette for the tracing. You can change the tracing accuracy and simplicity of the vectors by dragging the **Colors** slider when you choose **Automatic**. Setting it to **0** simplifies things at the cost of accuracy while setting it to **100** makes things more complicated without sacrificing accuracy.
- **Limited:** The output only makes use of a narrow palette of colors. To customize the output color scheme, you can adjust the number of colors using the Color slider.
- **Full Tone:** Makes use of every color in the output. If you want to make artwork that looks just like the original picture, this is the way to go. When this is checked, the fill area pixels' variability is determined by the Color slider. There are more paths with smaller color patches when it's set to **100%** since the variability is at its lowest. In contrast, the fill regions are both smaller and bigger when set to 0%.
- **Document Library:** You can specify the precise colors you like in the final product by using an existing color group in the Document Library. From the **Swatches** window, you can choose any color library that you've made.

Advanced options

To access the advanced tracing options, click the arrow next to Advanced.

Paths

Sets the distance in pixels between the traced and original shapes of pixels. With lower values, the path fitting becomes looser, while with larger ones, it becomes tighter.

Corners

The likelihood that a sharp curve will become a corner point and the focus on corners are specified. More corners are produced by increasing the value.

Noise

Indicates a region in pixels that will not be traced. There is less noise when the value is greater. **Tip:** You can get a better-quality picture by adjusting the **Noise** slider to a higher number, say, between 20 and 50. Choose a lower number (1–10) to get a picture with lesser resolution.

Method

Specifies a technique for tracing. You can choose from the following:
- **Abutting:** Cutout paths are created by abutting. One path's edge is identical to the edge of the path just across from it.

- **Overlapping:** Makes paths that are stacked. Different paths touch one another only a little bit.

Create

- **Fills:** Creates filled regions in the trace result.
- **Strokes:** The trace result is enhanced with paths that have been stroked. The maximum width that features in the source picture can be stroked is specified. When the feature width exceeds the maximum, the trace result will show highlighted regions.
- **Gradients:** When you set **Color** or **Grayscale** as **Mode** and choose **Automatic** or **Full Tone** as your **Palette**, it will find and trace linear gradients in your picture. If the **palette** is already defined, **gradients** will function in **grayscale** mode.
  - To get a more gradual gradient, increase the value of the **Smooth** slider, which controls the gradient detecting strength.
  - When you're satisfied with the expanded trace, use the **Gradient** tool to tweak the gradients.

Shapes

Rectangles, squares, and circles can be found in the picture and traced as live shapes for simple manipulation. The only shapes it can identify are perfectly round and square. It can also identify somewhat twisted rectangles, albeit it's not as precise.

Options

- **Snap Curves To Lines:** If somewhat curved lines are replaced with straight lines, and if lines that are near 0 or 90 degrees are snapped to absolute 0 or 90 degrees, then snap curves to lines is the option to use. If the shapes in your source picture are slightly rotated or if you're creating geometric artwork, you can use this option.
- **Transparency:** When you set **Color** as **Mode**, the image's transparent background will not be traced as white. Choose four or more colors using the **Colors** slider if you've set the **Palette** to **Limited**.
- **Ignore Color:** Ignores a specific color while tracing. To disregard certain colors, use the color picker. When the **Mode** is set to **Grayscale** and the **Method** is set to **Overlapping**, this option is not accessible.

CHAPTER 5
COLOR, GRADIENTS, AND PATTERNS
Exploring color modes

The way colors are seen, understood, and used in digital artworks is greatly affected by the color modes in Adobe Illustrator. To accurately portray colors and operate efficiently, designers and artists must be familiar with various color modes. There are some color options available in Adobe Illustrator, and they all have their unique uses. Adobe Illustrator's two main color options, RGB (Red, Green, and Blue) and CMYK (Cyan, Magenta, Yellow, Key/Black), each have their unique uses.

1. RGB Color Mode:

RGB is a commonly used additive color model in digital displays, including screens, cameras, and computer monitors. Mixing the three primary colors of light—**red, green, and blue**—creates an array of shades. In RGB mode, the intensity of each color is specified for each channel (red, green, and blue) using a combination of **0 to 255** numbers. It's great for screen-display designs and digital artwork since the combination of these three colors at different intensities provides a large range of colors.

2. CMYK Color Mode:

Printing uses the CMYK color model, which is a subtractive approach that uses varying amounts of cyan, magenta, yellow, and black inks subtracted from a white background, to generate colors. Printing and other industries that use the process of creating colors by selectively absorbing light from a white surface (often paper or similar materials) make extensive use of it. CMYK inks do not use light to generate colors but rather remove light wavelengths. This is in contrast to RGB inks. When all color is taken away, what remains is black. Printing using black ink, sometimes called the "**key**" color, is easier and produces a deeper black. Each of the four ink colors—cyan, magenta, yellow, and black—is represented by a percentage in the CMYK color mode, which may be anywhere from zero to one hundred percent. While working on a drawing in Adobe Illustrator, you can easily choose between various color settings. However, be aware that while converting between RGB and CMYK, colors may not seem identical. This is because there are differences in the color spectrum and the rendering of colors on displays compared to print. Because it more precisely displays how the colors will appear when printed, CMYK mode is essential for design projects. However, since it displays colors more faithfully on computers and other digital displays, producing in RGB mode is preferable for digital creations that will be seen on screens. Before you start a new project, you will pick the color setting for the art from CMYK or RGB.
NOTE: It's possible that the designs shown in the New Document window box won't match the ones in the photo.

Each new document option, such as Print or Web, has its color mode, and you can access them all via **File > New**. One example is the default usage of the CMYK color option in the **Print settings.** After selecting **Advanced Options** in the **New Document** dialog box, you can easily change the color mode by selecting a new option from the **Color Mode** menu.

You can display and create solid colors on the website by adjusting the color settings. By navigating to **File > Document Color Mode** and selecting either RGB Color or CMYK Color, you can alter the color mode of an already-created document.

Basic Adobe Illustrator Color

Color can be worked with in a variety of ways in Adobe Illustrator, as it can with many other things. The color tools in the Control Panel and the Toolbar work well together; I find that they complement each other. Equally useful to the Control Panel's drop-down options is the Swatches Panel, where you can manipulate colors. Illustrator uses what are known as **"swatches"** to represent colors; each colored box in the image represents one swatch. A circle can be drawn on the artboard (**L**). By default, your shape will be filled with white and outlined with a 1-point black stroke.

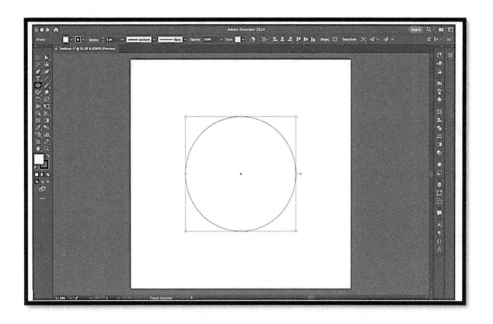

In the top left corner of the control panel and on the left side of the toolbar, you can see the fill and stroke swatches. The color swatch on the left represents the fill, while the one on the right represents the stroke. Using an "**empty**" stroke swatch is my general recommendation for SVG files, particularly for novices. This rules out the possibility of a stroke occurring. I can alter the fill and stroke colors accordingly. Choose the circle (**V**) and then use the color pickers in the top right to change the fill to color (I chose the teal swatch). Then, choose the white swatch with the red line across it to change the stroke to empty.

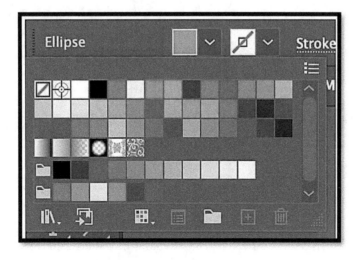

As you can see, the outside of the teal circle is now free of strokes.

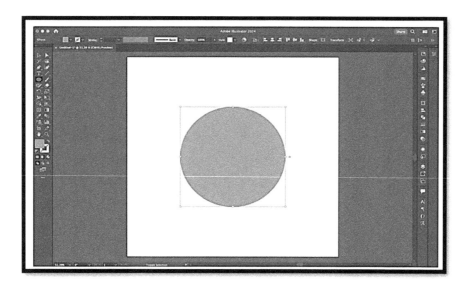

So there you have it, the bare minimum of how to alter colors in Illustrator! Additionally, you can double-click the swatches located at the left-hand bottom of the Toolbar, which will launch the Color Picker.

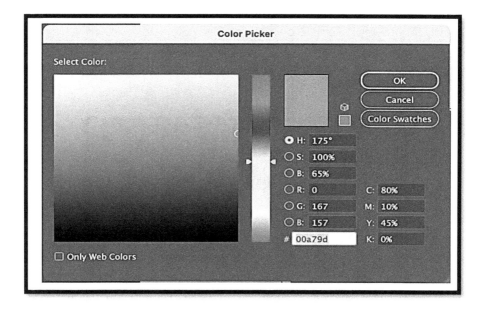

Here are a few other choices for you. In the gradient picker located on the right, you can choose a color by dragging the mouse. You can input the values of the desired Hex, HSB, RBG, or CMYK colors in the appropriate boxes on the right side of the screen. As a result, you can choose precise colors, which is ideal if you have a preferred brand or other color scheme in mind.

Default Swatches in Adobe Illustrator

Your default swatch library in Adobe Illustrator can be accessed using the Control Panel menu or the Swatches Panel. There is a vast array of color swatches available; if you choose to use just them, that is quite OK.

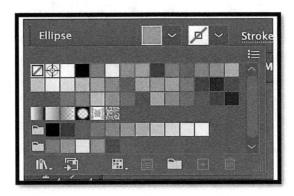

To access more default swatch libraries in Adobe Illustrator, you can click the Swatch Library button located at the panel's bottom.

So, let's say I went to **Color Properties** and chose **Bright** as an example. A new swatch library would open with coordinating bright colors.

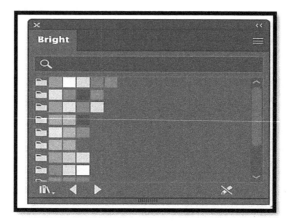

You don't need to make your color palette if you use this method to discover suitable color combinations.

Creating and Saving a Color Palette

Now it's just as simple to build your color palette. Alternatively, you can create a color palette that suits your tastes by experimenting with the color tools up top. I used the Color Picker to experiment with different combinations of colors until I found one I liked, based on my intuition about what would look well together. This is how my color palette was born. **My recommendation is to make a little circle (L) for each color. Accordingly, this is my color palette:**

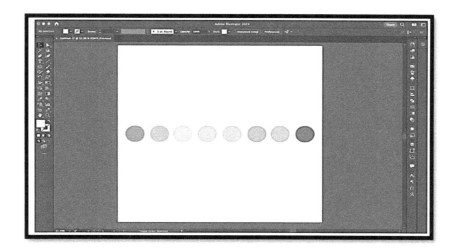

No limit on the number of colors you can use. About eighty percent of the SVGs I create end up using this method. On occasion, I'll add a splash of another color—like orange for Halloween or various browns for fall—but for the most part, I adhere to this palette. Coming up with a consistent color palette is important if you want to establish a store, but it's not as important if you're simply creating for yourself. After you've organized your color palette on your artboard using circles like this, I can remove any unnecessary swatches by returning to the color swatch menu. They will be back the next time you launch Illustrator, so there's no need to worry about permanently removing them. Pick out all the swatches you want to remove using the mouse. I usually keep black and white to make them easy to access from my new palette.

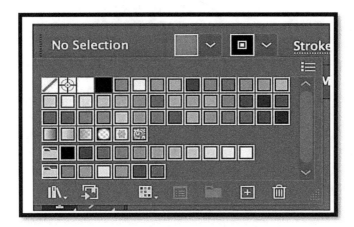

To delete the swatches, go to the bottom right and click the trash can symbol.

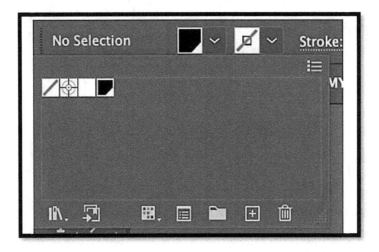

After that, select all of the circles on your artboard by dragging and dropping the Selection Tool (**V**). To create a new color group, return to the Content Panel's color picker in the upper left corner and choose the small folder icon.

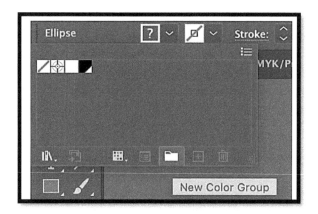

Doing so will generate a new color group using your chosen colors. Give your collection of color swatches a name and hit OK. After that, you can see your new colors in a new row when you return to the color dropdown. You should save this palette so that you can continue to use it even after you exit Illustrator. Select "**Save Swatches**" from the menu that appears when you click the Swatches Library icon (bottom left). After you give your swatches a name, you can access them whenever you want by going to the **same dropdown** menu, selecting **User Defined**, and then choosing your palette. Your new palette will always be available to you, but your regular swatches will revert to their original state in the dropdown!

Use the Generative Recolor Tool

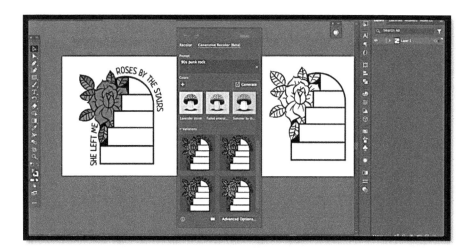

Adobe Illustrator's generative AI update, which was announced in June 2023, includes AI Generative Recolor. You can use the text prompt to choose a color scheme and then use this tool to recolor any vector artwork. New colorful art possibilities can be quickly and easily generated without requiring any mental effort on your part. You can rebrand your user interface and user experience icons, try out various color schemes for vector graphics, and play about with hue to get beautiful monochromatic effects using Generative Recolor. There are many more fantastic applications for Generative Recolor; these are just a few examples.

How to Use Illustrator's Generative Recolor Tool

There is little difference between utilizing Generative Recolor in Adobe Illustrator and the Adobe Firefly Vector Recolor tool now that it is available as an Adobe Illustrator tool. The Firefly tool is only compatible with vector files saved in the SVG format. Learn how to utilize Illustrator's Generative Recolor tool with this detailed tutorial.

Step 1: Open or Create Your Vector in Illustrator

You can either use Illustrator's built-in vector drawing capabilities or import an existing vector file in the .ai, .svg, or .eps formats. You can directly utilize Generative Recolor with these formats. Because you can change the color of both filled shapes and paths, you won't need to draw path outlines if you plan on making changes to the shapes afterward. Additionally, the Live Paint tool can be used on vectors that have already been colored. You can also import .tiff files and other formats, such as Procreate drawings, however, to recolor the graphics, you will need to use Illustrator's Image Trace tool. Make sure that RGB or CMYK, not Grayscale, is your vector color format.

Step 2: Open Generative Recolor

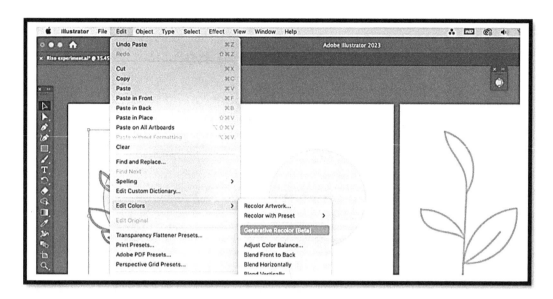

Choose the whole graphic or only the areas you want to recolor when your vector graphic is prepared to be placed on the Illustrator artboard. Following that, choose **Edit > Edit Colors > Generative Recolor.**

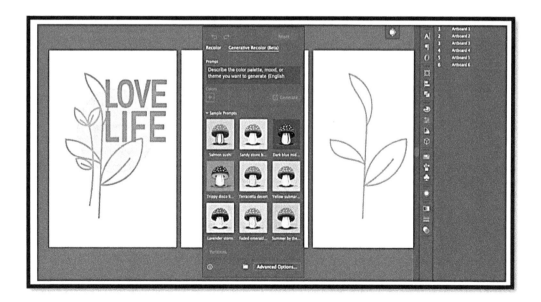

The Generative Recolor window will open. There is a prompt box, sample images, different outcome variants, and some complex recoloring choices in the window.

Step 3: Type a Prompt or Choose a Sample

A color scheme can be created in two different methods. Both are quite easy. First, in the text box, you can enter your prompt. You can apply any theme or style prompt that comes to mind by typing it in and then clicking the **Generate** button. Focusing on the details will enhance your outcomes. **The following are a few examples of valid prompts:**

- Retro American Diner
- Living Coral
- Beautiful Pink Sunset
- Country Fields
- Barbie Girl

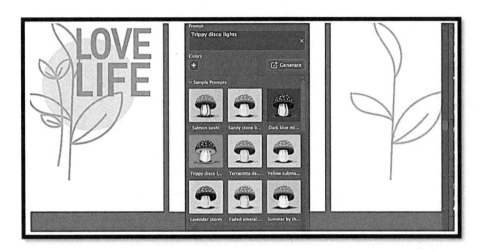

Two, if you're stuck for a theme description, you can use one of the nine offered examples as a starting point. They come with images of the samples, so you can see how your color scheme will seem. Just choose a prompt and your vector will take on that prompt's style.

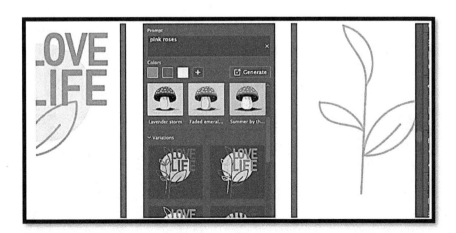

After you've written a prompt, click the plus sign to add a certain color under the prompt box. Along with the question, this guides the AI to think about those colors further. No limit to the number of colors you can use

Step 4: Apply Your Generative Recolor Result

The Generative Recolor tool takes your prompt and returns four different versions after it's produced. Without duplicating your vector, you can just choose one of the four and apply it to your work in progress. You can redo the question by selecting **Generate** again if you are unhappy with the output. In most cases, AI will not provide the same findings more than once.

After applying the Generative Recolor to your vector, you can simply dismiss the window and return to editing your vector as before. Using Fill and Stroke and other tools, you can make standard color adjustments. All of your vector paths and shapes can be edited in the usual way.

Creating and Applying Gradients

You can't have a gradient fill without a starting color and an ending color; these are the building blocks of any color gradient. If you have Adobe Illustrator, Photoshop, or Microsoft Paint, you can make gradient fills. There are three different gradient fills that can be created in Illustrator. Here they are outlined in their most basic form:

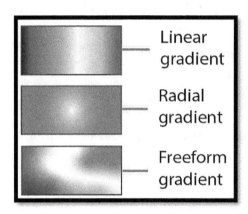

- **Linear:** As you go along a line, the color transitions into another color.
- **Radial:** The radial pattern is characterized by the gradual transition from one color to another as it radiates outward from a central point.
- **Freeform:** This graded color combination can be organized in either a sequential or a random fashion, as long as it stays within a shape. Because of this, the blending seems seamless and fluid, much like real colors.

Unless you're working with freeform gradients, you can either utilize one of Adobe Illustrator's premade gradients or create your own and store them as swatches. A light and shadow effect, the impression of depth, or dimension can be achieved in your artwork by using gradients. This will further increase its aesthetic value. Alternatively, you can use the Gradient tool on the toolbar or the Gradient panel (**Window > Gradient**) to apply, generate, or modify gradients. You can find both of these panels and tools on the toolbar. You can see what sort of gradient was used for the object's fill or stroke in the Gradient Fill box and what colors were used for the current gradient in the Gradient Stroke box in the Gradient panel, respectively.

How to Make a Gradient in Illustrator

Step 1

You need to be able to access the **Gradient** panel before you can make a gradient. On the right side of the toolbar, you should see this. Additionally, you can get to this by selecting **Window > Gradient.**

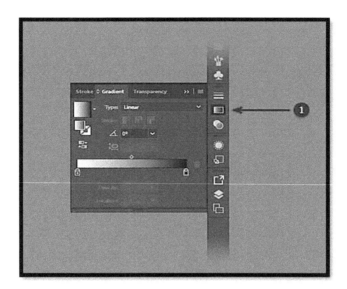

Step 2

When you initially click on the Gradient panel, a white and black gradient will be selected. If you don't want to change it, the previous gradient you used will be applied. Before you can apply a gradient to an object, you need to click on it to choose it. After that, in the **Gradient panel,** find and click the **Gradient Box or Gradient Bar**. The object will be automatically given the gradient. Redesigning the gradient's appearance in the Gradient panel will also alter the object's gradient.

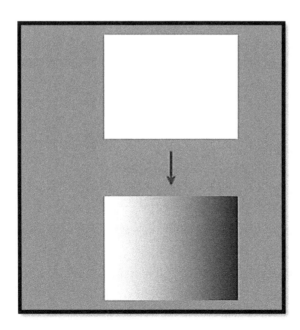

Step 3

To define the gradient colors, **double-click** on one of the color stops under the gradient bar. Selecting a color will be made easier with these options. When you choose a color, it will automatically be applied to the gradient.

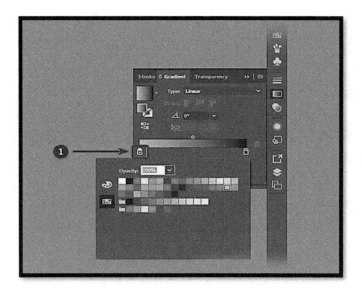

Step 4

Define an ending color by clicking on the color stop on the right of the bar.

Step 5

When you've defined the colors, you can change the beginning and ending points as you want. Because of this, the gradient's appearance and smoothness will be altered. To do this, just click and hold the color stop on the screen until you're satisfied with the outcome.

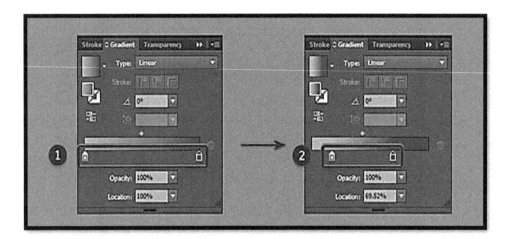

Step 6

The diamond symbol represents the midway, and you can move it to change the gradient's appearance. Where the gradient exhibits a balanced blend of the beginning and ending colors occurs at this point. Just move the diamond to the left or right to do this.

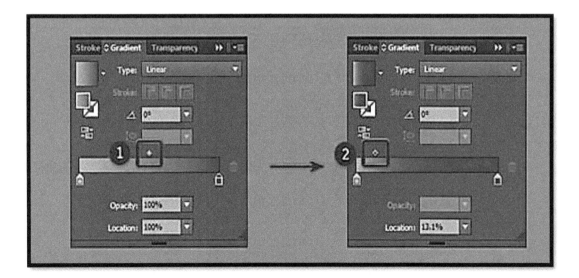

Step 7

You can also customize your gradient by adding more colors. To add a new color stop, click underneath the gradient bar. Just as before, choose a color and then click and drag the mouse to set the color stop. To make more color stops, just repeat the previous step.

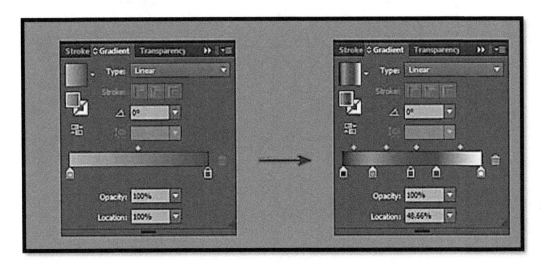

Step 8

Pick out the color stop you want to delete, then either click and drag it to the bottom of the screen or use the **Delete Stop** option.

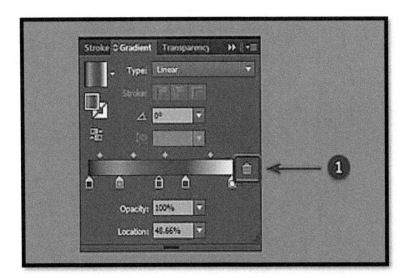

Step 9

Alternatively, you can input a value or choose one from the **Angle Dropbox** to change the gradient's angle. Once you have an object chosen, the angle will be applied automatically.

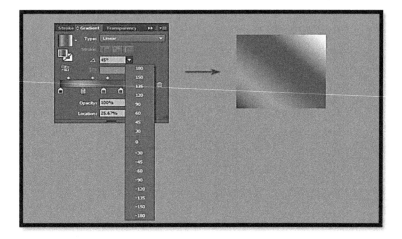

Step 10

Simply click on the color stop you want to change the opacity of, and then utilize the **Opacity Drop Down** menu that appears underneath the Gradient Bar. On the panel, you should see an **Opacity** slider; alternatively, you can enter a value into the box. When a color's opacity is less than 100%, a checkered pattern is shown.

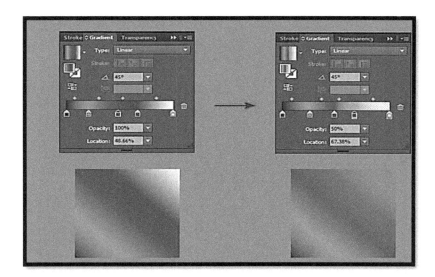

Step 11

Alternatively, you can choose the **Gradient Type** from the menu that appears at the top of the **Gradient** panel.

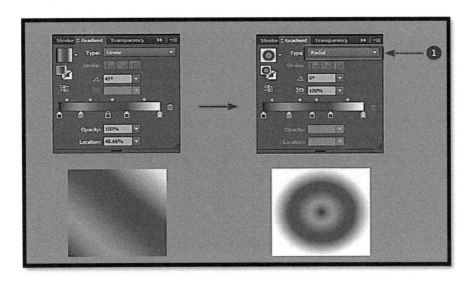

How to Save a Gradient in Illustrator

Step 1

You need to add a gradient you've made to the **Swatches** in Illustrator before you can save it. Launch the **Swatches** panel (**Window > Swatches**) to do this.

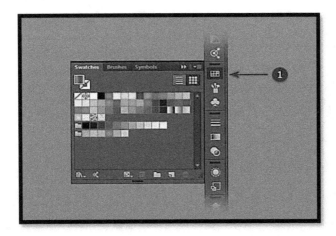

Step 2

The second step to save a gradient in Illustrator is quite straightforward. Press the **New Swatch** button while keeping the gradient chosen.

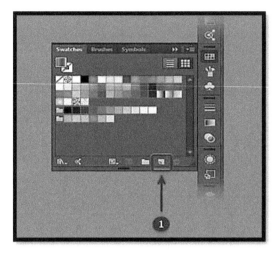

Step 3

Now let's move on to another Illustrator example that shows how to save gradients. After giving the swatch a name in the pop-up box, click **OK**. The gradient you just made will be applied to a new swatch. Additionally, the **Gradient** panel's gradient fill box can be dragged and dropped into the **Swatches** panel. I have given the new gradient the name "**Dark Bronze**" as an example. Every new swatch you create will appear at the end of the list.

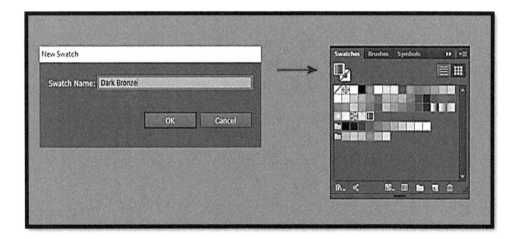

Step 4

Click the library button on the bottom left and choose **Save Swatches** to save the swatch library. Enter a filename and hit the "**Save**" button. You can change the default location for Illustrator's swatch library, but this will store your existing library anywhere you choose. This concludes the process of saving gradients in Illustrator.

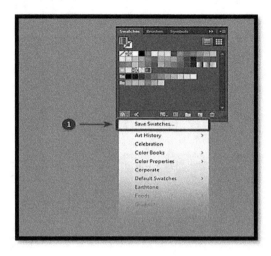

How to Load a Gradient in Illustrator

Step 1

A variety of gradients are available in Illustrator's presets, which can be accessed using the Gradient or Swatches panels. Even your custom gradients will be accessible in the Swatches panel. Navigate to **Window > Swatches** to open the **Swatches** panel.

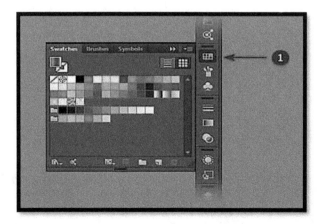

Step 2

Locate the library button on the bottom left and click on it. When you do this, all the available swatches will be shown. You can find a large variety of predefined gradients, including metals, seasons, sky, water, and earth tones, under the **Gradients** menu.

Step 3

To load your Illustrator swatch library, go to the **User Defined** menu and choose the name of the saved file.

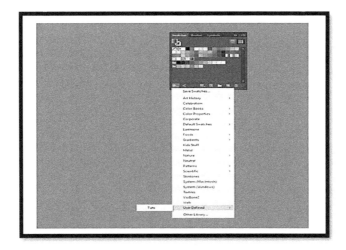

Saving a gradient as a swatch

To make a swatch of the gradient you just made, go over to the Swatches panel. Not only does saving a gradient make it quicker to apply it to subsequent artwork, but it also ensures that all of that artwork has a consistent gradient appearance.

Here are the steps:

1. Get the **Gradient menu** open. Next, click the **Add to Swatches button** at the bottom of the panel that appears after clicking the arrow.

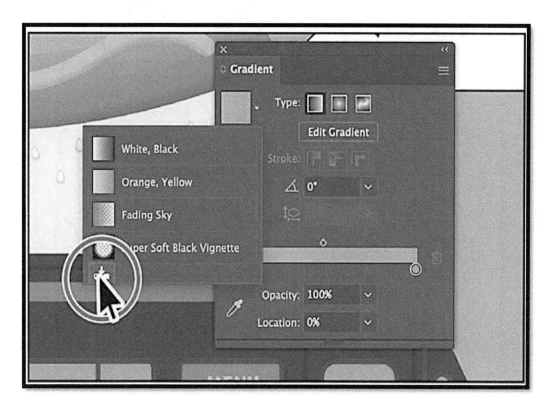

If you want to save a gradient but don't know where to put it, you can choose an object with a gradient fill or stroke, go to the **Swatches** panel, click the **Fill or Stroke** boxes, and finally, click the **New Swatch button** at the bottom of the panel. Doing so will create a new swatch with the gradient saved.

2. You can close the Gradient panel by clicking the **X** located at the top of the panel.
3. Select the background rectangle and then click the Fill box in the Properties tab. When the Swatches option is selected, opening **the Swatch Options dialog box** can be accomplished by double-clicking the **"New Gradient Swatch 1" thumbnail.**
4. Type "**Background**" into the "**Swatch Name**" field of the Swatch Options dialog box, and then hit the **OK** button.

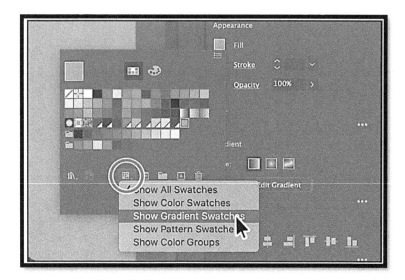

5. Click the **Show Swatch Kinds Menu button** at the bottom of the Swatches panel to bring up a menu. From there, choose **Show Gradient Swatches** to display only gradient swatches in the Swatches panel. In the Swatches panel, you can sort colors into different groups, such as gradient swatches.

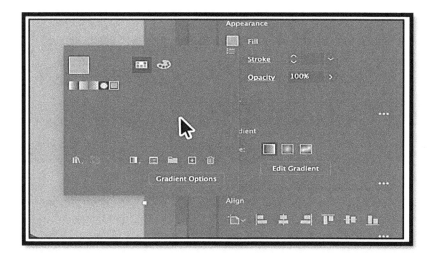

6. In the Swatches panel, choose the gradients you want to use as the shape's fill while the shape is still chosen on the artboard. After that, fill the shape with those gradients.
7. To ensure that the gradient is applied, go to the Swatches panel and click on the gradient that says "**Background**." The gradient you just saved is this one.
8. Select the **Show Swatch Kinds Menu** option at the bottom of the Swatches panel. Next, choose "**Show All Swatches**" from the pop-up menu.
9. Select the shape before going to the **File menu** and choosing **Save**.

The New Generative Shape Fill (Beta)

You can fill shapes with color and detail in your manner with Generative Shape Fill, which is powered by Adobe Firefly. Choosing a shape is as easy as describing the fill you want and adjusting the necessary creative settings. Illustrator quickly creates some variants for you to examine. Pick the one that works best with your artwork once you've tried them all. The variations are neatly organized in groups, making it easy for you to make additional modifications.

Fill a shape with vector graphics

1. To fill a shape with vector graphics, use the **Selection** tool.

Open and closed paths, basic shapes, grouped objects, and compound paths are all shapes that you can apply. Multiple shapes can be selected as well.

2. Select **Gen Shape Fill** in the **Contextual Task Bar** that appears.

From the **Properties** panel's **Quick Actions** section, the shape's context menu (when you right-click it), or the **Object** menu, you can also access **Gen Shape Fill**.

3. Describe the fill you're seeking in the prompt field. Prompt recommendations assist you in providing additional depth as you write.

Although it is not required, the fill will be determined solely by the shape's contour if the prompt is not provided.

Choose **View all settings**, and then turn off **Suggestions**, to disable prompt suggestions.

4. Adjust the **Shape strength and detail** settings as necessary:

Shape Strength: You can change the fill's required proximity to the shape's outline by using the **Shape Strength slider.** The fill will completely cover the outline when set to **High**. The fill's contours will resemble real-life objects when set to **Low**, however, they won't always perfectly match the outline.

Detail: You can adjust the fill's degree of detail by using the detail slider.

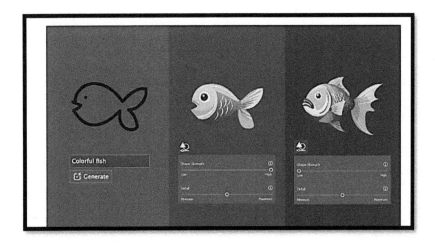

5. **As required, make use of the Style Reference options:**

Style reference: To have the fill style reflect the surrounding objects' style (vector or image), leave **Auto** enabled in the style reference. This applies to the chosen shape as well. **Choose asset or Replace asset** will allow you to choose a style from an individual object in your artwork. A lasso or selection of the object may be drawn next.

Effects: Apply a preset effect or effects from the effects menu. To erase the effects, choose **Clear All.**

To eliminate the reference to the style and its effects, click Clear all next to Styles.

6. After that, choose **View all settings** ⚙. Then, in the **Gen Shape Fill** dialog box that appears, you can adjust the fill colors by selecting Color and Tone.

Color Presets: Apply a color preset.

No. of colors: Either leave it at **Auto** or enter the desired amount of fill colors.

Specify Colors: Specify up to 12 colors. Pick a color to modify or delete, and then use the pop-up menu to make the necessary adjustments. To erase the chosen colors, click the **Clear all** button next to **Specify Colors**.

For a complete removal of all color and tone settings, click **Clear all** at the **Color and Tone** panel top. Similarly, in the **Gen Shape Fill** dialog, click **Clear All** to remove all settings.

7. When prompted, choose **Generate** in the **Gen Shape Fill** dialog box. In the **Properties** panel, you may see several fill options. A generated object, denoted by ✶ on its bounding box, fills the shape on the canvas with the initial variant automatically. No matter what you do with the fill, the shape will stay on the canvas. In the **Layers** panel, you may also create a **Generative Object** layer.

8. To choose the version that works best with your artwork, utilize the arrows in the **Contextual Task Bar** to evaluate the options.

Manage the generated variations

In the **Properties** panel, you can handle generated objects contextually by selecting one from the canvas. Its connected variations, or the group of variations from which you picked one, will display in the **Variations** section. Under the **Generated Variations panel (Window > Generated Variations)**, you can centrally manage all the variants that are created in your document using Generative Shape Fill and Text to Vector Graphic. Nothing happens in the **Generated Variations** panel when you remove a generated object from the canvas or its associated variants from the **Properties** panel. Conversely, a variation cannot be used as a connected variation for the canvas object after its deletion from the **Generated Variations** panel. By using **Ctrl + Z or Cmd + Z**, you can always undo the deletions. Variations created using Generative Shape Fill do not have the option to use Generate Similar.

Repeat shape fill generation

An object that has been generated using Generative Shape Fill can be subjected to the Generative Shape Fill process. The new output will preserve the shape's contour until you ungroup the object. Suppose you generate fill-1 on a shape with **Shape Strength** set to **Loose**. Then, you generate fill-2 on fill-1 with **Shape Strength** set to **Tight**. Fill-2 will match the outline of the original shape, not that of fill-1. If you want the output to match the outline of fill-1, you need to ungroup fill-1, and then generate.

Manage linked variations

Any linked variations in a generated object will be lost when you ungroup it. Any linked variations in an object that was generated using Generative Shape Fill are passed on to the new object when you use Generative Shape Fill on that object. A created object's linked variants are passed down to any copies made of that object. Both instances of a linked variant will remain unaffected if one is deleted. Provide feedback on your output. **To access further options, just hover over a variant, click on "More options ●●●," and then choose:**
- **Good result** or **Poor result**: Rate its quality
- **Report variation**: Report it if it's harmful, illegal, or offensive

Working with Patterns

This definition of pattern has evolved to include: "any regularly repeated arrangement, especially a design made from repeated lines, shapes, or colors on a surface." A pattern, from a design aspect, is made up of overlapping tiles of repeated artwork to form a continuous whole. Having said that, patterns have become ubiquitous across many sectors and an integral part of our everyday lives, piquing the curiosity of many about their creation.

What Makes a Good Illustrator Pattern?

To make a graphic pattern "work," you need to take a few things into account.

Make It Seamless

The secret to a well-designed graphic pattern is to have the transitions between the repeated tiles blend into one another without noticeable seams or breaks.

In most cases, this is accomplished by making sure that your repeated parts are uniformly spread around the tile's boundaries. To avoid seeing white spaces between tiles while working with a backdrop color, you must ensure that they are "glued" to one other.

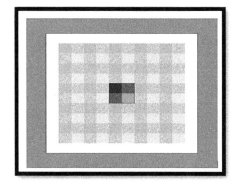

This shouldn't be too much of an issue if you're only trying to create a basic pattern. However, you may need to reconsider the placement of some of your compositional shapes or components if you're working on something somewhat more intricate.

The overlapping of the artwork's composing shapes or pieces is another detail to watch out for; this will be more noticeable when the tiles are placed close to each other, so you don't want any design irregularities brought about by incorrect shape overlapping. So long as you're making extensive use of Illustrator's **Pattern Options** panel while designing your patterns, this shouldn't be an issue. When positioning an element along one edge, be careful to place a copy onto the opposing edge if you prefer to work by hand. Keep the same distance and trajectory from the boundaries of your reference surface and the original shape.

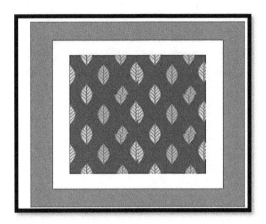

If you're going for a harmonic composition, **color** is another factor to think about. You wouldn't want a shape that has one hue on one side and a different value on the other.

This is unlikely to occur if you offset the tiles using the **Pattern Options** panel, but if you prefer a more hands-on approach and place each repeating element on a clipping mask, be sure to review your graphics pattern well before proceeding.

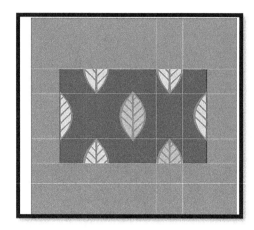

Be that as it may, there will be instances when the **Pattern Options** tool in Illustrator just cannot generate the precise pattern design you have in mind. As a result, be on the lookout for any unusual behavior when that occurs.

Strive for Balance

You need to pause after you've verified that your Illustrator pattern satisfies the first criterion. You can tell whether your design requires tweaking by carefully examining the composition's balance. **There are three factors to think about when you want to create a balanced pattern in Illustrator:**

    1. **Size**

For them to live together and avoid creating the impression that they are fighting for attention, each component's shape or element should be designed for its neighbors. To rephrase, it's not a good idea to make one element small and then place it next to a large one; this will cause the viewer's eyes to focus on the large element and ignore the little one.

When repeating the tile, you should aim for a clear, legible pattern, thus it's important to spread out pieces of varying sizes in a natural manner.

2. **Color**

Always use complementary colors while you're working on the primary recurring tile of your Illustrator patterns. To avoid having two or more colors that are too similar, it's important to appropriately spread out your colors.

3. **Layout**

Are you confused about how to create a logical pattern in Illustrator? Try out a few alternative arrangements before you settle on the perfect place for each of your ornamental shapes and components. Just as with colors, it's best to avoid stacking identical shapes or parts too closely together lest an unnatural pattern emerge in the final product.

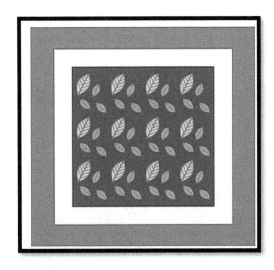

How to Access the Default Adobe Illustrator Patterns

After going over the basics of patterns, let's take a closer look at the pattern designs in Illustrator and see how I can put them to use. By navigating to the **Swatch Libraries** menu in Illustrator's **Swatches** panel, you can access the program's built-in collection of attractive patterns.

A new dropdown menu will appear, towards the bottom of which you'll find a category called **Patterns**, which itself is divided into three subcategories.

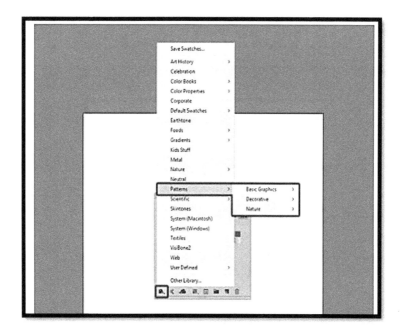

To see all of the Illustrator pattern swatches, a new swatch library window will pop up as soon as you choose a subcategory.

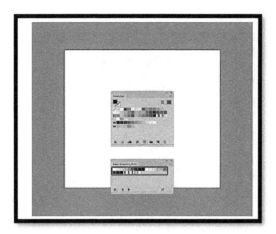

How to Use the Default Adobe Illustrator Patterns

Illustrator comes with a variety of background patterns to choose from. To use one, just click on the pattern design you want. It will be added to your **Fill** instantly. After that, take the **Rectangle Tool (M)** and make a new shape using the click-and-drag or the more accurate window prompt approach. Illustrator automatically adds patterns to the **Swatches** panel of active documents whenever you use them, as you can see above. Put it there so you can find it easily and utilize it when you need to.

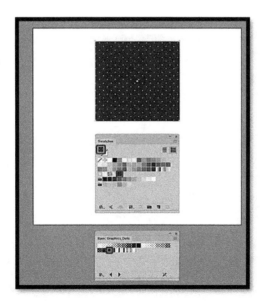

Quick tip: you can use any of Illustrator's geometric shapes to create patterns, depending on your goals. To start from scratch, you can use the **Pen Tool (P)** to make a new one. Then you can add the pattern design to it.

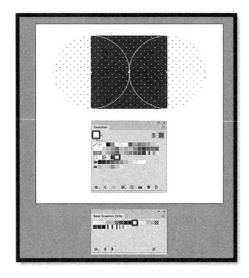

How to Apply Illustrator Patterns to an Existing Shape

At this point, we've shown how simple it is to make a patterned shape using the shape tools, but what if you want to apply the same pattern to an already-made shape? By the way, the procedure is the same; you can use the pattern on any preexisting shape by picking it out and then assigning the desired pattern as its **Fill**, just like any other swatch.

How to Apply Illustrator Patterns to Text

Would you want to apply an Illustrator pattern to some text? Are you ready for this? The truth is that you can, and doing so is a breeze. Start by making a text segment using the **Type Tool (T)**. Then, just choose the pattern you want to use as its **Fill**.

How to Use the Illustrator Pattern Options Panel

Everyone has been learning about Illustrator patterns and has seen them in action up to this point. But what if we'd rather figure out how to use Illustrator to create patterns independently? Well, let's spend a few minutes learning how to use Illustrator's pattern tool before I get into it. You can find Illustrator's pattern-building tool, in the form of the **Pattern Options** panel, which can be accessed by heading over to **Window > Pattern Options**. Choosing the artwork to convert into an Illustrator pattern is the first step in using the panel's many features since it is dormant by default. Now that we know what the Illustrator pattern tool is, let's go on to using it.

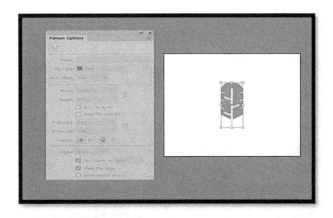

Now that we have our artwork chosen, we can easily make a pattern in Illustrator. Simply enter the panel's advanced menu and click on **Make Pattern.**

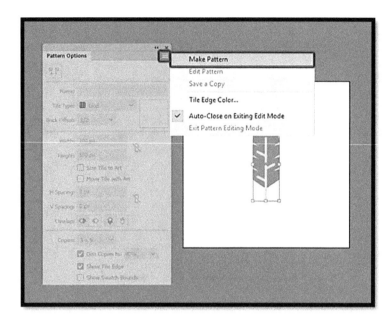

The program will launch **Editing Mode** and make all of the panel's features available the second I click the option. After I switch to this mode, the original artwork tile will keep its full **Opacity** while the duplicates around it are reduced to **40%.**

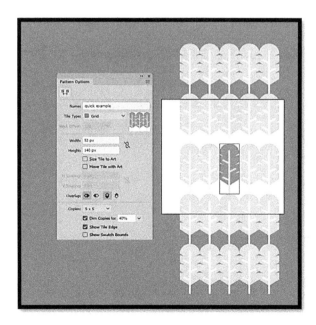

A quick tip: you can get the same effect without always having to have the **Pattern Options** panel displayed. Select the shape, then go to **Object > Pattern** and tap **Make**. This will put you into the pattern **editing mode**.

Tile Type

When you create a new pattern, the first choice you'll notice is **Tile Type**. This determines the arrangement of the tiles that make up your pattern and is affected by the shape of the tiles itself. Tiles are like the big canvas on which you'll be laying your artwork. You can choose from five different tile layouts based on your pattern design.

Grid: The artwork tile takes on a rectangular shape due to the grid structure, which guarantees that the centers of neighboring tiles are aligned with each other horizontally and vertically.

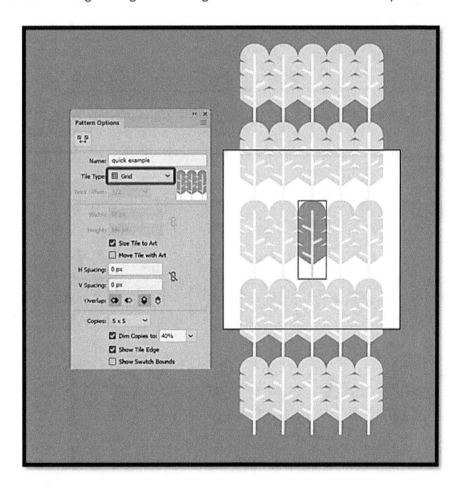

Brick by Row: The tiles are put in rows with their rectangular shapes, with the centers of each row aligned horizontally and the centers of alternating columns vertically.

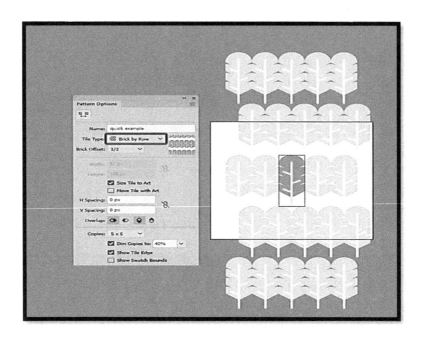

Brick by Column: In the brick-by-column layout, the tiles are organized in columns with their centers vertically aligned and their edges aligned horizontally. The tiles are shaped like rectangles and are arranged in this way.

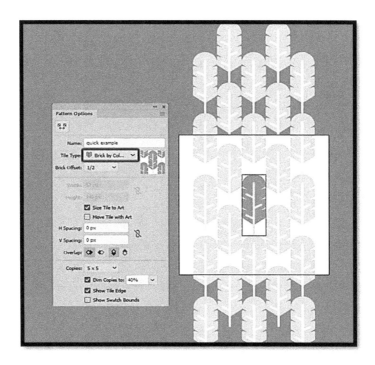

Hex by Column: The tiles are put in columns with their centers vertically aligned and ones with opposite columns with their centers horizontally aligned; this arrangement is called "hex by column." The tiles are shaped like hexagons and are stored in columns.

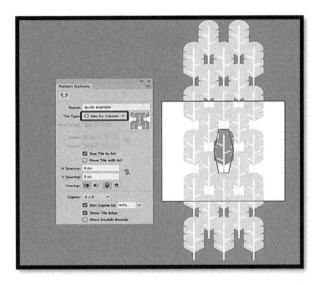

Hex by Row: In Hex by Row, each row of tiles is considered to be hexagonal, and the centers of each row are aligned horizontally; in alternating rows, the centers are aligned vertically.

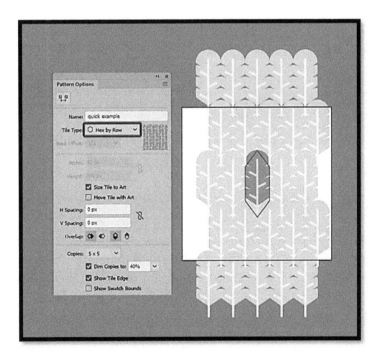

The Pattern Tile Tool

You can change the shape of the basic **Tile Types** by using the **Pattern Tile Tool**, which is located in the top left corner of the panel. It will bring up a bounding box around the tile's real shape. Then, by clicking and dragging the composing boundary points in any direction, you can change its size and shape.

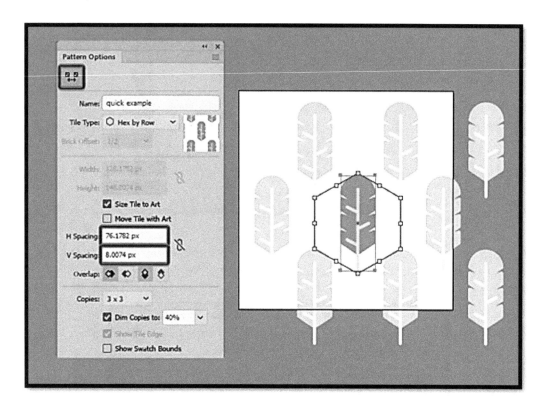

A quick tip: As you can see, this option will always produce decimal numerical values, thus it may not be the best choice if you want your shapes to be pixel-perfect.

Brick Offset

Brick Offset is an additional subsetting that, as its name implies, allows you to offset your tiles. You may have seen this if you've swiftly experimented with the various Tile Type choices, particularly the "Brick by" ones. The amount by which the centers of tiles in neighboring rows are not vertically aligned can be adjusted while working with the **Brick by Row** tile type, as stated by Adobe. You can pick from eight different values, each of which will have a unique effect, with **1/2** being the default.

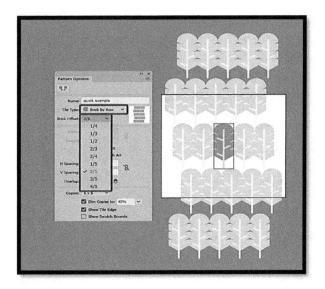

If you want to know how much space there is between the tile centers of neighboring columns, you can use the **Brick by Column** option to find out.

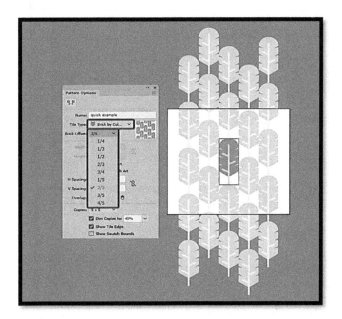

Width and Height

Following that, I have **Width** and/or **Height**, which provide us control over the tile's total dimensions. The program will create more space between the tiles if I make them larger than the artwork, thus the spacing between them will be greater; conversely, if I make the tiles smaller than our artwork, the neighboring tiles will overlap; and so on. Since neither the backdrop nor the clipped ornamental components will link properly thereafter, this would break the pattern in the case of seamless repeating patterns, particularly those that employ a background. There is a better way to do this, as we will see in a minute, but if I was to utilize the settings on the current feather example, I could make the tiles bigger to increase the gap between the artwork.

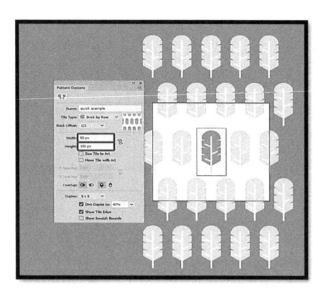

Size Tile to Art

Every time you start making a repeat pattern in Illustrator, you'll see that if you resize one of your tile's composing artwork, the software will begin to overlap the adjacent tiles. This is because the tile itself has kept the same **Width** and **Height** values.

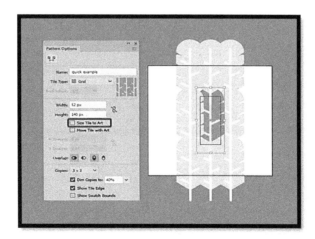

Simply turning on the **Size Tile to Art** option will solve this problem and eliminate the overlapping right away. **Quick tip:** I've found that this choice isn't always functional, so you may need to rearrange your artwork before selecting it again.

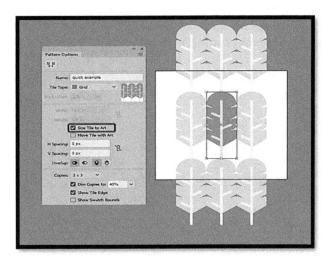

You can resize the design as whole or individual shapes in your artwork with this option selected, and the pattern will automatically adjust each time.

Move Tile with Art

When you make changes to the artwork's position while making the pattern, the tile will also move to reflect those changes. This saves you the trouble of having to use the **Size Tile to Art** tool after the fact to put the tile back where it belongs.

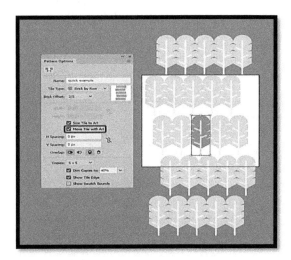

H Spacing and V Spacing

I said before that expanding the tile's **width** and/or **height** isn't the best way to increase space between the artwork in our pattern, therefore I should look into other options. Here you'll find **H Spacing** and **V Spacing**, which let you adjust the distance between adjacent tiles. To create a more harmonious pattern, you can see it as inserting a padding zone that allows you to spread out your artwork. You need to activate the **Size Tile to Art** feature for the choices to become available; by default, they are grayed off. You can see that by modifying the **H** and/or **V Spacing** of the tile, a more balanced design can be achieved in the feather example that was used to demonstrate the different **Tile Type** options.

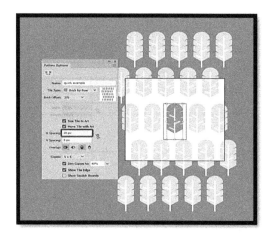

Because it doesn't clip, you can use any number greater than 0 without worrying that it would overlap your artwork, which is why this approach is preferable to altering the tile's **width** and/or **height**. Improperly adding the padding value to the existing tile value(s) while using the **Width** and/or **Height** technique can cause your artwork to be overlapped.

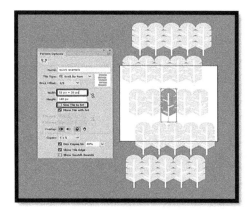

Overlap

The second choice is related to overlapping tiles; it enables us to choose which tiles are shown first when neighboring tiles overlap, so I can flip any pattern upside down. The **Pattern Options** panel gives you a simple method to adjust the default values; however, I have never needed to do so since I seldom use overlapping tile patterns. By setting the **Overlap** to **Right in Front** from **Left in Front** and then providing a negative **H Spacing** value, you can manage the horizontal overlapping of your tiles.

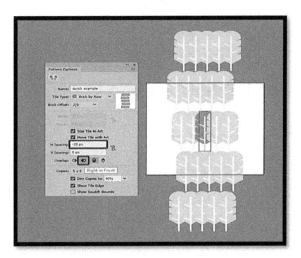

Similarly, you can achieve a similar effect with the vertical overlapping of your tiles by setting the **Overlap** from **Top in Front** to **Bottom in Front** and putting a negative number in the **V-spacing** input box.

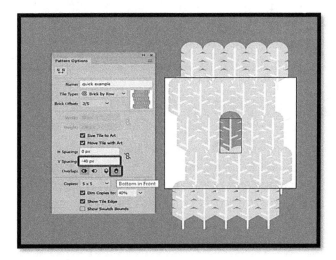

Copies

Following that, I have **Copies**, which is like a preview mode for patterns; it allows you to adjust the amount of horizontal and vertical tiles that are displayed as you create or revise a pattern. Changing the values will not change the pattern itself, so you can choose a greater or lower tile count as needed for your intricate design. Using only odd numbers ensures that your original tile design will always take center stage in your copies, as you can see.

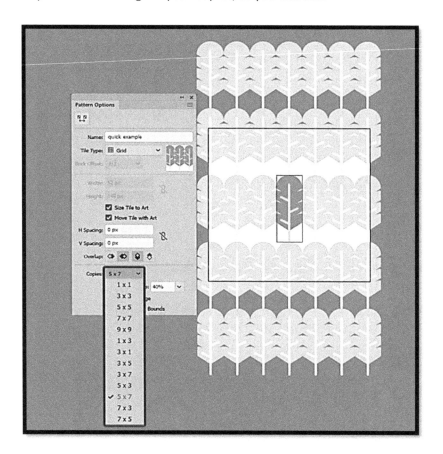

Dim Copies To

In the **Dim Copies to** input field, you can change the **Opacity** level of the copies. You can use one of the predefined values or enter a custom one. The intensity of the copying will determine how well you can see your original artwork tile as you create and refine the pattern. You can always deselect it entirely if you choose. You can choose any value that suits your requirements since this will just influence the Illustrator preview of the patterns and will not affect the final design.

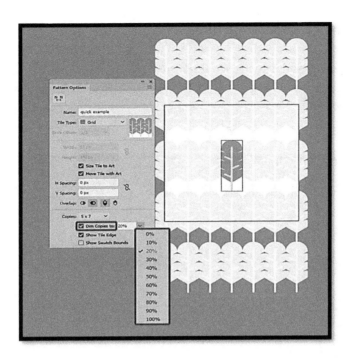

Show Tile Edge

If you want to see how your pattern will appear without any unwanted distractions, you can use the **Show Tile Edge** option in conjunction with the unchecked **Dim Copies to one** to disable the box around your artwork tile and see how it will look. This function might save you a lot of time compared to repeatedly entering and exiting the pattern **editing mode**.

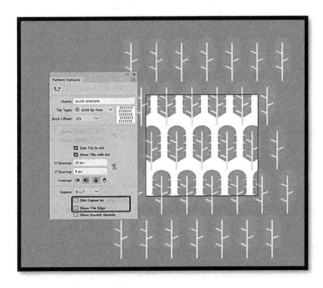

Show Swatch Bounds

As a last choice, I have the **Show Swatch Bounds**, which, as its name implies, will show a unit piece of the artwork that is repeated to get the pattern design. If you're new to creating patterns, this option could help you grasp how the repeating process works by showing you precisely where your shapes should be for a smooth tile transition.

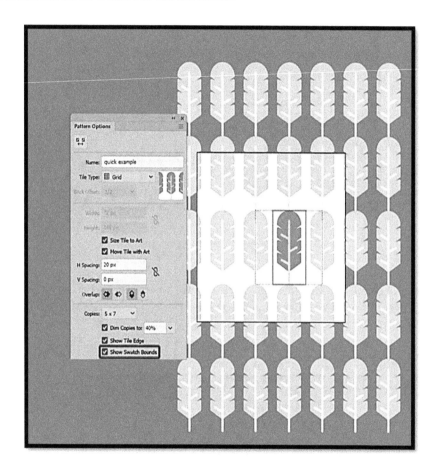

How to Make a Pattern in Adobe Illustrator

Although the provided Illustrator patterns aren't terrible, you'll likely encounter a requirement to make your pattern in Illustrator at some point. So, if you're currently in that position, let's dive into Illustrator pattern design. I'm going to presume that you've already made the repeating tiles artwork; if so, I can use it to make the pattern swatch. In this case, I'll be using a wave pattern I made earlier; it's completely perpendicular to the Artboard's perimeter, as you can see, so the change will look great in any orientation.

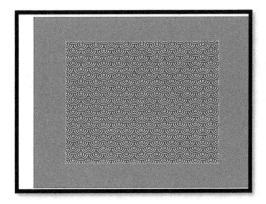

Step 1

To begin, choose a tile. Then, open up the **Pattern Options** panel by going to **Object > Pattern** and hitting **Make**.

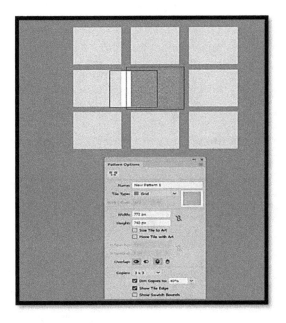

Step 2

As you can see, Illustrator will show us a preview of the repeating pattern tiles, but it will space them out since I haven't told it their **width** and **height**, which makes the whole thing seem a little disorganized. First, I'll use the **Align** panel to make sure our original tile is centered on the Artboard. Then, I can rapidly repair it by using the **Size Tile to Art** option.

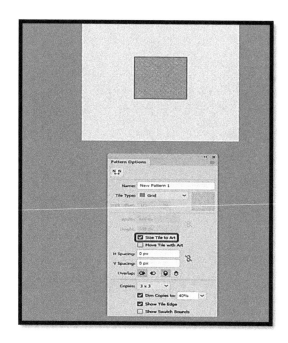

Step 3

Now that I have a better preview, I can start fine-tuning our pattern. To accomplish this, I will first give it a custom name.

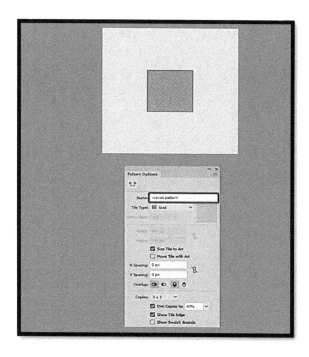

Step 4

Choosing a **Tile Type** is the next step in creating our pattern. For my particular scenario, I've decided to utilize **Grid** as my wave pattern design is square and incorporates a background. I want the program to replicate it horizontally and vertically to achieve that smooth transition.

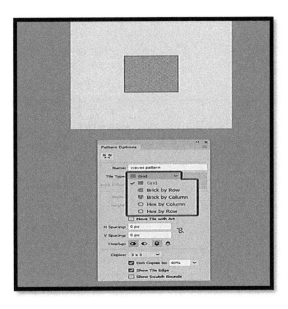

Step 5

To ensure that my tiles exactly fit with each other's edges, I will leave the **H Spacing** and **V Spacing** choices alone as I am utilizing a square design for my artwork's tiles. Now that I've taken care of it, selecting **Done** will add my seamless Illustrator pattern as a separate pattern swatch to the **Swatches** panel.

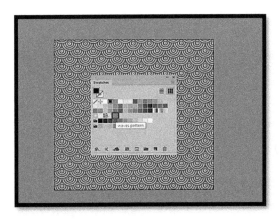

How to Edit an Existing Illustrator Pattern

Making changes to a pattern design is rather easy, whether you're using an Illustrator-built pattern or have your custom-made one.

Step 1

After launching the **Swatches** panel, double-clicking on a pattern swatch will open the **Pattern Options** panel.

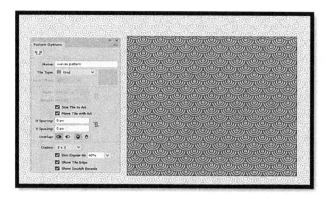

Step 2

You can see that this functions like an **Isolation or Pattern Editing** mode; here you can make any change to your design, like changing the size of your composing shapes, changing their color, or adding new shapes and elements; these changes will be reflected in the copies of the repeating tiles right away. When you're through making adjustments to your Illustrator pattern, press the **Done** button.

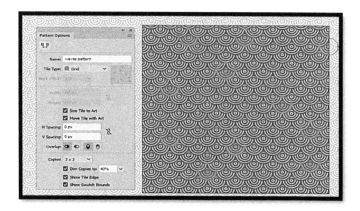

How to Scale an Illustrator Pattern Fill

What if, after applying a pattern to a shape, we wanted to change its size? We've covered the basics of pattern creation and learned how to construct repeating patterns in Illustrator. Because the shape will keep its original proportions when you attempt to adjust it using the click-and-drag approach, resizing an applied pattern can be a real pain. So, how do we go about scaling an existing Illustrator pattern fill? To apply the pattern to a shape, first choose it. Then, **right-click** and choose **Transform > Scale.** This will open the **Scale** panel.

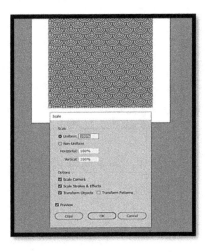

Once the panel appears, you can easily scale your shape using the **Uniform** or **Non-Uniform** techniques by entering a specific percentage. After that, just make sure the Transform Patterns option is selected. After you click **OK**, the pattern should automatically adjust its size to fit the shape you've applied it to.

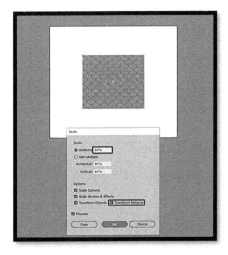

How to Rotate a Pattern in Illustrator

Just now I covered scaling patterns in Adobe Illustrator; but, what about when I need to rotate them? It's not that hard; when you've applied the pattern to a shape, you only need to **right-click** on it and choose **Transform > Rotate**. Before you can enter a custom value in the **Angle** input box, toggle the **Transform Patterns** option. When you click **OK**, both your pattern and the shape it was applied to will become subject to the rotation process.

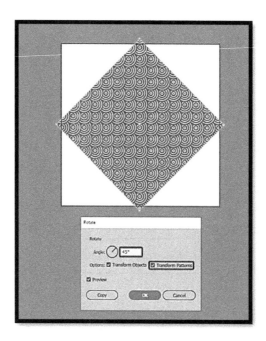

Text to Pattern Feature and Customization

Create one-of-a-kind vector patterns to enhance your artwork effortlessly with Text to Pattern, powered by Adobe Firefly. To create a pattern, just describe it briefly and provide the necessary creative controls. Illustrator can swiftly produce a variety of pattern variants for you to experiment with. Simply add the one that you think would work best for your design requirements as a swatch and make changes whenever you want.

Generate and apply a pattern

1. If you want to apply the pattern to an object on the canvas, make use of the **Selection** tool. Next, go to the toolbar and choose **Fill or Stroke** ⬚.
2. Navigate to **Object > Pattern > Generate Patterns**. The **Generate Patterns** window opens.

You can also access **Text to Pattern** ⠿ from **Fill** or **Stroke** in the **Properties** or **Control** panel, or from **Window > Generate Patterns.**

3. Please specify the desired output in the **Prompt** area. **Choose from a sample prompt** if you need ideas or aren't sure how to create your own.

4. Use the options in **Add colors or choose from color presets** as needed:

Color presets: Apply a color preset.

No. of colors: Leave it at **Auto** or enter the desired number of colors for the output for the "No. of colors" field.

Specify Colors: Specify up to 12 colors. Pick a color to modify or delete, and then use the pop-up menu to make the necessary adjustments. To erase the chosen colors, click the **Clear All** button next to **Specify Colors**.

To remove your color settings, go to the **Color & Tone** menu and choose **Clear All.**

5. Choose "**Add effects to your creation** ▦" and, if necessary, apply an **Effect** from the preset.

6. To modify the density of the pattern, choose **View all settings** and then drag the **Density** slider.

7. Tap on **Generate**. The **Generate Patterns** panel displays pattern variants. It applies the first variant automatically to the object.

8. Experiment with the different goals until you find the one that works best for your design needs.

Every preview is saved as a pattern swatch in the **Generated Patterns** folder in the **Swatches** panel **(Window > Swatches)** so you can utilize them later. Just like any other pattern swatch, you can utilize them as well.

Edit a pattern variation

To launch the **Pattern Options** panel, double-click the pattern swatch you want to edit in the **Swatches** panel **(Window > Swatches).** From there, you can change the **width, height**, and **copies** of the pattern. **Brick Offset** and **Tile Type** cannot be changed for a pattern that has already been generated. If you choose a variant in the **Generate Patterns** panel and then go to **Edit Pattern**, the matching swatch will still be updated. There has been no modification to the variation in the **Generate Patterns** panel.

Manage pattern variations and swatches

From the **Generate Patterns** panel, you can see and control all of the document's created pattern variants. In the **Generated Variations** panel, you cannot see them. You can remove one swatch of a pattern variant without removing the other swatch. The deletion of a variant cannot be undone, but a swatch can be undone. The canvas's applied pattern is unchanged in both instances. Both the variation and the swatch will be impacted if you remove an applied pattern from the canvas. None of the canvas-applied patterns have linked variants, unlike the objects produced by Text to

135

Vector Graphic and Generative Shape Fill. Text to Pattern variants also does not include **Generate Similar** functionality.

Provide feedback on your output

A variant can be rated by hovering over it, selecting More options, and then choosing **Good Result** or **Poor Result.**

Frequently asked questions

Who can access Text to Pattern in Illustrator?

The Illustrator app includes Text to Pattern, which is accessible in all regions where Adobe offers services (except mainland China). It is commercially safe because of its design.

Is Text to Pattern in Illustrator a part of users' existing subscription or do they have to pay an additional fee for this capability?

As part of their licensing, Illustrator users can utilize the app's Text to Pattern feature and earn generative credits for processing generative AI material more quickly.

Why did you bring Text to Pattern into Illustrator?

Adobe Firefly, a robust generative AI system developed by Adobe, is directly integrated into many Creative Cloud tools, including Illustrator. With the integration of Adobe Firefly, users can now enhance their creative processes and outputs without ever leaving the Illustrator program.

How is Text to Pattern different from other tools in Illustrator?

Adobe Firefly powers the generative AI capabilities known as Text to Pattern. In contrast to Illustrator's other features, this one lets you build editable vector patterns from text prompts, which you can then add to your swatch collection.

Will Text to Pattern replace existing tools in Illustrator?

The goal of the generative AI-powered Text to Pattern feature in Illustrator is to augment the current toolset.

What are the system requirements to use Text to Pattern?

Since Text to Pattern is an Illustrator program, it requires the same software as the main Illustrator application.

Do you need to be connected to the Internet to use Text to Pattern?

Yes, you do need an active Internet connection to utilize Text to Pattern.

What regions and languages is Text to Pattern in Illustrator available in?

Except for mainland China, you may access Text to Pattern in the Illustrator app wherever Adobe offers services. It supports more than 100 languages.

What are generative credits and are they applied when using Text to Pattern?

Text to Pattern applies generative credits.

What are Content Credentials and do they apply to Text to Pattern in Illustrator?

When you export your Text to Pattern assets as.jpg,.png, or.svg files, be sure to include Content Credentials, a new kind of tamper-evident metadata. They provide clarity to the past and present of the assets to which they are applied.

Applying Strokes

Select **Window > Stroke** from the menu bar to access the Stroke panel. From there, you can specify a line's solid or dashed status, the dash sequence, and other dash adjustments (if dashed), the stroke weight and alignment, the miter limit, arrowheads, width profiles, and the styles of line joins and line caps.

With Live Paint groups, you can apply different strokes to certain boundaries within an object, or you can apply stroke choices to the whole object. You can choose between the two options.

Apply a stroke color, width, or alignment

1. Verify that the object has been chosen. (Two edges that are part of the same Live Paint group can be selected using the Live Paint Selection tool.)
2. From the toolbar, Color panel, or Control panel, choose the desired stroke type by clicking on the corresponding box. Doing so indicates that you would like to use a stroke over a fill for that particular location.

Select a color from the "**Color**" panel, a swatch from the "**Swatches**" panel, or control from the "**Control**" panel. Alternatively, you can utilize the Color Picker by double-clicking on a color in the Stroke box.

- Choose a weight in the Control or Strokes panels.
- To align the stroke along a closed path, choose an option from the Stroke panel if the object is not a Live Paint group. You have the choice between the following options:
  - *Align Stroke To Center*
  - *Align Stroke To Inside*
  - *Align Stroke To Outside*

Notes:

- The "**Align Stroke to Inside**" option will be used automatically whenever you start a web project in Illustrator 2023. Illustrator used to provide the option to center the stroke as its default behavior in prior versions.

- Probably, the pathways won't line up exactly when you try to align them using different stroke alignments. Make sure the path alignment settings are the same if you want the edges to line up properly when you align them.

Create strokes with variable widths

Using the Width tool on the toolbar, you can create a stroke with a configurable width and then save it as a profile to apply to future strokes. With fewer anchor points, you can now adjust or extend the variable-width strokes in Illustrator thanks to its simplified routes to the strokes. A hollow diamond with handles will show on the path when you hover the mouse over a stroke that was made using the Width tool. The stroke width can be adjusted, the width point can be moved or copied, or the width point can be removed. When dealing with many strokes at once, the Width tool only changes the active stroke. Before you can make any modifications to a stroke, ensure it is the active stroke in the Appearance window. If you hold down the **Width** tool and double-click the **stroke**, a dialog box will appear called Width Point Adjust. Here you can make or change a width point. You may do this by adjusting the width point values. Modifying the currently chosen width point will also affect the adjacent width points if the **Adjust Adjoining Width Points** box is checked. To quickly alter the adjacent width points, double-click a point while holding down the **Shift key,** and the box will be checked. As you adjust the variable width, the Width tool could pick up points of continuous and discontinuous width.

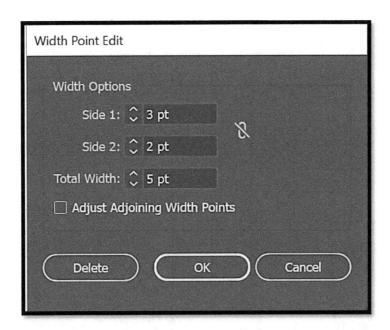

Do this to create a point of discontinuous width:
1. Make two points on a stroke that have different widths.

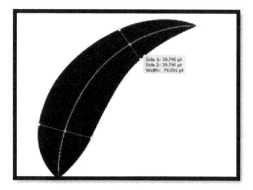

You can create a discontinuous width point for the stroke by dragging two width points onto one other.

The dialog box for editing discontinuous points in Width Point Edit shows the widths on both the left and right sides.

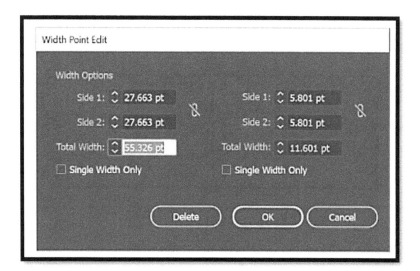

Width tool controls

Do any of the following:

- Drag the handles to the left or right to modify the stroke width at a specific point along the path. Points of width that were generated at corners or direct anchor selections will stay connected to those points throughout the basic path alteration.
- You may move the width point by simply dragging it along the path.
- Select several width points by holding down the **Shift key** and clicking the mouse. The Width Point Edit dialog box will need you to enter values for Side 1 and Side 2 of some points. No matter how you modify the width points, it will reflect on all of the defined points.
- From the Stroke panel's **Weight** drop-down menu, choose the required stroke weight to apply globally to all of the width points.

Fill a Shape with Color

Adobe Illustrator offers a wide variety of fill methods. With a color hex code or by navigating to the Swatches panel in the Properties panel, you can change the color right from the toolbar. As an additional option, you can bring in sample colors and utilize the eyedropper tool. To get a sample color from this picture in two steps, let's fill the triangle using the Eyedropper Tool.

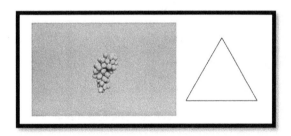

Step 1: First, open Adobe Illustrator and place the picture with the color sample you choose.
Step 2: The second step is to select the triangle and then, using the shortcut I on your keyboard, pick the Eyedropper Tool from the toolbar. The triangle will transform to the color of the selected region when you click on it in the image.

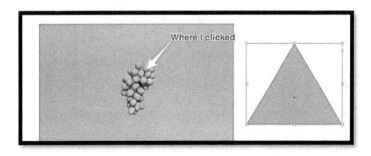

To choose your favorite, you can make a copy of the object and experiment with several samples.

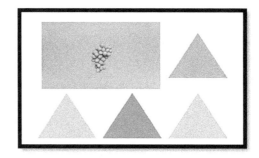

How to Fill a Shape with Pattern in Adobe Illustrator

If you're wondering where the pattern panel is, it's not there. However, the Swatches panel is where you can access the patterns you've saved in the past.

Step 1: Choose the object that you want to fill. For example, let's fill this heart with a pattern.

The **Properties > Appearance** panel will display the appearance attributions of the chosen object.

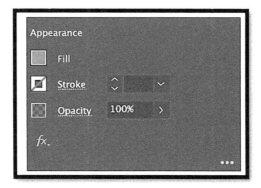

Step 2: The Swatches panel will appear when you click the color box next to **Fill**.

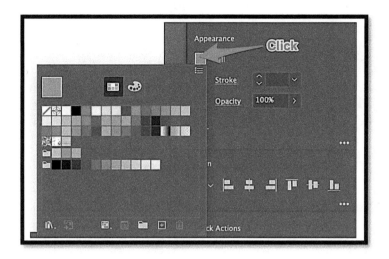

Step 3: Choose the pattern, and the shape will be filled with the pattern.

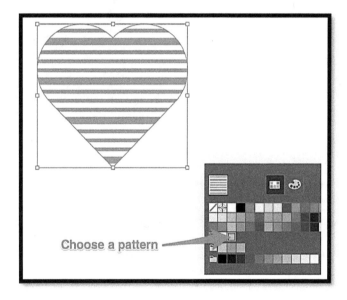

How to Fill a Shape with Image in Adobe Illustrator

The creation of a clipping mask is the only method for filling an object with an image; positioning the object above the mask is also required. Here we can see an example of filling a moon with a glitter image.

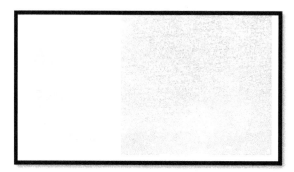

Step 1: Place and embed the image in Adobe Illustrator.

Choose the picture, right-click, and then choose **Arrange > Send Backward** in Illustrator if you already have a shape or object that you want to fill in before you add the image.

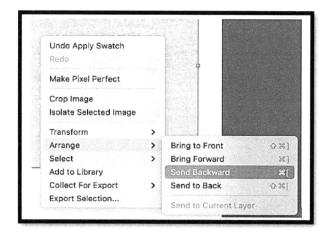

Step 2: Place the object you want to fill the picture with on top of the selected region.

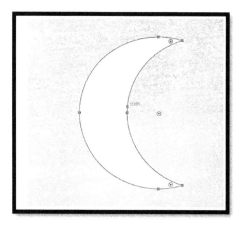

144

Step 3: Choose the picture and the object or shape. Select "**Make Clipping Mask**" from the context menu.

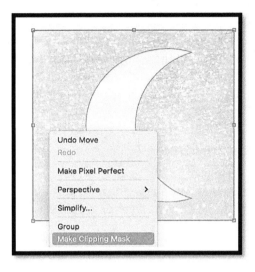

And that's all!

The space underneath the object is used to fill the picture. By doubling-clicking the object, you can reposition the picture underneath if you are unhappy with the chosen region. Outlining the text is an additional step that can be added to the previously mentioned approaches to fill it with color, pattern, or picture. You can alter the text as an object or shape once you've drawn its outline.

Adjusting Transparency and Blending Modes

Change the opacity of content

At the object, group, or layer level, you can change the opacity (the degree to which the content is see-through). Choose the artwork and then modify the Opacity value in the Properties window to alter the content's opacity. **Note:** If you adjust the opacity of a group and then ungroup it, the adjustment will be undone, but the opacity settings of the individual objects inside the group will remain unchanged.

Understand blending modes

With the use of blending modes, you may change how an object's colors mix with those of nearby objects. Any objects underneath the object's layer or group will also be affected by the blending mode when you apply it to the object itself.

Copy and rotate artwork using the rotate tool

1. Once you have the shape chosen, go to the toolbar and choose the rotate tool.
2. The artwork can be automatically rotated by pressing **Option (MacOS) or Alt (Windows)** and clicking anywhere around the bottom center of the shape. This will display the rotate dialog box, where you can specify the rotation point.
3. Set the rotation angle and click **Copy** to make a copy.

Apply a blending mode to the copied shape

1. After you've made your selection, open the Transparency panel by clicking the Opacity option in the Properties panel on the right.
2. The **Blending Mode** option will appear when you click **Normal**. The menu is organized by function, so you can easily find the blending option you're looking for. By default, "**Normal**" does not apply any interactivity between artwork colors. **Darken, Multiply, and Color Burn** are some of the dark blending modes that may be used to get a darker final shade. **Lighten and Screen** are two of the several blending modes that lighten the final product.

Note: Be sure to attempt View > Preview on CPU or View Using CPU if you're having trouble previewing blending modes.

Create more copies of the shape

To make further copies of the circle, just use the Transform Again command in Illustrator to apply the same copy and rotation as before.

- Select the circle again, and then go to Object > Transform > Transform Again. Using the same relative rotation point, Illustrator makes a copy and rotates it. To add enough circles to finish the artwork, choose that command many times.

Apply an opacity change to the artwork

On the artwork, you can alter the opacity and use blending modes.
- Move the cursor over the circles using the Selection tool. You may change the transparency of the chosen artwork by adjusting the Opacity value in the Properties window.

Working with blended objects

By blending two separate objects, you can make new shapes and distribute them uniformly. Any two shapes, same or otherwise, can be blended. You can also mix color blends with objects to make color transitions in the shape of an object, or you can blend between two open paths to make a seamless color transition between objects. **You can build a variety of blended objects, some examples of which are:**

Blend between two of the same shape.

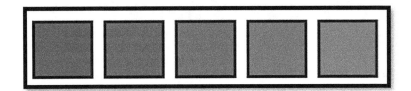

Blend between two of the same shapes, each with a different color fill.

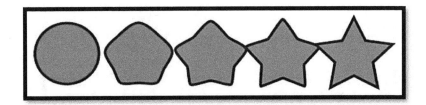

Blend between two different shapes with different fill colors.

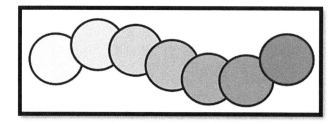

Blend between two of the same shape along a path.

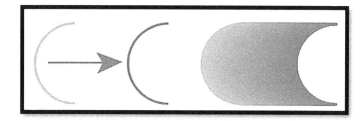

Smooth color blend between two stroked lines (original lines on left blend on right).

When a blend is established, the merged objects are treated as if they were a single entity and given the label "**blend object**." If you move one of the original objects or change its anchor points, the blend will adjust to the new state of the item. To further divide the mixture into its parts, you can also enlarge it.

Creating and editing a smooth color blend

There are many options available when you wish to create a new object by combining the shapes and colors of preexisting objects. By using the **Smooth Color Blend** option in the **Mix Options dialog box**, Illustrator will merge the objects' shapes and colors into many intermediate levels. As you can see in the picture on the right, this causes the original objects to merge in a gradual, seamless fashion.

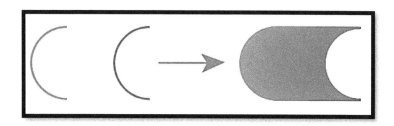

The steps are calculated to provide the optimal number for a seamless color transition when objects are filled or stroked with different colors. Optimal color transition sequences are used to accomplish this. In cases when the objects share colors, gradients, or patterns, the number of steps is determined by finding the maximum distance between the two items' bounding boxes. The sesame seeds on the hot dog were created by fusing two different shapes, as you will see now.

1. Make sure you can see two tear-drop shapes underneath the stars you just blended by either zooming out of the window or panning in with the **Hand tool**. The goal is to make these two shapes seem more three-dimensional by merging them into one.

2. Pick out the smaller shape on the left side of the workspace using the Selection tool. By clicking the larger shape on the right and holding down the Shift key, you can choose both options.
3. Select **Object > Blend > Make**.

If you ever find that making a blend using the Blend tool is too challenging, this other way could be just what you need.

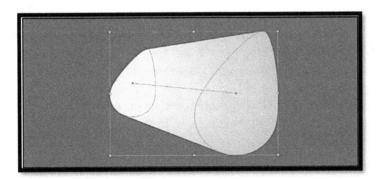

It can be difficult to achieve flawless color transitions across paths in certain cases. If the lines intersect or are excessively curved, for example, an unexpected result might occur.

4. To keep the blend object selected, double-click the Blend tool in the toolbar. Verify that the **Smooth Color** option is chosen from the Spacing menu in the Blend Options dialog box. Choose the **OK** option.

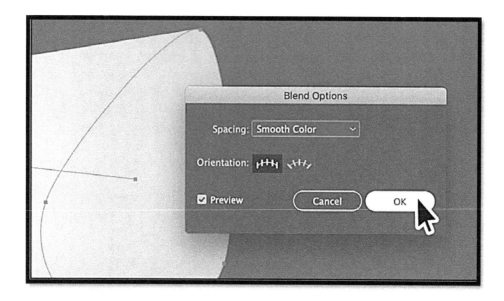

5. **Select > Deselect menu option**. Modifying the pathways that make up the mixture.
6. After you've chosen the Selection tool, double-click anywhere in the color mix to activate the Isolation mode. To choose it, just click on the compact path on the left.
7. When you want to go out of isolation mode, use the **Escape** key.
8. Click the **Select > Deselect menu option**.
9. Pick **View > Fit Artboard in Window** from the main menu to bring the artboard back into view. Once you've blended some artwork off the right side of the artboard, you can zoom out to see it by hitting the Command and — key combination on a macOS keyboard or the Ctrl and — key combination on a Windows keyboard.
10. Choose **Object > Arrange > Bring to Front** to move the star artwork to the front if it's behind other artwork.
11. By dragging with the **Option (macOS) or Alt (Windows) key**, releasing the mouse button, and pressing the key, you can make a copy.
12. To flip the artwork horizontally, go to the Properties tab and find the **Flip Horizontally button.** Click on it.
13. Simply drag the mouse to slowly rotate the stars once you take the cursor off one of the corners and see the arrows that indicate rotation.
14. Arrange the stars the way you choose.
15. Go to the **"File" menu** and choose "**Save**," return to the "**File**" menu and click "**Close**."

CHAPTER 6

WORKING WITH TEXT AND TYPOGRAPHY

Typing Basics in Illustrator

Adobe Illustrator has a powerful collection of tools and options for working with typography and text, allowing users to design high-quality text elements with intricate details. Some text-adding options will appear when you right-click the **Type** tool or the text tool button on the toolbar:

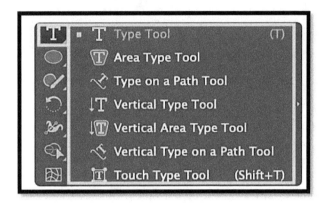

How to Edit Text in Adobe Illustrator

In Adobe Illustrator, you can make edits to pre-existing text by **double-clicking on the text box** or placeholder text. Furthermore, the **Type** tool can be quickly and easily used by simply hitting the **T** key on your keyboard. After that, to update the existing text, click once within the bounding box of the text object or anywhere you want to make changes. You can erase text by using the delete button, or add new text by typing. Adobe Illustrator also has a Character panel, glyphs, and other tools for editing text. You will need to either add new text, import a design template with existing text, or open an Illustrator file with a text-based design before you can alter the text.

Method 1: Add, Delete, Or Change Text

Here you can find an AI text editor that is easy to use for adding, removing, or changing text in your creations. It's the quickest and simplest approach to begin working with text components in Illustrator that you can find.

Step 1: Type Tool

Pressing the **T** symbol on the toolbar will bring up the **Type** tool, which you can use to begin entering basic text into a text box. Alternatively, you might use the **T** keyboard shortcut.

Step 2: Highlight the Text

Now that you have the **Type** tool at your fingertips, just move the mouse to the text box and click once to make any changes you like. The text box will display a thin vertical line that blinks. The term for such is a text cursor.

To add additional text, start typing. To remove words, delete text. On the other hand, if the black arrow-shaped **Selection** tool is already visible, you can use it. When you double-click within a text box, the text cursor will appear so you can make fast edits.

Method 2: Edit Text Styles

Among Illustrator's text style options include the ability to alter fonts, sizes, and weights, as well as modify the typeface itself. You can easily distinguish between headers, body text, and quotations as well as apply basic styles and formatting to both the **Character** and **Paragraph** panels. Here, I'd like to make some changes to the text in my artwork so that it reads better than it does right now.

Follow these steps:

Step 1: Open the Character Panel

To begin, go to **Window > Type > Character** to bring up the **Character** panel. The **Control** panel and the **Properties** panel are other ways to reach it.

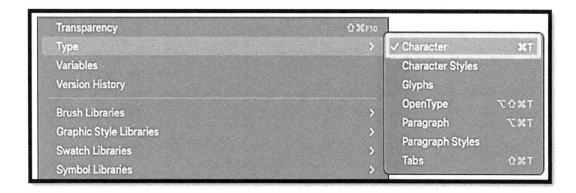

Still another option is to utilize the **Command + T (Mac) or Ctrl + T (Windows)** keyboard shortcut.
Step 2: Edit and Style Your Text
Here, I'd want the infographic's title to be more noticeable than the rest of the text.

The title, in this instance, can have its font changed to something other than the sub-title and its font size increased. Go to the part where you can "**Set the Font Family**" once you've selected the title text box. Click the button with the arrow pointing down, and then select your preferred font in the drop-down menu.

I thought it would appear better in the body text if the sentence spacing might be broader. More space between lines can be achieved by raising the value in the "**Set the Leading**" box. Given that the title simply contains a single line of text, I will not be doing this task.

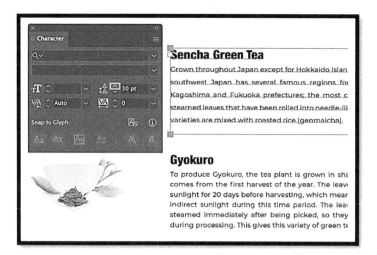

Step 3: Increase Text Size

Now that the title text style has been changed, it seems that the size can be bigger. Make sure you can see the bounding box by selecting the text. After that, go to the toolbar and choose the **Free Transform** tool. (Alternatively, you can press the **letter E** on your keyboard).

Then, until you see four arrows, navigate to any corner of the bounding box. Pressing and holding the **Shift** key while dragging the corner outwards will magnify the text.

The size may not seem to be in place, even if it looks excellent. To make the necessary adjustments, switch to the black arrow cursor by using the **Selection** tool. The next step is to align the text in the title text box so it complements the infographic style.

Method 3: Change Text Colors

The most recent color applied to the **Fill and Stroke** area will be carried over to the text color. In the toolbar, you can locate it. Because you should select a color that works for your design, you may or may not desire to leave the text in that color. Black is my default text color in this case. In addition to changing the fill color to blue, I'd like to highlight the title text with a stroke color. **The process for changing the color of text is as follows:**

Step 1: Use Appearance Panel

Pick **Window > Properties** from the top menu bar to access the **Properties** panel, where you'll find the **Appearance** panel.

Step 2: Change Colors

Pick out the text you want to change the color of, and then locate the square color box next to **Fill** in the **Properties** panel's **Appearance** section. Pick a color from the palette that appears to change the font color of your text.

Next, you may choose to add color to the text's edges by selecting the arrow pointing up next to **Stroke**. To alter the **Stroke** color, use the left-hand stroke icon.

Method 4: Use Glyphs

Glyphs are special characters or symbols that are part of a font. You can utilize them to make your designs more special and distinctive. Following this procedure, you will learn how to use glyphs in Adobe Illustrator for text editing, including how to open the **Glyphs** panel, choose and insert glyphs, and modify your designs. Using glyphs effectively can help you create more polished designs, give your text more character, and make your projects seem more professional.

Step 1: Open the Glyphs Panel

To begin, go to **Window > Type > Glyphs** to bring up the **Glyphs** panel.

Step 2: Select Glyph

The letter "G" in the word "Green" is very difficult for me to read in this example. So that the whole title remains in the same font and I can just make the "G" glyph legible, I've opted to convert it to glyph format. You can accomplish this by bringing up the **Glyphs** panel and then selecting the letter using the Type tool pointer. The letter I want to alter is "G," and as you can see, the "G" button has an arrow pointing to the right on its bottom right. More possibilities are available because of this. Hold down your cursor as you click the "G" button. Additional choices are shown in a drop-down menu. Hold down the cursor while dragging the cursor to the desired glyph; release it when it is highlighted.

156

After applying a glyph to the text, this is the result:

If you want to select a glyph without more options or the arrow, just double-click the glyph button and your selected text changes.

Creating columns of text

The following procedures will allow you to create text columns:

1. In Adobe Illustrator, find the "**Type**" tool and click on it. To specify the boundaries of an area-type object, just click and drag the box.

You can also use the Type tool to transform pre-existing objects like rectangles and polygons into area containers by clicking on them. Illustrator removes any fill or stroke applied to the object's inner or exterior paths when it transforms it into a type area.

2. Just type your text or paste it from a word processor or text file. You can change its font, style, size, tracking, and more in the Character panel. Inserting indents and adjusting alignment are both possible in the Paragraph panel.
3. Navigate to the "**Selection**" tool and choose the region text object you want.
4. Open the "**Type**" menu and choose "**Area Type Options**."
5. The Area Type Options dialog box's Columns section is where you can configure various settings.

Note: Take note that "**Gutter**" determines the spacing between columns, "Span" specifies the width of those columns, and "Number" regulates the total number of columns.

6. Illustrator automatically **adjusts the Span** with the Gutter value whenever you modify the Number value. If you increase or reduce the Span, Illustrator adjusts the Gutter.
7. If you set the Span to a number that calls for a broader box than your existing area-type object, Illustrator will automatically expand it.
8. To verify the settings' outcomes, click "**Preview**"
9. Finally, to apply, tap the "**OK**" button.

Working with Panels

Using the Character Panels

The first thing we need to know is how to bring up the **Character** panel in Illustrator. You can do this in one of two ways: either by going to **Window > Type > Character** or by using the **Control-T** keyboard shortcut. You will sometimes only get a limited sample of your options when you open the Character panel. To see all of them, go to the panel's top right and click the burger menu. Then, choose **Show options**.

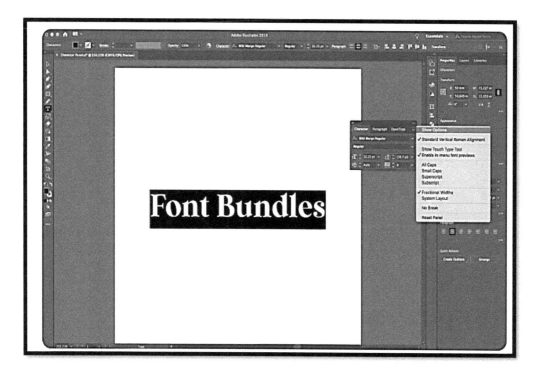

With the Character Options window open, you can now adjust your character's settings. For each setting, you have three options: either use the up and down arrows to adjust the value, use the drop-down menu that offers bigger increments of settings, or enter your settings manually. As you adjust the slider or mouse over the menu selections, the font will change accordingly.

Set the Font Style

Different fonts will have different font styles, which may include regular, bold, italic, and a plethora of additional possibilities beyond these basic ones. The font I used, for instance, only had a regular option.

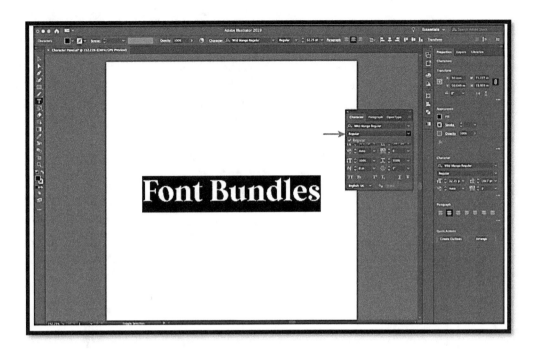

Leading

The leading is the gap between each line of type. For instance, with this option, the distance between the baselines of the text (blue lines at the base of the type) will increase and decrease. Use the arrows or the drop-down menu to alter the settings once you've highlighted all of the text.

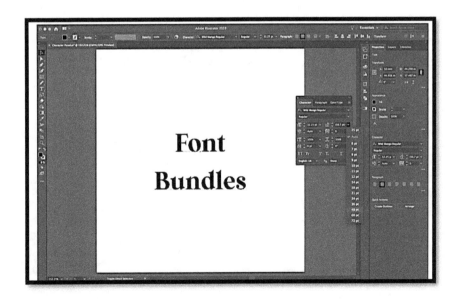

Kerning

Because the spacing between letters shouldn't always be the same—the kerning depends on the shape and curve of the letters that sit next to each other—it may be necessary to change each letter individually. This setting is important because it will make the text more visually appealing. I have inserted a little space between the **'d'** and **'l'** of Bundles,' so it should be easy to see where to put your cursor to modify the letters.

Tracking

Your tracking setting will modify the space between your whole words rather than your letters after you are satisfied with your kerning. Use the arrows or the drop-down menu to alter the settings once you've highlighted all of the text.

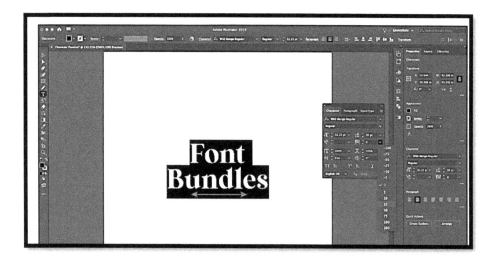

Vertical and Horizontal Scale

This setting will enlarge the text by a percentage. You can change these settings individually by highlighting your text and going to the settings, or you can set both the vertical and horizontal settings to the same percentage; for example, I set both to 50%.

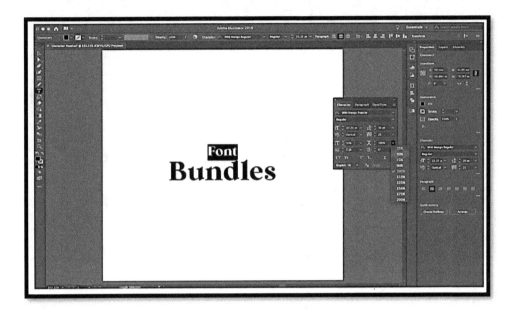

Baseline Shift

When you use this setting, the blue line serving as the baseline will be raised or lowered relative to the highlighted area of text.

Character Rotation

When you pick this option, the individual letters in your highlighted area will be rotated.

All Caps

Your highlighted text will be converted to all caps by clicking this button.

Small Caps

Any text you've highlighted will be converted to sentence case when you click this button.

Super Script

Clicking this button will make the highlighted selection lie lower on the text, which can be helpful for things like trademark icons or certain mathematical situations.

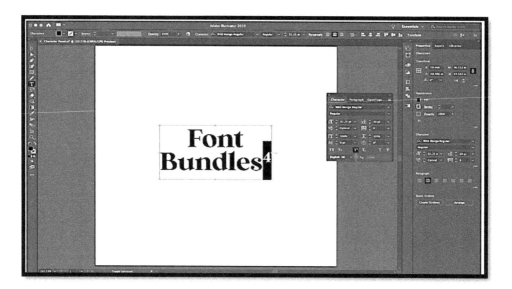

Sub Script

In contrast to Super Script, Sub Script will shrink the size of your highlighted selection and set it below the text baseline.

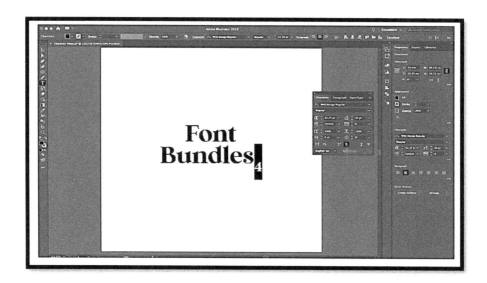

Underline

All of the text you've selected will be underlined when you click this button.

Strikethrough

A line will be drawn across all of the text you have highlighted when you use strikethrough.

Type on a Path: Advanced Techniques

Step 1

I'll begin with the badge scenario, where you can use any image you like. To make the text follow it, draw a circle or a portion of a circle inside the badge; the size of the circle and the amount of text you want to wrap around it will determine your choice.

In Illustrator, you must have a path before you can attach text to it.

Step 2

Once you have your path generated, you can click on it using the **Type Tool** or the **Type on a Path Tool**. The Type on a Path tool is your only choice when dealing with a closed path, like a circle. A blinking cursor will appear when you click on the path, and then you can enter your text. When the text exceeds the path, a square box will appear with a plus sign within; this is a common occurrence, but it's easily fixable.

Step 3

By clicking on the text with the **Selection Tool**, you can see the left, center, and right alignment brackets. Then, using the Selection Tool again, drag the left bracket to the far left of the path and the right bracket to the far right. This will give you access to the entire path, which is the first thing I do when starting to work with text.

Step 4

You will need to adjust the size, spacing, or horizontal scale of the font to fit it along the path if your text is still falling off the path (indicated by the square box with the plus (+) symbol that stubbornly refuses to disappear). Now that the text is there, you will probably want to tweak it a little more. Should it be centered? Right-aligned? Left-aligned? With a simple selection of the text and its formatting applied in the usual manner using the **Control**, **Paragraph**, or **Character** panels, or by grabbing the alignment brackets and sliding them until the text fits precisely where you like it, you can even add spaces and change the kerning.

How to Modify the Shape of Text on a Path in Illustrator

Here are some samples of how each of the many effects can be applied to text on a path: Select the path, then go to **Type > Type on a Path > Type on a Path Options**.

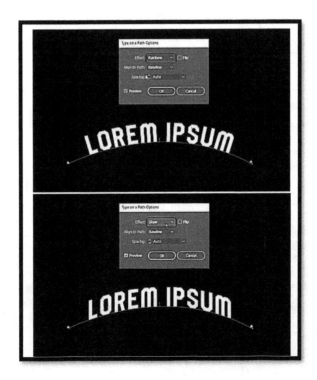

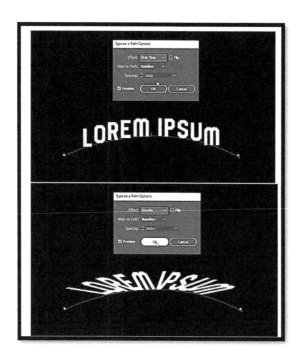

How to Change the Position of Text on a Path in Illustrator

What if you don't like where your text sits on the path? No problem! Select the path. Then, choose **Type > Type On A Path > Type On A Path Options**. In the **Align To Path** menu, choose one of the following options: **Ascender**, **Descender**, **Center**, or **Baseline** (the default alignment).

How to Flip Text on a Path in Illustrator

To have your type run below the text path instead of on top of it, you can simply reverse the alignment brackets so they are on the other side of the path. Alternatively, you can go to **Type > Type On A Path > Type On A Path Options** and choose **Flip**.

After you've used the Type on a Path Tool, flip the text by dragging the marker.

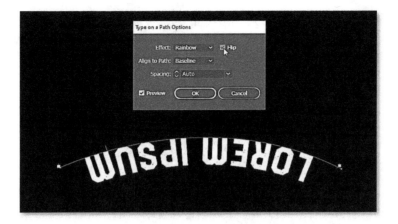

A frustrating issue is that text can sometimes flip when you don't want it to. To prevent this, hold down **Control (Windows)** or **Command (macOS)** as you move the text.

How to Adjust Character Spacing Around Sharp Curves

In some cases, text does not flow smoothly down a path; this is particularly problematic when dealing with tight curves; in such cases, you will need to rectify the curve or the text. After you've chosen the path, go to **Type > Type On A Path > Type On A Path Options**. In the Value field, enter a value or choose one from the drop-down menu; a larger value removes more space between characters. When you're dealing with very sharp angles, fine-tuning can be a real pain. Sometimes it's simpler to merely tweak the curve or move the text along the path until it fits snugly.

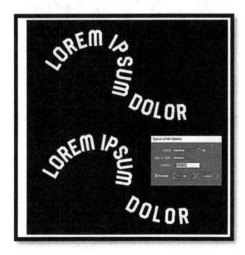

How to Write Vertical Text in Illustrator

To put vertical text on a path, you can use the same tools as horizontal text, such as the **Vertical Type Tool** or the **Vertical Type On A Path Tool**, and then click on the path you want to use as a guide to begin typing.

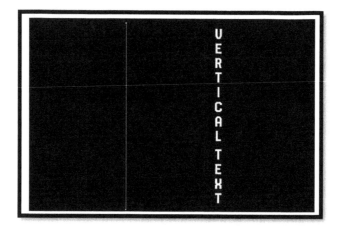

How to Use Illustrator's Text-to-Path Function

Okay, but what if you want to return to the path after producing the text, say, to style it? To do this, select all the text using the **Lasso Tool (Q).** Then, copy the selection and paste it. To paste it in the same spot as before, use **Control-F.**

Outline Text in Illustrator

Mastering the process of text-to-outline conversion can be quite helpful when dealing with text in Illustrator. Once you've converted text to a shape in Illustrator, you can no longer change it as text. However, you do have complete flexibility to shape and style the outlines. In this part, I'll demonstrate how to vectorize text in Illustrator and address a potential issue that can arise.

Convert Text to Outlines in Illustrator

Step 1

We need to understand how to size our document before we can learn how to transform text to a shape in Illustrator. To make a shape out of text in Illustrator, follow these steps. First, create a **New Document**. You can use any size you wish.

Step 2

To add text to a shape in Illustrator, use the **Type Tool (T)**. Change its position and size, and choose a lovely font.

Step 3

Make sure you give Illustrator enough time to transform text into a path. Go to **Type > Glyphs** and swap out a few letters for their variants to ramp up the impact.

Step 4

You can't undo the changes you made once you converted the text to a path, so be careful before you continue with Illustrator's shape conversion. Before you transform the text into outlines, make sure you have a backup copy in case you decide you want to make changes later. Press the menu on the **Layers** panel and then choose **Duplicate Layer**. Keep the original **hidden**.

Step 5

Creating vectorized text in Illustrator is something I'll demonstrate now. To outline, select the text and then go to **Type > Create Outlines**.

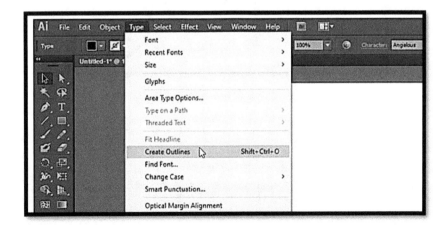

Step 6

This will usually work, but there are situations when you'll need to add another step. Recognize how these paths intersect. Then let's get rid of them. Go to **Window > Pathfinder**, select your outlines, and select **Unite**. The text will seem more cohesive after this.

Step 7

Once you've mastered Illustrator's text outlines, you can use the **Direct Selection Tool (A)** to change the letters' appearance by dragging the anchor points, just as you would with any other vector shape.

Step 8

You can also shift the letters individually if they aren't already linked. **Object > Ungroup** is all that's needed after selecting the text. Everything that a single path outlines will be considered its shape.

Step 9

Now that your text is a shape, you can simply add an inner or outside stroke to it. Think about it this way: if the text were still text, the stroke would appear on the crossing paths, and you'd be stuck with the solution of centering it. Even while you can't alter the text anymore once you transform it into a curve, you do have greater control over how the text appears as a shape.

Good Job!

The process of turning text into a shape in Illustrator is now clear to you. Use everything you've learned to transform text into shapes in Illustrator and make some breathtaking artwork!

Text to Vector Graphic Feature

How to Add Text-to-Vector AI to Illustrator

It is easy to integrate this new AI into your illustrator. Adding AI to your creative process is as easy as updating to the current version of Illustrator. If the update isn't showing up, it's probably because your Creative Cloud client needs updating. To find the update button, look at the very bottom of your Creative Cloud. This is, of course, supposing that you have previously paid for a Creative Cloud membership.

How to use Text-to-Vector in Illustrator

To begin, draw a rectangle to indicate the desired size and placement of your artwork. Then, go to the Contextual Task Bar and select the "Generate" option. From there, choose the sort of vector graphic you want to create: icon, subject, scene, or pattern. Finally, write your prompt into the Task Bar and hit generate!

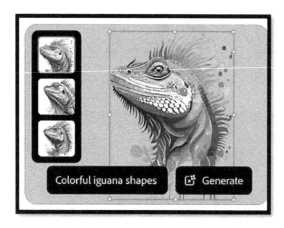

It's as easy as that!

Once Illustrator establishes an online connection to the Firefly engine, it will produce many possibilities for your selection. To utilize **Text-to-Vector, you will need to have an active internet connection.** In the properties panel of the Text-to-Vector Graphic, you will see three possibilities after the AI has finished generating.

Make sure your rectangle is still selected, and then use the properties window to see the full-sized illustration by clicking on each option. In the properties panel, you can make as many edits and iterations as you want on your prompt. After making your selection in the textbox, hit generate again.

Expert Hint: If you want to avoid having the AI references to an earlier version and suggest same color schemes and compositions, my expert tip is to remove the alternatives that aren't near to your desired appearance.

Everything on the artboard is seen by Adobe as a context for what you want to create in the end. You can use AI recolor to quickly change the color palette of one option and then try regenerating if you're still caught in a color loop after that. Finally, feel free to experiment with the detail slider and the settings!

As you move the number to the left, the level of detail that the AI will create when you hit the button decreases, and as you move it to the right, the level of detail increases. From what I can see, this is the primary factor that determines the brightness and contrast of an image.

How to Match a Style in Illustrator Vector AI

In my opinion, this is one of Text-to-Vector's most impressive new features from Adobe. Think of it as the eye-dropper tool, but it can also help you create something entirely new by using the styles you eye-dropped! Now that you have your main character for your children's book produced, the next step is to generate some friends. You'll want the other characters to be unique but share the same illustrative style as the main character. To achieve this, just make a new artboard, draw a rectangle, and enter your prompt as normal. However, before pressing generate, click the style picker located in the properties panel beneath the prompt area.

After that, choose the picture whose style you want to copy and then hit the generate button. Now the updated picture choices should look just like the original. That's all there is to it!

What are Vector Graphic Types and When to Use Them?

It's tricky, but Adobe uses various AI models to produce different types of vectors. It has dedicated AI for icons, characters, scenes, and patterns. There is a certain area of composition in which each of these AIs has been trained.

Icons

Producing really basic, flat icons suitable for use on websites is what the Icons AI excels at. Anything with substantial detail cannot be produced by it well. For instance, the Icons AI wouldn't be able to handle the level of complexity needed for an icon representing a vintage logo.

Character

Conversely, the Character AI is fantastic at paying attention to detail! From designing characters to creating brand icons to creating items, this AI has my full support. To put it simply, the Character Graphic Type is what you should use to create a focused object. Although it often produces the specified object with a transparent backdrop, this graphic type has difficulty generating whole scenes.

Scene

In this case, the Scene AI is useful. The Scene graphic type excels at creating comprehensive illustrated scenes, as its name implies. Is the character you made up a backdrop you're looking for? In need of a landscape image to accompany your social media post? If so, you'll love this style of graphics! You could get better results by combining scenes from the Character type with images from the Scene type, as it isn't always good at producing the scene's subject.

Pattern

Lastly, the Pattern AI is good at generating seamless patterns! It's as simple as that. ¯\(ツ)/¯ In the properties pane or the contextual taskbar, you can choose Vector Graphic Type. The prompting text box for each region is next to the dropdown.

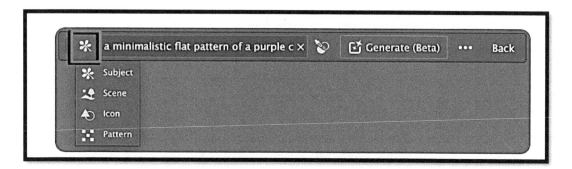

Using Text Effects

Adobe Illustrator's text effects can transform ordinary text into visually appealing design components. From basic shadows to advanced 3D and gradient effects, Illustrator's built-in effects and customization tools let you stylize text to your heart's content. Learn more about these effects and how to exploit them to their full potential with this comprehensive guide.

1. **Warp Effects**

How It Works: Warp effects let you shape text to fit certain shapes or give it a different flow by bending, curving, or distorting it.

Applying Warp Effects: After selecting your text, go to **Effect > Warp** to apply a warp effect. Some warp styles are available in Illustrator, including **arc, arch, bulge, wave, fish, rise, fisheye,** and **twist.**

Customizing Warp Settings: A **Bend** slider is available for each warp parameter, allowing you to adjust the effect's strength. There are sliders for **horizontal** and **vertical** distortion that you may use to change the text's compression and stretching.

Practical Example: You're making a poster in the manner of a vintage badge, and you want the text to curve upwards. To get the required curve, apply the **Arc** warp and tweak the **Bend**. To add dimension, increase or decrease the **Horizontal Distortion** and stretch the letters outward.

2. **3D Text Effects**

Overview of 3D Text Options: You can find tools like **Extrude & Bevel, Revolve,** and **Rotate** under Illustrator's **3D and Materials** panel. With them, you may make text that seems three-dimensional by making it angular, elevated, or looped around an axis.

Extrude & Bevel

- Transform your text into a three-dimensional object by adding depth using the **Extrude** tool. Select **Effect > 3D and Materials > Extrude & Bevel** to apply this.
- You may adjust the **Depth, Rotation, and Perspective** in the options.
- The thickness or thinness of the extrusion will be determined by its **depth**. Raising this makes the 3D effect more noticeable.
- You can adjust the viewing angle by **Rotation**. The text can be made to appear from either above or side perspective by dragging inside the box or by providing values for the X, Y, and Z axes.
- Options for Bevels: A stylized edge may be added to your 3D text by adding a bevel to its edge. You can choose between **Classic, Rounded,** and **Convex** versions.

Revolve: This effect makes your text seem round or semicircular by wrapping it around an axis. Logos and badges with a 3D appearance benefit greatly from this.

Lighting and Shading: Play around with the **Light** settings to get those photorealistic shadows and highlights. To get a realistic, three-dimensional effect, you can manipulate the light source's positioning, brightness, and shading.

3. **Drop Shadow**

How Drop Shadows Work: To make text stand out from its backdrop and give it a subtle or dramatic feeling of depth, drop shadows create a realistic shadow effect. This is how they work.

Applying Drop Shadows: Choose your text and then choose **Effect > Stylize > Drop Shadow** to apply a drop shadow. You will be able to modify the **color, blur, offset,** and **opacity** once a panel appears.

Opacity: The opacity slider determines how see-through the shadow is. If you want a subtle shadow, set the opacity to 30% or lower; if you want a strong shadow, set it to 70% or higher.

Offset: To change the shadow's orientation, use the **X Offset** and **Y Offset** parameters. The shadow stays close to the text with small offsets and seems lifted off the page with high offsets.
Blur: Adjust the blurring effect to make the shadow's edge less sharp. With smaller values, the shadow remains crisp, while with higher numbers, it becomes more dispersed.
Color Customization: The shadow can be whatever color you like, so you can express your creativity or match it with your brand's colors.

4. **Outer Glow and Inner Glow**

Outer Glow: To make text stand out on a darker backdrop, you may apply the following effect: Outer Glow, which adds a glowing effect around the text edges.

- Go to **Effect > Stylize > Outer Glow**.
- You can adjust the brightness and width of the glow using the **opacity** and **blur** settings.
- Based on your taste, you have the option to make **Color** selections ranging from bright neons to delicate pastels.

Inner Glow: Applies a glow inside the text edges, creating a softer, illuminated look.

- Make use of **Inner Glow** by navigating to **Effect > Stylize > Inner Glow.**
- The **Blur** and **Opacity** settings, which are similar to Outer Glow, let you tweak the effect's strength.
- **Edge vs. Center**: For a glow around the inside edge of the text, choose **Edge**. If you want the light to fill the inside area of the letters, choose **Center**.

5. **Gradients and Gradient Overlays**

Applying Gradients to Text: Illustrator lets you fill text with gradients, so you can add depth and visual appeal with a seamless transition between hues.

Creating a Gradient Text Fill

- Pick out some text and go to the **Swatches Panel** or **Gradient Panel**.
- Give your text a **linear** or **radial** gradient. Radial gradients radiate outward from a central point, in contrast to linear gradients, which change in a straight line.
- **Color Stops:** The gradient's colors can be adjusted by dragging the gradient bar to add or remove color stops. More contrast or softer transitions can be achieved by moving the color stops around.

Gradient Overlay Effect

- To create a layered effect, you can use the **Appearance Panel** to add gradients as an overlay over other effects, such as shadows or outlines.

6. **Text Effects with the Appearance Panel**

Adding Multiple Fills and Strokes: Using the **Appearance Panel**, you can apply several fills and strokes to text, each with its own set of parameters.
Stacking Effects: To layer multiple colors, gradients, or effects on your text, use the **Add New Fill** or **Add New Stroke** options.

Opacity and Blending Modes: Layer-specific opacity and blending mode controls in the Appearance Panel let you do things like create a secondary gradient layer or make a faint shadow behind a stroke—all of which are possible with complicated text effects.

7. Using Image Masks and Textured Fills

Image Masks on Text: You can clip an image inside your text for a unique effect. To do this:
- Place the image on top of your text in the Layers Panel, select both the text and the image, then go to **Object > Clipping Mask > Make**.

Adding Texture Fills: For textured text effects that mimic wear and tear, try adding texture fills. Just import a texture (such as a grunge or distressed picture), place it over your text, and then use the same **Clipping Mask** approach as before.

8. Transform Effects for Unique Layouts

Using the Transform Effect: To use the Transform Effect, click on **Effect**, then **Distort & Transform**, and finally **transform**. With this effect, you can create dynamic or circular patterns by repeatedly rotating or repeating text.

Rotation and Scaling: To create captivating recurring patterns, you can use Transform's **Rotation** and **Scale** tools. Another creative layer is added when you combine this with blend or transparency settings.

9. Expanding Appearance for Customization

Expand Appearance: To make the effects into vector shapes that you can modify, go to **Object > Expand Appearance** once you've applied them. Because of this, you may modify certain parts of the text to make it your own.

10. Saving and Exporting with Effects

Preserving Quality: Use **PDF or SVG** for vector output when storing or exporting text with effects. This will preserve the crisp quality. To preserve the intricacies of any text effects, make sure your resolution is high enough before exporting to web formats like **PNG or JPG.** When you get the hang of using Illustrator's text effects and combinations, you can create stunning, high-quality text designs that are ideal for both digital and print media. The Appearance Panel is a great place to play around with layering effects; try combining shadows, 3D, and gradients to give your text more dimensions and make your designs pop.

CHAPTER 7

TRANSFORMING AND MANIPULATING OBJECTS

Using the Selection Tools

With Illustrator, the selection tool is among the most basic and important tools available. You may use them to highlight a certain part of the object. You may target a particular section of the object using the selection tool's array of approaches, which include the Lasso Tool, Direct Selection Tool, Group Selection Tool, Magic Wand Selection Tool, and Perspective Selection Tool. There is a distinct function and set of characteristics for each selection tool. Depending on the situation, the user may utilize the selection tool to reposition, flip, scale, skew, or deform the object. **Graphic designers and artists often and frequently utilize six selection tools in Adobe Illustrator. These tools for selection are:**

1. **Selection Tool** (▶) :

Users can interact with objects inside the canvas with the basic Selection Tool.

Basic Selection

- An object can be selected by clicking on it.
- A selection box can be dragged around objects to make several choices.
- You can easily move, scale, rotate, and transform the objects you've chosen.

2. **Direct Selection Tool** (▷) :

The Direct Selection Tool allows for fine-grained anchor point and path editing.

Precise Editing

- Selects individual anchor points or segments within an object.
- Allows modification of specific anchor points or entire paths.
- Useful for adjusting curves, shapes, or paths within vector objects.

3. **Group Selection Tool** ▷⁺ :

When working with grouped objects, you can utilize the Group Selection Tool to pick out individual elements.

Selecting Grouped Items

- Assists with picking out certain items from a group without having to ungroup them all.

- You can toggle between the Direct Selection Tool and the Group Selection Tool by holding down the Alt key (Option on a Mac).

4. **Lasso Tool** ✋:

The Lasso Tool facilitates freeform selection of anchor points, segments, or components.

Freeform Selection

- Users may circle objects or paths to pick out certain elements.
- Great for picking out parts of an object that aren't perfectly flat or have odd shapes.

5. **Magic Wand Tool** ⁄:

When using the Magic Wand Tool, you may more easily choose objects with shared characteristics.

Color-Based Selection

- Color, stroke, opacity, and other comparable properties can be used to select objects.
- It's useful for picking out objects with the same properties fast.

6. **Perspective Selection Tool** :

When it comes to objects in perspective grids, the Perspective Selection Tool shines.

Working with Perspective

- Using a perspective grid, it's easier to choose and manipulate objects.
- It's crucial for precisely positioning and resizing objects in a perspective view.

Selecting and editing with the Direct Selection tool

To edit the object, I can add or remove points or segments. When working with Adobe Illustrator, this is the tool to use. This tool is used in conjunction with all other tools to create the outcome.

Step 1: The initial step in using this tool is to sketch a shape. Using the toolbox on the left side of the screen, I can build a rectangle as our shape. The shortcut for your system's Direct Selection tool is Keyword A. Once you've clicked on the rectangular command, a toolbox will pop up on the top of the screen. It will show you the color of the rectangle's inner/fill, outline, line thickness, line profile, opacity, and graphic style panel. Using the transform tool, you may relocate the rectangle. Using the isolate chosen object tool, you can separate a rectangle from any other shape.

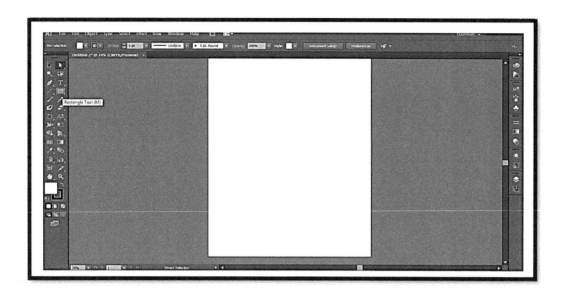

Step 2: I will use the characteristics of a rectangle to create a rectangle shape that meets our needs.

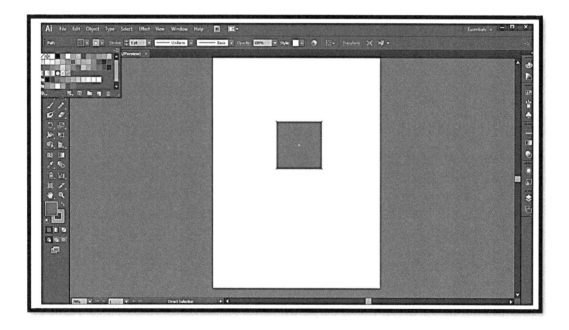

Step 3: The nine points can be seen using the Selection tool, which is accessible in addition to direct selection. They are seen below as four points in the center of the line, four points on each corner of the rectangle, and one point in the middle of the rectangle.

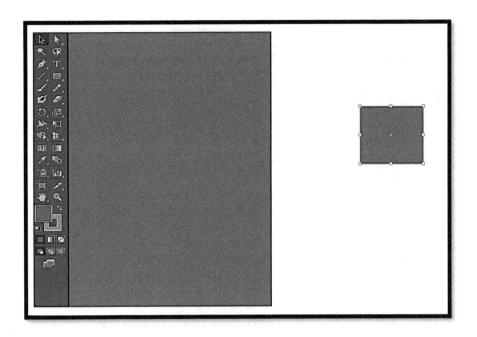

Step 4: However, if I select Direct Selection Tool, I will only be able to view 5 points—4 at the corners and 1 in the middle of a rectangle, as seen below.

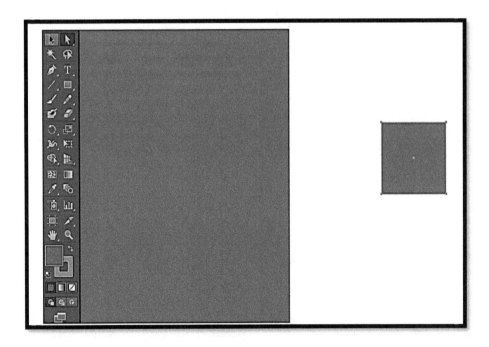

Step 5: I can move the rectangle by pushing and dragging the right mouse cursor using the Direct Selection Tool.

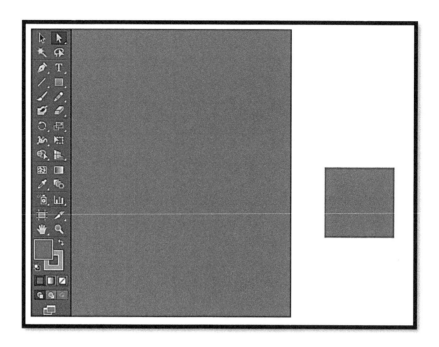

Using the right mouse button, I can now click and drag any corner of the rectangle to change its placement relative to the center of the rectangle.

Returning to the rectangle command, I will now generate a fresh rectangle.

Using the Direct Selection tool, I will modify the four corners of the basic rectangle to create a geometric pattern. Each of the initial rectangle's corners will be matched.

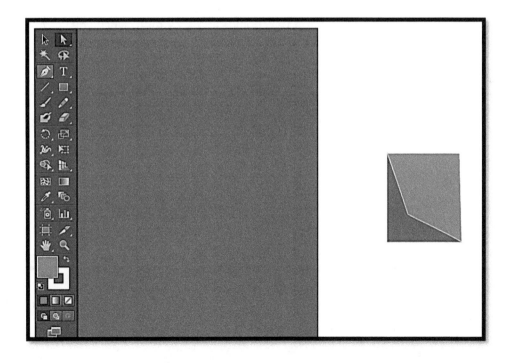

Selecting with a marque

Next, you'll use a technique called a marquee selection to pick information by dragging it across the screen.

1. Take the Selection tool from the toolbar. Using the left and up arrow keys, you can move the leaf shapes. You can make a marquee that covers some or all of them by dragging it over them. Release the mouse.

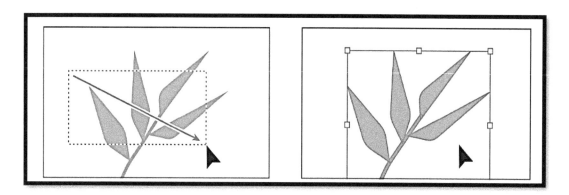

- The Selection tool only needs to cover a small area when dragging an object.
- Either choose **Select** > **Deselect** or click in the area where no objects are shown.
- Using the Direct Selection tool, you will now choose several anchor points within the circles by dragging a marquee around the anchor points.
- Find the **Direct Selection tool** on the toolbar and click on it. Once you've dragged the cursor over the upper leaves in the first section of the image, you can release the mouse button.

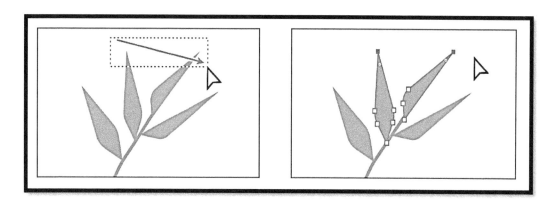

- Position the cursor over one of the chosen anchor points at the top of the leaves. Drag the word "**anchor**" to see how it moves with other words when you see it.

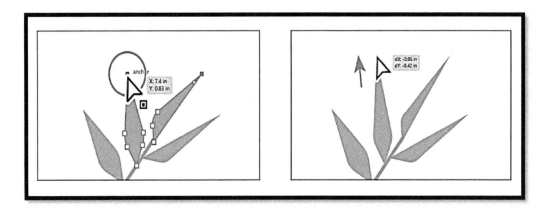

To avoid accidentally clicking on the wrong anchor point, you can use this technique to choose points instead. Go to **File > Save** once you've picked **Select > Deselect**.

Hiding and locking objects

- Locking, grouping, and hiding artwork will make it easier to pick and modify content.

Hide content to make selections

- To make selecting other artwork simpler, hide selected artwork by choosing Object > Hide > Selection, or pressing Option+3 (macOS) or Alt+3 (Windows) on the keyboard.
- Select **Object** > **Show All** to see all hidden artwork.

Lock content to make selections

- Go to **Object > Lock > Selection** to lock selected artwork.

View artwork in Outline mode

- To make content selection easier, pick **View > Outline** to display the artwork without fills, as outlines.
- **View > Preview** (or GPU Preview) will display the artwork in its original form.

Group artwork

- To group chosen contents, go to the Properties panel and click the **Group** button.

Select content in the group

- To activate Isolation mode and choose content within a group, just double-click the group while using the Selection tool.
- Press the **Escape** key to leave Isolation mode.

Unlocking objects

You can unlock objects on the canvas without going to the Layers panel by using the lock icon. Pick out a single option:

- To enable this feature, set **Preferences** > **Selection & Anchor Display** > **Select and Unlock Objects on Canvas**. A lock icon is displayed on the canvas for the lock objects. Click this icon to unlock objects.
- Choose **Unlock > object-name** from the context menu after you right-click the locked object.

The Layers Panel is the only place where layers can be unlocked. The lock symbol is not shown for objects on a locked layer.

Selecting similar objects

By comparing the fill color, stroke color, stroke weight, and other attributes, you can choose artwork using the **Select > same command**. The stroke denotes the outline of an object, whereas the stroke weight denotes its width. Finding a set of objects whose fill and stroke are identical is the next stage.

- Choose **View > Fit All in Window** to see all the artwork simultaneously.
- Use the Selection tool to click on one of the larger green "**bamboo**" shapes on the right.
- From the menu, choose **Same > Fill Color**.

Now we've chosen all the shapes that share a fill color.

- With the shapes still chosen, go to **Select > Save Selection**. After you've given your selection a name, such as Bamboo, in the Save Selection dialog box, click OK.

When you're ready to use a saved selection, you can retrieve it effortlessly from the bottom of the Select menu.

- After you've chosen **Select > Deselect**, go to **File > Save**.

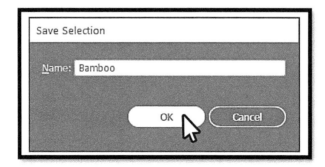

188

Aligning objects

To align objects in Illustrator, go to **Window > Align**. This will open the Align panel. Following your selection, either a key object or the artboard can be used to arrange the objects you want to align in the Align panel. The Align panel is accessible via the "**Align**" option in the Window menu's dropdown. To access the Align panel quickly, use **Shift + F7**.

You can dock the Align panel to any workspace window or sidebar. When docked, the icon will take on the appearance of a row of rectangles stacked vertically to the left.

Align Panel Options

You should know that the Align panel has a few hidden options. To access them, you need to click the hamburger menu icon in the top right corner of the Align Panel.

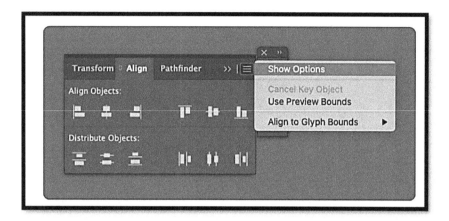

Show/Hide Options: The Align panel, including the "**Align To**" options and the distribution by certain units, can be seen by toggling the show/hide options toggle.

Use Preview Bounds. There are bounding boxes on Illustrator objects. With these bounding boxes, you can align objects with ease. Components of a shape or object may sometimes extend beyond the path of the shape itself. A stroke placed outside of a shape is used as an example. In the absence of the "**Use Preview Bounds**" option, the Align panel will make use of the bounding box linked to the object's path. With "Use Preview Bounds" turned on, the bounding box will go all the way to the edge of the shape, shielding it from things like outside strokes and other imperfections.

Align to Glyph Bounds. This option is similar to "**Use Preview Bounds**" for different types of text; it aligns with glyph boundaries. Here, you have the choice between two types: point type and area type. Point Type is a typeface that lacks wrapping and text boxes; it is injected into your page at a specific spot. Wrapping around it as it approaches its border is a text box called an area type. When either option is selected, objects will be aligned to the visible border of your editable text. With this feature turned off, the alignment tools will use their bounding box instead of the one you've specified for your editable text. This works well with Area Type but poorly with Point Type.

Align To Selection, Key Object, and Artboard

Before you begin to align objects in Illustrator, be sure you understand how they will align. One might choose to align to the selection, another to the key object or the artboard. To change them, check the box that says "**Show Options**" in the hamburger menu.

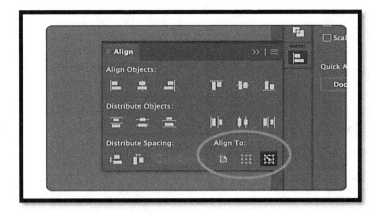

In the lower right corner, you can see three icons: artboard, selection, and key object.

- **Align to Artboard** – Throughout your whole canvas or work area, you will have at least one artboard. To ensure that everything is aligned with that artboard, choose this option.
- **Align to Selection** - Using Align to Selection, you can usually get two objects to line up with each other. You can adjust to fit a variety of products with this choice.
- **Align to Key Object**: To have additional objects automatically align to a designated "key object"—one that you can change at any time—use the "align to key object" feature. This may be accomplished by selecting several objects, and then clicking on the one you want to align to. If an object is significant, its darker contour will show it.

How to Align to Selection in Illustrator

Now that we've had a look at the two choices for vertical and horizontal alignment in the **Align panel**, I can move on to the actual alignment tools. When you pick numerous objects in Illustrator, **"Align to Selection"** is a common option. But before you do that, make sure you're aligning to the correct parameter. If you want to align to a selection in Illustrator, you must click the center box inside the "**Align To**" icons. Using the **horizontal align** tools, you can position your objects such that they are left, center, or right of their bounding boxes.

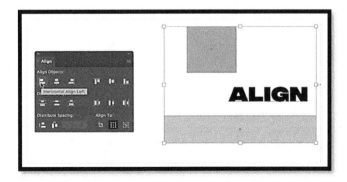

You can align objects with their bounding boxes' top, middle, and bottom with the **vertical-align** tools.

Align to Artboard in Illustrator

I'm not in the mood to coordinate our efforts. Like, maybe you want to put some text or anything else right in the middle of your artboard. Your "**Align To**" options must have "**Align To Artboard**" chosen for this to work.

How to Align to Key Objects in Illustrator

Moving objects isn't always the best option; there are times when aligning them are. If you want to align objects without repositioning them, choose "**Align to Key Object**" from the menu. Select all of the objects you want to align by clicking and dragging them, or by selecting one object while holding down the Shift key. Once all the objects have been chosen, click on the one you want to be the main object. Because of this, the region around that object will be more noticeable. Once that is done, you can use the align tools normally and everything will be aligned to your key object.

Working with groups

Any two objects can be joined to form a new one. Using this method, you can move or modify a set of objects without affecting their characteristics or their interdependencies. Furthermore, it might simplify the process of selecting artwork.

Editing a group in Isolation mode

In Adobe Illustrator, you can modify paths or objects that are inside a sublayer, compound path, group, or symbol by switching to Isolation Mode. The visibility of objects outside of the isolated one is diminished when the Isolation Mode is turned on. On top of that, the document window will display a gray isolation bar at the very top.

1. Isolation Mode can be activated in two ways. One way to make changes to an object is to double-click it. Extra access points are provided via the Layers Panel. When you're ready, choose "**Enter Isolation Mode**" from the panel's drop-down menu.

At the very top of the document window, you can see a gray isolation bar with a left-pointing arrow. Click the arrow until the bar separating the objects vanishes once you have finished editing the isolated object. To exit the mode, you may have to hit the arrow button many times since, as you make modifications, you are "**diving down**" into deeper degrees of isolation. Hitting the **Esc** key on your keyboard might be your savior in this predicament.

Exploring object arrangement

The objects you make in Illustrator are stacked in the order they were generated, with the most recent one at the top and the oldest one at the bottom. The stacking order, or the sequence in which objects are stacked, dictates how overlapping objects are shown. You can always change the stacking order of your artwork's objects using the Arrange commands or the Layers panel.

Arranging objects

Using specialized tools, the arrow keys on your keyboard or entering precise numbers into a panel or dialog box are just a few of the methods you can use to move objects. When repositioning objects, you can achieve more exact placement by using the snapping option. You can snap the pointer to anchor points and guides, and you can snap the limits of an object to gridlines, for instance. You can also utilize the Align panel to position objects relative to one another. Then, when the x and y axes are in their present positions, you can use Shift to limit the movement of certain objects to a certain horizontal, vertical, or diagonal direction. This can be done for each object separately or for all of them at once. Another feature is that the Shift key can be used to rotate objects in increments of 45 degrees.

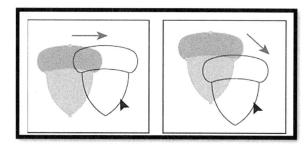

Working with Enclosed Selection Mode for Rectangular Marquee

Selecting just objects completely encircled by your selection rectangle1 is now possible with Adobe Illustrator 2025's **Enclosed Selection Mode** for the Rectangular Marquee tool. **Follow these steps to utilize it:**
1. **Select the Rectangular Marquee Tool**: On the toolbar, you should see the Rectangular Marquee tool.
2. **Drag to Create a Marquee**: To pick several objects at once, just click and drag to draw a rectangle marquee around them.
3. **Toggle Enclosed Selection Mode**: To toggle enclosed selection mode, hit the **E** key once while holding down the mouse button. When the **Enclosed Selection Mode** is activated, the cursor will show brackets.

4. **Continue Dragging**: To adjust the selection, keep dragging the marquee. The marquee will only choose objects that are completely inside it.

To swiftly choose objects without inadvertently choosing sections that are partly within the marquee, this capability is quite helpful.

Using the Free Transform Tool for Perspective Modifications

In Illustrator, you can access Free Transform in two different methods. After you've chosen an object to transform using the **Selection Tool (V)**, go to **Object > Transform** to choose a particular transform mode. The next step is to choose the desired transform mode.

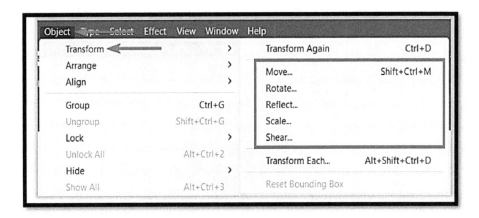

Select the **Free Transform Tool** from the toolbar or press **E** on your keyboard to utilize the Free Transform to further edit the object. The transform controls will be shown as handles around the chosen object.

To transform an object, click and drag the anchor points. Various handles will have various effects as you drag them.

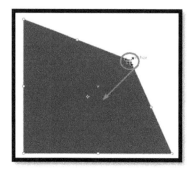

You can also adjust the object using the Free Transform Tool extended menu.

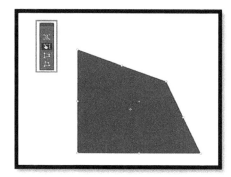

Free Transform Modes in Illustrator

Various transformations can be achieved by dragging the anchor points. Using Free Transform, you can do the following common transformations:

- **Rotate:** Locate the curved arrow and drag it outside the object's bounding box to rotate it. Next, you may rotate the object by clicking and dragging. To limit the rotation to increments of 45 degrees, you can also hold down **Shift**.

Scale: To scale an object, hover your cursor over one of its corner handles until a diagonal arrow appears. To scale the object, just click and drag. As an additional option, you can hold **Shift** to scale the object proportionately, **Alt on Windows,** or **Option on Mac** to scale it from the center.

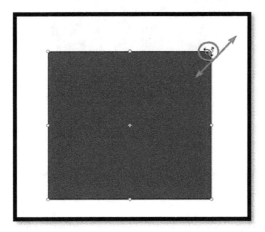

Skew: To make an object seem skewed, hover your pointer over one of the side handles until a straight arrow appears. To make the object skewed, just click and drag. You can also skew the object along the horizontal or vertical axis by holding **Shift**, or you can skew it from the other corner by holding **Alt on Windows** or **Option on Mac.**

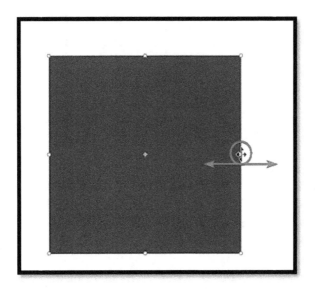

Distort: You can distort an object by dragging the pointer over one of its corner handles until a diagonal arrow appears. To further distort the object, hold down **Control (Windows)** or **Command (Mac)** while clicking and dragging. Additionally, you can symmetrically distort an object by holding **Shift**, or you can center-distort it by holding **Alt on Windows** or **Option on Mac.**

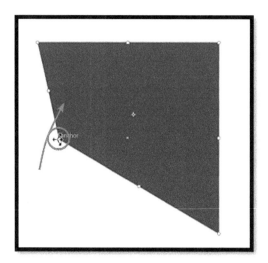

Perspective: Applying a perspective effect is as simple as dragging the pointer over a corner handle until a diagonal arrow appears. Then, to switch the object's viewpoint, press and hold **Control + Alt (Windows) or Command + Alt (Mac)** as you click and drag. To keep the object's original angle, you can also hold down **Shift**.

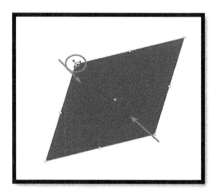

Shortcuts When Using Free Transform in Illustrator

You can undo all of your transformations by hitting **Control + Z on a Windows** computer or **Command + Z on a Mac**. This will reset the transformation. You can change the object's transformation mode by right-clicking it and selecting the desired mode from the context menu. As an additional option, you can choose the desired mode using the widget that displays next to the object.

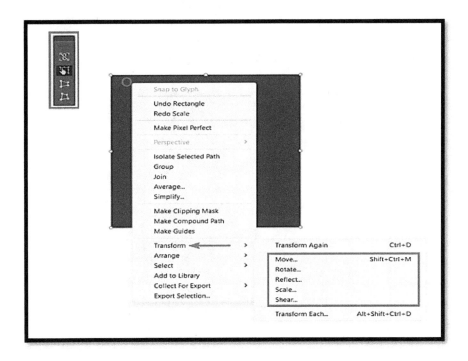

Select **Transform** from the menu at the top of the screen to input the transformation's exact parameters. To see and modify the transformation values, you can also utilize the Transform Panel, which is accessible via **Window > Transform**.

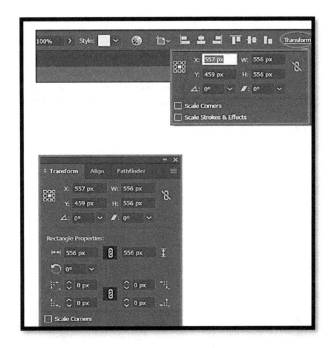

Use the **Selection Tool (V)** to pick numerous objects, and then use Free Transform as normal to transform them all at once. In addition, you can distribute and align objects before or after the transformation using the **Align Panel**, which can be accessed via **Window > Align**.

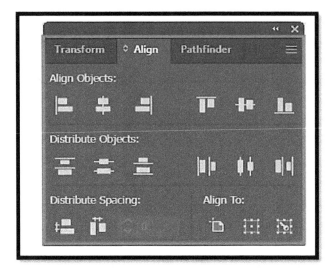

Applying the Puppet Warp Tool

The Puppet Warp tool will allow you to organically warp parts of your artwork and make variants on your artwork that blend in as you use it. Having a fresh viewpoint is crucial while making cartoons or when dealing with complex subjects.

- Select **Your Subject** and the **Puppet Warp Tool**
- Select your subject by using the **Selection tool** (V).

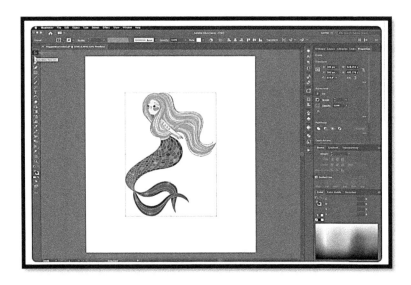

- Pick out the **Puppet Warp tool** from the left-hand toolbar.

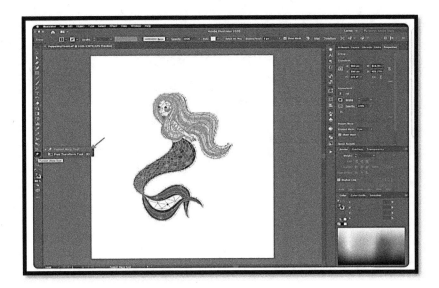

Occasionally, the illustrator may put pins where it thinks they would be most suitable. You can modify this option by going to **Edit > Preferences > General**. **Enable Content Aware Defaults** can also be unchecked. Manually adding all the pins will be a breeze with this.

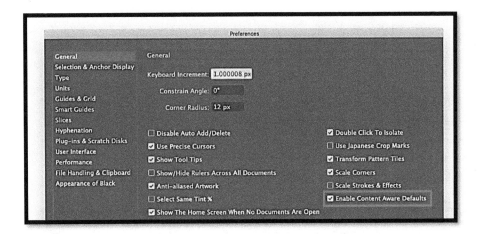

Adding pins

Using the mouse, you can place pins on specific regions that you want to transform or anchor. Using at least three pins will provide satisfactory outcomes. Select the pin you want to permanently delete and then press the **Delete** button.

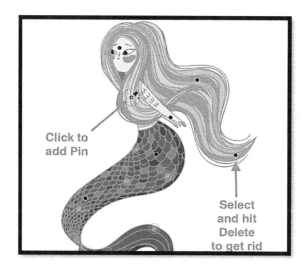

Modify Your Subject Using the Pins

Using pins, you can modify your subject. To change the outcome, just drag and rotate the pinned sections. Then, make the disjointed areas part of your selection.

Select a Pin and Move It

To transform a section of your subject, click on a pin to select it. When you have selected the pin, a dotted circle will appear around it. Then, try to reposition the selected section by dragging it around. The remaining ones will keep the rest of the subject in place.

Select More Than One Pin

Hold down the **Shift** key or use the **Control** panel's **Select All Pins** option to choose many pins at once. If you go to **Windows > Properties**, you'll see the **Properties panel** where you can alter the settings. **Note**: The control panel can be accessed from the top toolbar, as shown.

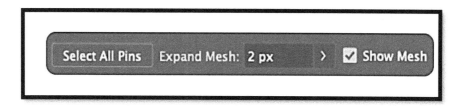

You can toggle the **Mesh's** visibility in the **Control** and **Properties** panel. Hiding the mesh will show only the pins.

Rotate a Pin to Twist the Selected Area

To twist a selected area, select a pin then hover with your cursor on it. Do so until a curved arrow appears close to the dotted circle. After this, you will be able to rotate the selection.

Use Expand Mesh to Modify Disjointed Objects

The **Expand Mesh** tool will allow you to expand the mesh that is positioned outside of the subject. For a change to take place, this will assist you in bringing together separate objects. Before making any changes, you may need to group them. **Note:** The **Control** and **Properties** panel allows you to adjust the mesh size.

CHAPTER 8
LAYERS AND ORGANIZING ARTWORK

Understanding Layers

Like invisible folders, layers let you hold and arrange all the components that go into making an artwork. The artwork in your stack will seem different depending on how you rearrange those folders. Your document's layered structure will be as complicated or simple as you want it to be. Illustrator creates a new project with all of the generated content in a single layer and arranges **it in that way. Similar to subfolders, you can arrange your artwork in layers by creating new layers and sublayers.**

1. Just open the document window and click the document tab at the top to display the document.
2. Get to the Layers panel by going to **Window > Layers** in the menu bar or by clicking the tab in the top right of the workspace.
3. After you finish reading the panel, you can close the file by selecting **Close** from the **File** menu.

Create a Layer in Illustrator

Step 1: To start using the Layers, open it from the Windows and select the **Layers** option. A layers panel will now appear in the lower right corner. To start listing, managing, and controlling things in your work, you can use the layers options. To make working with layers a breeze, you should always have that panel active in your project.

Step 2: Access the Layers panel and click the icon shown in the image below. A **new layer** will be generated by this. The name of the layer is **Layer 1** by default. You can rename it by double-clicking on the layer you want to rename.

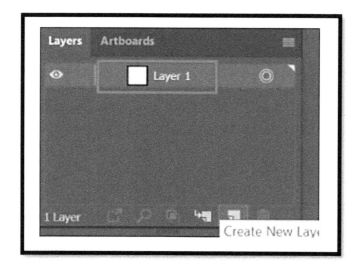

Step 3: This new layer will have the default color. By accessing the layer's options with a double-click on the layer, you can change its color. Look at the image below.

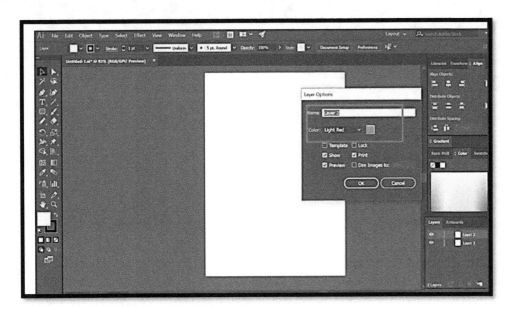

Step 4: Adjacent to the generated Layer, you will see Adobe Illustrator layers. Toggle its visibility to show or hide the Layer's contents.

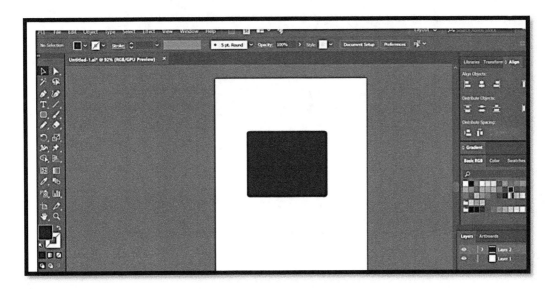

Step 5: When you press it, the Eye icon goes away and everything in it is hidden. Simply pressing the eye icon region again will bring up the Layer.

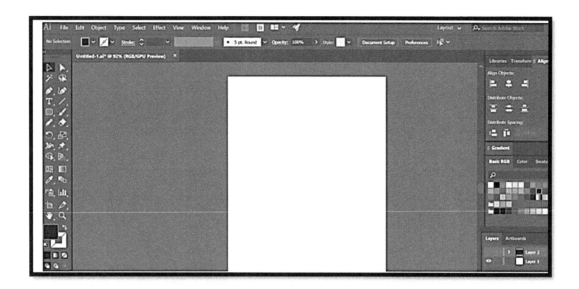

Step 6: Locate the spot to **lock your Layer**, which is next to the eye icon. A padlock icon will show up when you click it. Nothing can be done inside your locked layer; you are unable to move or select any of its contents. Once again, you can access the objects by clicking the lock icon; after that, you can return to working on the Layer.

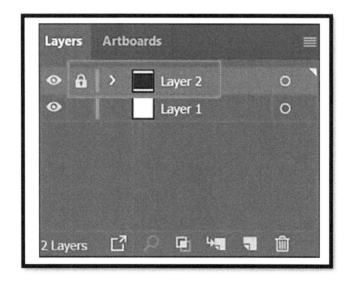

Set Layer and Sublayer options

Illustrator allows the users to further create objects and link them with the parent layers. Items will branch out from the initial layer, creating what are known as sub-layers.

Please proceed as instructed below.

1. From the layers panel, double-click the object.
2. After you've chosen the item, go to the layers panel and click on options.
3. The last step is to select New Layer or New Sublayer from the layers panel menu.

Move an Object to a Different Layer

After making an object in Illustrator, you may find that you need to move it to a new Layer. You can still move objects created in one layer to another by following these steps:

1. Select the items you'll need to move.
2. To move an item to a different layer, choose that layer.
3. Go to **Object > Arrange > Send to Current Layer**.

A simpler option is to drag the object directly to the desired layer. Just be careful that you are moving the object to the correct layer.

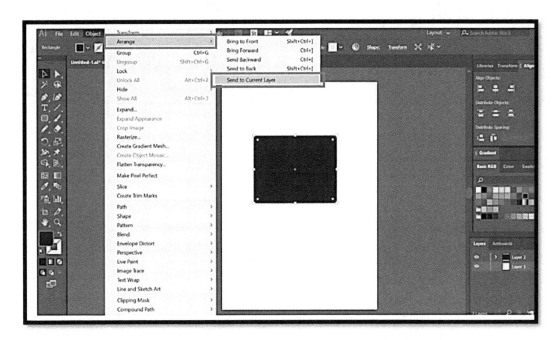

Consolidate Layers and Groups

You can fuse many layers or objects into one if you so like. We can combine or flatten many layers into one if that's what you need. When you flatten an image, all of the objects in it will merge into one layer, but when you merge, just the ones you've chosen will merge into one. Neither of these choices will mess with the stacking sequence, but they will remove all of the level elements from the layers.

- To merge items, press and hold the **Control key** on a Windows computer or the **Command key** on a Mac. Using the shift key, you can easily pick multiple objects from different layers. Then, pick **Merge Selected** from the layers panel menu. Based on the layer you selected last, a combined layer will be the result.

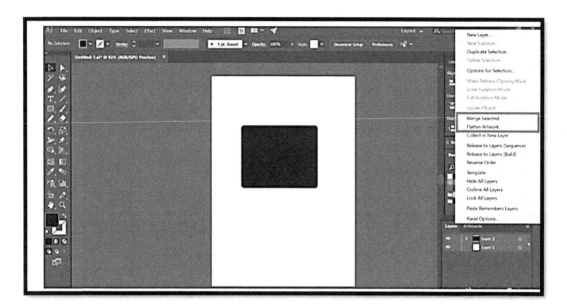

- Select the layer you wish to flatten if you want to do so. Then, select **Flatten Artwork** from the layers panel menu.

Locate an item in the Layers Panel

In certain instances, you could have lost track of the objects in your artwork while working on your document. To find these lost elements, Illustrator provides an easy method.

- In the document window, choose an object. When you choose several objects, the front-most objects in the stacking order will be located. Things in complex layers can be located with ease using this sequence.
- Select **Locate Object** from the options; if **Show Layers Only** is selected, the option becomes Locate layer.

Change the Display of the Layers Panel

How you choose to display the layers panel is entirely up to you. Depending on your requirements, you can make it simple or sophisticated. Typically, everything will be stored on the parent layer. You can further change the appearance, color, and other attributes like lock, hide, and more using the layers panel.

Step 1: Choose **Panel Options** from the layers panel menu.

Step 2: Select **Show Layers Only** from the panel options to hide the paths and clubbed objects.

Step 3: Select an appropriate row size based on your requirements. You can often fill in any number between 12 and 100. You have three options—**Small, Medium**, and **Large**—in the most recent versions of Illustrator.

Reordering layers and content

Here are the steps:

1. On the artboard, with the **Selection tool** selected, drag across the content at the top of the artboard to select the header content. Doing so will choose the content of the header. Although you first succeeded in selecting only the header material, you will soon discover that it also captures other elements. This is clearly shown by the fact that the artboard is covered by the bounding box that surrounds the selection.
2. Click the triangle with the disclosure label to the left of the Phone Body layer's name to view its contents. The chosen content should be shown to you. Some things need your consideration. There is also a rectangle shape with a gradient fill.

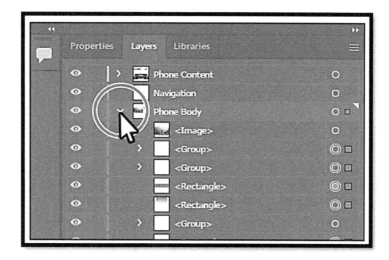

3. Click the artboard's rectangle while holding down the Shift key. The selection will be cleansed of the gradient-filled rectangle.
4. Opening the Layers panel and shifting-clicking the selection indicator to the right of the item will remove the bottom **"Rectangle" objects** from the selection. This will remove it from the selection.
5. To hide the information, hide the layer by clicking the disclosure triangle to the left of the Phone Body layer. Drag the selection indicator on the right of the Phone Body layer until it reaches the Navigation layer; then release the mouse button to move the chosen content to the **Navigation layer**. If a selection signal appears to the right of a layer, it means that the layer has contents that can be selected. Only the currently chosen content is moved when you drag it to another layer. However, it does not inform you what or how much is selected.

6. To de-select an item, use the Selection tool, and then click on a blank space that is far from any artwork. Using the **shift key**, move the image from its current location on the left side of the artboard to bring it closer to the center of the board. Let go of the mouse button then press the **Shift** key.

7. Since the picture has to be on the Phone Content layer, pick it and then drag the selection indication in the Layers panel up to the Phone Content layer. This will place the image on the correct layer. After that, you will rearrange the layers so that you can once again view the content of the menu bar.

8. By dragging it downward, you can position the **Phone Content layer** beneath the Navigation layer. By releasing the mouse button when a blue line appears beneath the Navigation layer, you can drop the Phone Content layer below it without risking anything. Now that it has risen above the Phone Content layer, the navigation content should be visible.

9. Pick the **Select > Deselect menu option**.

10. Go to the **File** menu and choose "**Save**".

Locking and hiding layers

1. First, choose your preferred picture on the artboard and click on it. Use the Locate Object button at the Layers panel's bottom to find it inside the layers.

2. From the menu bar, choose **Object > Hide > Selection**.

3. Find the location where the eye symbol was to bring up the image again in the Layers panel. In menu terms, it's the same as going to **Object > Show All**. Contrary to what the command does, you are not obligated to reveal anything that you have concealed under the Layers panel. One or more layers, sublayers, or objects can be shown or hidden, or all three can be hidden at once.

4. To reveal or conceal the other layers, press the **eye icon** (or **Option on macOS or Alt on Windows)** on the layer's left side. By hiding all layers except the ones you want to deal with, you can more easily concentrate on the current subject.

5. Find the rectangle on the artboard with a gradient fill and click on it. Once you've positioned the selection indicator above the **Phone Content** layer in the Layers panel, release the mouse button. The rectangle will be erased because it is now on a hidden layer.

6. Hold down the **Command+Y (macOS) or Ctrl+Y (Windows) keys** at the same time to view the artwork in Outline mode (Windows). On the artboard, near the center, you can see four smaller circles.

7. Once you've positioned the selection indicator above the Phone Content layer in the Layers panel, release the mouse button. The circles have disappeared since they were on a user-visible layer.

8. On macOS, use Command+Y, and on Windows, press Ctrl+Y, to exit Outline mode.

9. Return to seeing all of the layers by going to the Layers panel's menu and selecting **Show All Layers**.

10. Locate the Lock column to the left of the Navigation layer and click the unchecked box to lock all the content on that layer.
11. After you click **Select > Deselect**, a menu will open; from there, choose **File > Save**.

Using Clipping Masks

With a preset shape or path, you can control the visibility of artwork in Adobe Illustrator with clipping masks, a powerful and flexible tool. A wide variety of effects, from basic cuts to intricate patterns and textures, can be achieved using them.

What is a Clipping Mask?

By using a predetermined shape or path, you can regulate the visibility of artwork with a clipping mask. It controls which elements of your artwork are shown and which are hidden, similar to a stencil or mask. The object you wish to mask (the "**clipped object**") and the object that will serve as the mask are the two objects required to make a clipping mask. It is common practice to layer the clipped object with the clipping object, which can be any shape or path. Using the clipping mask will restrict the visibility of the clipped object to its immediate vicinity. Within the bounds of the clipped object, any portion that extends beyond those borders will be concealed.

Importance of Clipping Mask Illustrator

The adaptability of clipping masks is a major plus. They are a multipurpose tool for designers because of the myriad effects and designs they can create. You can make edits later without having to start over since they are non-destructive, meaning they won't permanently ruin your artwork.

- **Control Visibility:** The use of clipping masks enables precise control over the visibility of artwork to a predetermined path or shape. For more creative control, you can simply choose which aspects of your artwork to display and which to keep hidden.
- **Non-Destructive:** Clipping masks are non-destructive, meaning they won't permanently change your artwork when you apply them. Rather, depending on the shape of the clipping object, it selectively conceals portions of the artwork. As a result, editing the artwork in the future is a breeze, and there's no need to begin from square one.
- **Compatible with other Adobe applications:** Clipping masks are compatible with other Adobe apps like InDesign and Photoshop, allowing you to easily import or export your artwork across programs.

By letting you concentrate on particular areas of your artwork and by more efficiently arranging your layers and groups, clipping masks can also assist enhance your workflow. Additionally, you can easily import or export artwork across programs thanks to their compatibility with other Adobe apps like InDesign and Photoshop.

How to create a basic clipping mask in Illustrator?

In Adobe Illustrator, making a vector shape is the way to go for making a clipping mask. Then, before you cut an object, position this vector layer above it. After that, pick the object layer and the vector shape layer. Then, in the top menu bar, choose **Object > Clipping Mask > Make.** At your convenience, launch Adobe Illustrator CC and begin working on a new project, or choose an existing one to which you want to add a clipping mask. After that, just follow these steps:

Step 1: Create a Vector Layer

Pick out an object to serve as a mask first. To make a vector shape, use the **Rectangle** or **Pen** tools. Stack this shape over the layer you want to clip, and it will act as your mask. To manage your layers, go to the **Layers** panel (**Window > Layers**). To clip objects, position the masking object so it is on top of the other layers. Working efficiently in Adobe Illustrator relies on a Layers panel that is well-organized.

Step 2: Object Selection

Choose the masking object and the object (or objects) you want to clip using the selection tool. The masking object must be on top for it to function.

Step 3: Execute the Masking

To make the clipping mask, go to **Object > Clipping Mask > Make. Ctrl + 7** on Windows or **Cmd + 7** on Mac is another shortcut. At that point, a mask thumbnail will appear in Illustrator's layers panel, and the objects will be clipped to fit the shape of the masking object. A clipping group is essentially created by this action. Not happy with it? Enter Isolation Mode by double-clicking the masked object. Here you can modify the masked artwork with the use of tools like the pen tool, image trace, and gradient options in the transparency panel.

How to Release Clipping Mask

Simply navigate to **Object > Clipping Mask > Release** to release or edit your mask. Once again, your clipped objects appear as they were before. To begin over, you can remove a clipping mask.

Vector Paths in Clipping Mask Illustrator

For graphic design projects where scalability is essential, clipping masks in Adobe Illustrator are ideal since they are built on vector paths. You can zoom in and out of a vector-based clipping mask without sacrificing quality, unlike opacity masks or layer masks in Adobe Photoshop that are based on raster images. You can utilize shape masks for text, image trace elements, and even patterns in addition to shapes. From basic vector objects to intricate designs, the masked artwork can cover it all.

The Role of Layers Panel in Clipping Masks

Understanding Illustrator's layer structure is essential, particularly when dealing with clipping groups. Among the objects you wish to mask, the clipping path should be located at the very top of the layers panel. You may have to release the clipping mask and begin over if you mess up with the layers.

Tools for Creating Adobe Illustrator Clipping Masks

In Illustrator, you can make a clipping mask by combining many tools, such as the **Pen**, **Direct Selection**, and **Rectangle** tools. The clipping path that will mask your artwork may be made with the use of these tools. Clipping mask is a catchall word for "vector shape," "vector mask "and" clipping object" in typography. You can make precise alterations to your clipping path by selecting individual points with Illustrator's **Direct Selection tool**.

Why Use Clipping Masks in Adobe Illustrator CC?

Non-destructive masks are used for clipping. Because of this, you can edit them in Illustrator CC without erasing any of your work. When compared to Photoshop's layer masks, Illustrator's clipping masks are more versatile and scalable since they employ vector shapes to mask.

Why Not Just Crop or Delete?

You might be asking why it isn't possible to just remove unnecessary pieces using the **Selection Tool.** A clipping mask's non-destructive nature is its main advantage over, for example, a basic path operation. You may easily modify the masked object or objects with various paths by going back and forth. This comes in handy especially when dealing with items in the layers panel, where handling them can get complicated. Then how about the **Crop Tool**? Sometimes people ask why raster images can't be cropped using the **Crop Image** tool. You can crop off unwanted areas of a raster picture by selecting it and then using the Crop Tool. However, a vector drawing with paths and anchor points cannot be cropped with the **Crop Tool.** Only raster pictures may be used with it.

Editing a Masked Object

Do you wish to alter the mask in any way? In the layers panel, locate the mask and click on its thumbnail. You can change the mask's opacity, compound path, or compound shape using this menu. Adjusting a vector mask is a good analogy if you're familiar with Adobe Photoshop.

Working with Text and Backgrounds

For editing text and backgrounds, clipping masks are also quite useful. You can use a clipping mask and a pattern layer to give text a pattern. Just put the text layer behind the pattern layer. How the pattern relates to the text can be customized using the transparency panel.

Clipping Masks with Multiple Layers

Multiple objects or groups of objects can be clipped to a single shape object using clipping masks in Adobe Illustrator with multiple layers. Because of this, you may use a single clipping mask shape to selectively show or conceal portions of several objects or layers.

How to Edit Clipping Masks with Multiple Layers in Illustrator?

To build a clipping layer with several layers, you must first construct the shape object and place it above the objects or groups of objects that will be clipped in the Layers panel. Following that, choose all the objects or groups of objects together with the shape object. Then, either use the shortcut **Ctrl+7 (**Windows) or **Command+7** (Mac) on your keyboard to create the clipping mask, or go to **Object > Clipping Mask > Make.**
Here are the step-by-step instructions:
1. To edit a clipping mask with many layers in Illustrator, open the document and find it.
2. Use the **Selection tool** to click on the shape object, and then select it. In the Layers panel, align the shape object such that it is above the objects or groups that will be trimmed.
3. Various common Illustrator shape tools, such as the **Rectangle, Ellipse,** and **Pen** tools, can be used to modify the shape. To alter the shape, you can vary its size, location, or curvature, among other things.
4. After you've made your changes to the shape, hold down the Shift key and click on each of the objects or groups of objects that are clipped to the shape.
5. To access the Edit Contents menu, navigate to **Object > Clipping Mask**, or use **Ctrl+Click** on a Windows computer or **Command+Click** on a Mac. In isolation mode, the contents of the clipping mask will be shown.
6. Using the usual set of Illustrator tools and capabilities, you can modify individual objects or groups of objects independently in isolation mode. Not only that, you can edit the characteristics of individual objects or groups of objects, as well as move or resize them.

7. To escape isolation mode and apply your changes, click anywhere outside of it when you're done editing an object or collection of objects.
8. Press **Ctrl+Alt+7** (Windows) or **Command+Option+7** (Mac) on your keyboard to release the clipping mask and eliminate the shape effect. Alternatively, you may select the clipped objects and go to **Object > Clipping Mask > Release**.

Troubleshooting Clipping Masks

Designers can control the visibility of particular areas of an image or graphic using clipping masks, a crucial feature of Adobe Illustrator. Clipping masks are fantastic, but they can be a pain to deal with at times. Common difficulties include improper or incomplete clipping, missing masks, the wrong layer order, masks that are translucent or empty, and many more.

Issues that frequently arise while using Illustrator's clipping masks

- **Incomplete or incorrect clipping:** Parts of the picture may still be visible after applying the clipping mask, which might lead to incomplete or inaccurate clipping.
- **Mask not showing up:** The clipping mask could be on the artboard but not show up in the Layers panel. This can make mask editing and manipulation more challenging.
- **Incorrect layer order:** For the clipping mask to function properly, the layer housing it must be placed above the layer housing the target picture. If this is not the case, the mask will not be able to do its job.
- **Transparent or empty masks:** Clipping masks can sometimes seem to be functioning well, but in reality, the masked region is either transparent or empty.

When using clipping masks in Illustrator, how can one go about fixing issues?

- **Check the layer order:** Put the clipping mask layer above the picture layer that needs masking. Just choose the layer you want to rearrange and move it up or down in the Layers panel.
- **Check the mask shape:** Make sure the mask shape fully encases the region that needs to be disguised by checking its shape. After picking the mask, you can modify its shape using the Direct Selection tool or the Pen tool.
- **Check the mask mode:** To make sure the mask mode is set to "Clip" instead of "Opacity," you may go to the Transparency panel after selecting the mask. Switch to "Clip" from "Opacity" if that's the mask mode you're using.
- **Check the transparency:** Make sure the layer with the picture that needs to be masked is not set to 100% opacity. This will prevent the masked region from becoming transparent

or empty. Just pick the layer you want to see how it looks and play around with the opacity slider in the transparency panel.

- **Check for hidden layers:** Make sure the clipping mask isn't locked or hidden if it doesn't appear in the Layers panel. Look for the little eye symbol next to the layer name in the Layers panel to see whether any layers are hidden. This layer will not be visible unless you see the eye icon. Select the empty box adjacent to the eye icon to reveal the layer.

Introduction to artboards

By utilizing artboards, you can expedite the creation process and experiment with designs on an endless canvas. An artboard in Illustrator is similar to a blank piece of paper that you may use as a foundation for your artwork. You can construct custom-sized artboards to develop your artwork or utilize the presets that are offered for common devices. And you can print or export them, too. You can select your artboard's settings and dimensions when you start a new document or access an existing one in Illustrator. Multiple artboards can be added or created if you have multiple designs. To suit your needs, you can also delete, resize, rename, and duplicate artboards. To begin with the artboard, make sure you have your **Properties, Control, or Artboard panel** close at hand. **To activate the panels after creating or opening a document, use the following options:**

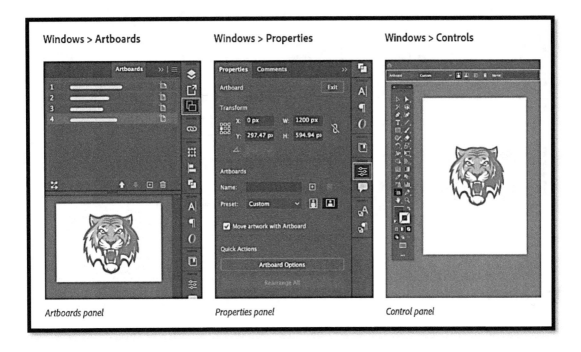

217

Managing Artboards

Create Individual Artboard Sizes for an Icon Set

With a single or double click of the Artboard tool, you can easily make a series of artboards in Adobe Illustrator that are proportional to each icon—ideal for exporting. In this way:

1. You can enter artboard editing mode by clicking the **Artboard Tool** or by pressing **Shift + O**.
2. You can view the existing artboard, which is Artboard 1 in this example, in the **Artboards panel**, which is accessible through the Window menu.
3. Simply **double-click your artwork** on Artboard 1 in the document window to resize it using the Artboard tool. Artboard 1 is now enlarged to accommodate the artwork.
4. Just use the Artboard tool to single-click on each of the remaining icons to make a new artboard for them.

At this point, don't stress over the artboard organization or order; we'll take care of that later.

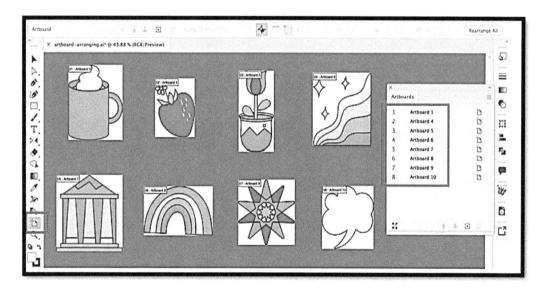

Above: the Artboard tool in the toolbar and confusing misnumbered artboard names in the panel

Managing Artboard Names

If you have more than one artboard in Adobe Illustrator, the program will automatically assign a unique number to each one. The names and artboard numbers can become confused when they are not in the correct sequence. Renaming the artboards in bulk is a fast remedy.

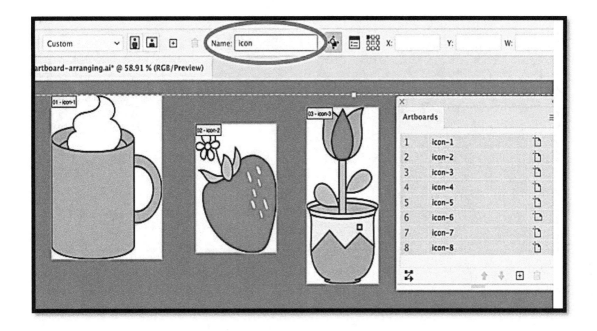

Renaming Illustrator artboards in bulk

You can rename numerous artboards in this way:
1. Click on the **Artboard tool** to enter artboard editing mode.
2. Hold down **Shift** and click on each artboard in the **Artboards panel** to pick them all.
3. Press the Enter key on the Control bar located at the top of Illustrator's window. In the Name field, type a popular prefix (for example, "icon").
4. Rearranging the naming of the artboards from first to last will ensure that the names of your artboards (Artboard 1, Artboard 2, etc.) correspond with their numbers.

Though I've already mentioned the quickest way, it could be more effective to give each artboard a meaningful name. **In the Artboards panel, double-click on an artboard name to change it.** Let's move one of our artboards to the top of the order in the Artboards panel.

Changing the Order of Artboards

Verify that the sequence of the artboards in the panel is right before attempting to rearrange their appearance in the document window. **My two-step procedure for rearranging and reordering them is as follows:**
1. To choose an artboard on the Artboard panel, just click on it.
2. To change its position on the order, use the arrow buttons located at the panel's base. You can also rearrange them by dragging and dropping, just as in the Layers panel.

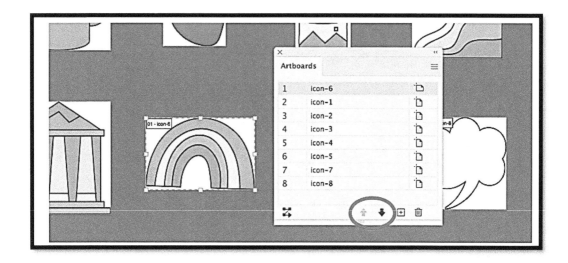

The position of the artboard you have chosen in the document window will not be visually altered when you move it to the first place in the panel. Artboards in the document window must be reorganized for them to appear in the same visual order as they do in the panel. In this way:

Rearranging Artboards

1. Press the **Rearrange Artboards** button on the Artboards panel.
2. Make any necessary adjustments to the layout, spacing, and checkboxes for **Move Artwork with Artboard**. Select **OK**.

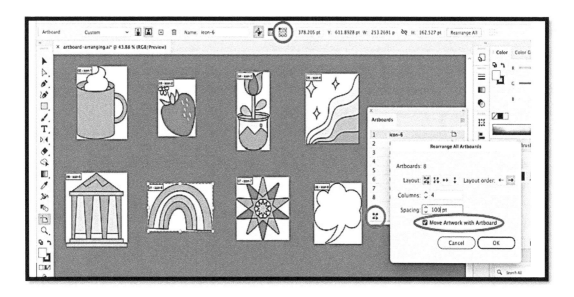

A quick tip: Default positioning for artboards is from the top left corner, so keep that in mind. Before you rearrange anything, go to the Control bar and click the reference point symbol to alter it. You might have to rename them once more after rearranging them to make sure the numbers remain in the correct sequence.

Creating a Margin for the Art

Slightly resize the icons so they don't touch the artboard edges. You can do all of the artwork at once with the help of the Transform each function.

1. Select the icons, then go to **Object > Transform > Transform each** after exiting Artboard mode.

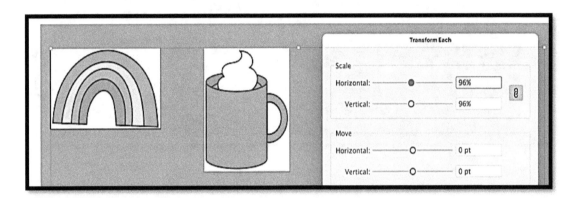

2. To center the panel, move the reference point from the bottom to the middle.
3. To get the best results with your artwork, lock proportional scaling and set the scale to 95%. Select OK.

Just a heads up: if you work with strokes like the art above, set your stroke scaling in Preferences before scaling. (**Edit > Preferences/Settings**.) Check **Scale Strokes and Effects** as needed.

New Feature: Scale Artwork with Artboards

Maintaining layout integrity and proportions and ensuring a similar experience across platforms is important when designing for numerous screen sizes, such as desktop, tablet, and mobile. **To do this, scale the artboard and artwork together.**

1. Before you can scale an object, choose it and then select the **Artboard tool** .
2. Choose "**Scale artwork with Artboard**" from the **Properties** panel.

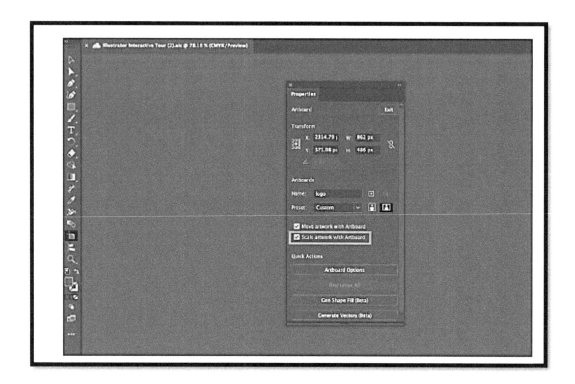

3. Adjust the dimensions of your artwork and artboard by dragging the bounding box.

CHAPTER 9

EFFECTS, FILTERS, AND APPEARANCE

Overview of the Effects Menu

The Appearance panel is where you can see the effects you've applied to objects. This effect can be edited, moved, duplicated, deleted, or saved as a graphic style. The object has to be expanded before the additional points can be accessed when an effect is used. You can find vector effects in the Effects menu's upper half. You can only use these effects on vector objects or bitmap objects' fill or stroke in the Appearance panel. In the Effects menu, raster effects make up the lower half. These can be used on bitmap or vector objects.

Apply an Effect

After you've selected an object, go to the Effects menu and pick an effect. The Appearance panel will display the effect after it has been applied. From the Appearance panel, you can also apply effects by clicking the *fx.* button and selecting an effect from the list.

Modify or Delete an Effect

- Click the Effect link in the Appearance panel to edit the effect.

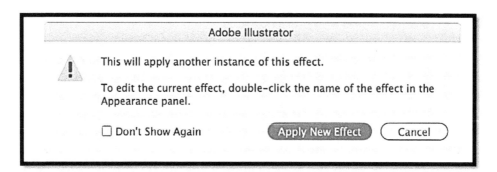

A dialog box will popup to alert you that this approach will produce the same effect twice on the same object if you pick the same effect from the Effect menu to alter the original. The **Appearance panel** will display a second instance of the effect when you click the **Apply New Effect** button. Pick out the effect you want to remove in the Appearance panel, and then hit the **Delete** button. Pressing the eye icon to the Effect's left will disable it, but it will not remove it entirely.

Applying Multiple Effects

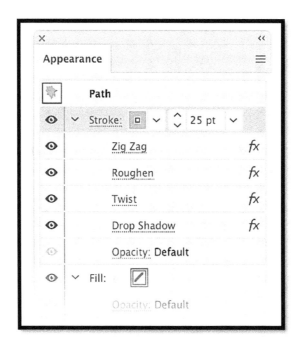

In the Appearance panel, you can apply several effects to a fill, stroke, or object. To apply an effect to the entire object, simply click on its name at the top of the Appearance panel. To apply the effect, click on either the path or the fill. Effects stack on top of one another when applied. One effect will have an impact on the one before it. In this example, the **Zig Zag Effect** was applied first, the Roughen Effect second, the Twist Effect third, and the **Drop Shadow Effect** last. By sliding the effects up or down the list, you can alter the appearance of the object by changing its order.

Scaling Effects

The default behavior of Illustrator's effects is to not scale with the object when the object is added to them. The effect will be applied to the full object when an object is scaled with an effect, but the effect itself will not scale. Select the box in the Transform panel to activate the **Scale Stroke & Effects** as required. To change the default settings of this feature, choose **Illustrator > Preferences > General (Mac)** and select **Scale Strokes & Effects,** or choose **Edit > Preference > General (PC).**

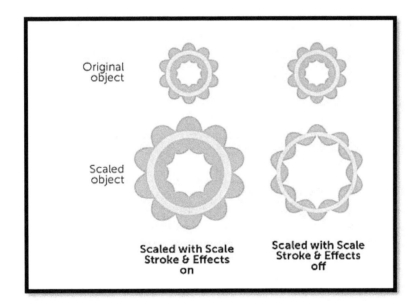

The object can be resized while the Scale Stroke & Effects is disabled. There will be no change to the stroke weight and the effects will be spread out throughout the whole shape. Whatever the object's initial shape was, the effect's appearance could alter drastically depending on the size. The effects and stroke will scale proportionally to the original shape when Scale Stroke & Effects is switched on. As a result, the object's appearance will remain unchanged regardless of the scale.

About raster effects

Instead of producing vector data, raster effects produce pixels. You can find raster effects under the Effect menu's bottom part, in SVG Filters, and in the **Effect > Stylize** submenu's Drop Shadow, Inner Glow, Outer Glow, and Feather commands. **This is all made possible by Illustrator's Resolution Independent Effects (RIE) feature:**

- To ensure that the effect's look is unaltered or barely changed when the resolution in **Document Raster Effects Settings (DRES)** is changed, the effect's parameters are interpreted to a new value. In the Effect dialog box, you can see the updated numbers for the parameters.
- Illustrator reinterprets the parameters of effects that are relevant to the document raster effects resolution setting, regardless of how many parameters the effect may have.

The Halftone Pattern dialog box, for instance, has several settings. Changing the DRES just affects the Size value, though.

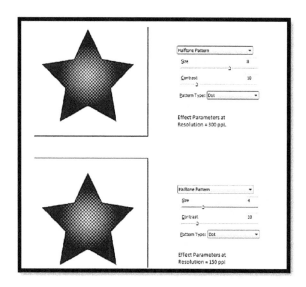

Halftone Pattern effect before and after the resolution value changes from 300 ppi to 150 ppi. By going to **Effect > Document Raster Effects Settings**, you may configure the document's rasterization parameters. **Note:** Raster effects might seem great on screen, but when printed, they can lose detail or look jagged. To fix this, just raise the resolution of the page.

Applying effects to bitmap images

With effects, you can give bitmap images and vector objects a unique style. You can create a wide variety of captivating visual effects, such as an impressionistic style; alter the lighting, warp pictures, and much more.

When dealing with bitmap objects and their effects, keep the following in mind:

- When working with linked bitmap objects, effects will not apply. Instead of the original, an embedded copy of a linked bitmap is affected when an effect is applied to it. You have to insert the original bitmap into the document so you can apply the effect on it.
- Adobe Photoshop and other Adobe applications, as well as third-party developers' plug-in effects, are compatible with Adobe Illustrator. Most plug-in effects, once installed, look like the built-in effects in the Effect menu and function similarly.
- When applied to a high-resolution bitmap image, some effects can be memory-intensive.

Improving performance for effects

It takes a lot of memory to implement some effects. When using these effects, the following methods can boost performance:

- To save time and avoid unexpected effects, use the Preview option in the effect dialog boxes.
- Change the settings. Some commands, such as Glass, are extremely memory-intensive. Try different settings to increase their speed.
- Before adding effects to a bitmap picture, convert it to grayscale if you're planning to print on a grayscale printer. It should be noted, nevertheless, that there are situations when the outcome of applying an effect on a grayscale version of a color bitmap picture could differ from the outcome when the image is converted to grayscale directly.

Modify or delete an effect

Through the use of the Appearance panel, you can alter or delete an effect.

1. Make your selection of the affected object or group, or utilize the Layers panel to zero in on the specific layer.
2. **Pick one option out of these:**
   - In the Appearance panel, you can change the effect by clicking on its name, which is blue and underlined. Edit the effect as needed in the dialog box that appears, and then hit the OK button.
   - In the Appearance panel, find the effect you want to remove, and then click the Delete button.

The Appearance Panel

The Appearance panel is already open; there's no need to open it! The **Properties** panel's Appearance panel appears on the selected object by default. When no object is chosen, it won't be seen. Because it is so much easier to change objects from the **Properties > Appearance panel**, I seldom ever use the real Appearance panel. Indeed, it has persisted throughout the years amidst the panels on your right-hand side.

How to Use the Appearance Panel in Illustrator

Step 1

The **Appearance** panel is a good place to begin. I need to know where the Illustrator **Appearance** panel is located first. You can access it by either hitting the **Shift-F6** keyboard shortcut or by navigating to **Window > Appearance**. The fill will be white and the stroke will be black by default.

A thumbnail displaying the current **Appearance** settings may be found in the top-left corner **(1)**. If it's not visible, you can access the Appearance panel's fly-out menu and choose **Show Thumbnail**. To hide the thumbnail in the Appearance panel, just choose **Hide Thumbnail**. To apply the current **Appearance** settings to an object in your design, just drag the thumbnail onto it. You may see the title bar **(2)** next to the thumbnail. In addition to showing whether a graphic style is applied, this bar also displays the type of object that is now chosen (No Selection, Path, Type, Group, Layer). If you want to make sure that the selection gets affected by an effect, rather than simply a single fill or stroke, you can click on it.

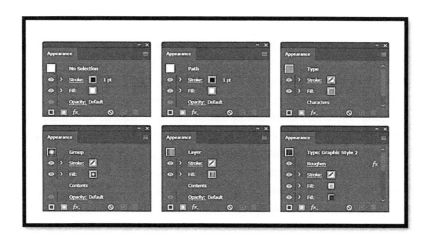

At last, the **Opacity** bar **(3)** is presented. You can change the **Opacity** and **Blending** Mode settings in the **Transparency** fly-out panel, which is accessible by clicking the underlined Opacity text. Rest assured, these modifications will have an impact on the entire object, not only on a fill or stroke.

Step 2

To access the **Swatches** or Color fly-out panels, respectively, to modify the color of a **fill**, pick the fill and click on its thumbnail. Alternatively, you may hold down the **Shift** key and click on the same thumbnail to access the **Color** fly-out panel. Changing the color of a **Stroke** is as simple as following the same commands.

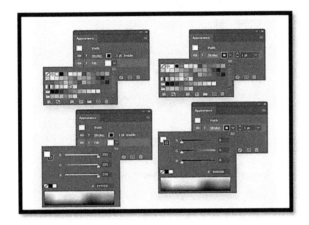

Step 3

The **Stroke Weight** can be adjusted by selecting a **Stroke**; the **Stroke** fly-out panel allows you to further stylize a **Stroke**. You can access the **Stroke** fly-out panel by clicking the underlined text.

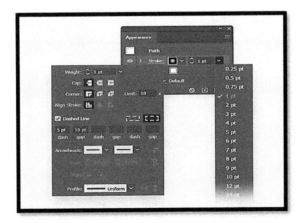

Step 4

Let's focus on the buttons at the bottom of the panel now that you've learned the fundamentals and how you can use them. The **Add New Fill button (2)** and the **Add New Stroke button (1)** are the first options. You can use them to create a new **Fill** or **Stroke**. Be aware that when you deselect all traits, the new one is superimposed on top of the others. It is possible to add a new characteristic on top of an existing **Fill** or **Stroke** selection.

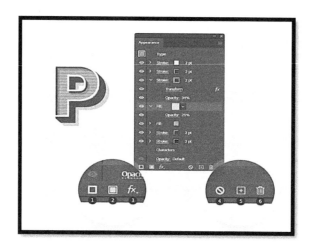

Press the **Add New Effect (3)** button to add an effect to the object as a whole, to a specific **Fill** or **Stroke**, or both. You can also access the same settings by selecting **Effect** from the menu bar. You can swiftly tidy up the **Appearance** panel by clicking the **Clear Appearance (4)** button. Aside from effects, it gets rid of fills and strokes. When you want to make a copy of a **Fill, Stroke**, or effect, just click the **Duplicate Selected Item (5)** button. By selecting the desired **Fill**, **Stroke**, or effect in the **Appearance** panel and then clicking the **Delete Selected Item button (6),** you may delete it. Remember that the **Control or Shift** keys can be held down to choose many attributes at once in the **Appearance** panel.

Not only can you get the **Add/Duplicate/Remove/Clear** commands from the fly-out menu, but you can also find them at the bottom of the **Appearance** panel.

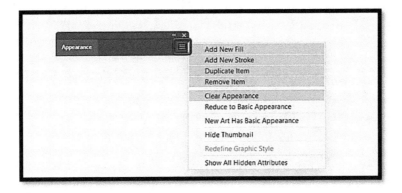

Step 5

Let's have a look at a more intricate design and some other options that can be changed before we dive into the remaining instructions from the fly-out menu. First of all, using the tiny arrow icons **(1)**, you can expand any Fill or Stroke. Once expanded, you will get access to a separate **Opacity** button **(4)** which can be used to adjust the Opacity and Blending Mode of that particular element. You can apply an effect **(3)** to a specific element when you pick a **Fill** or a **Stroke**. Finally, you can toggle the **Fill, Stroke,** effect, and **Opacity** settings on and off using the eye icons on the left-hand side **(2).** If you disable **opacity**, the default settings will take the place of the current ones. **Show All Hidden characteristics** are the option you'll find in the fly-out menu if you want to activate all hidden characteristics.

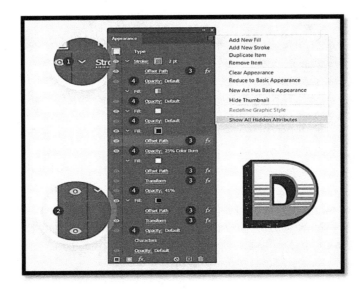

Step 6

Open the fly-out menu from the **Appearance** panel and go to **Reduce to Basic Appearance** whenever you wish to remove the existing attributes and keep just a single **Fill** and **Stroke**.

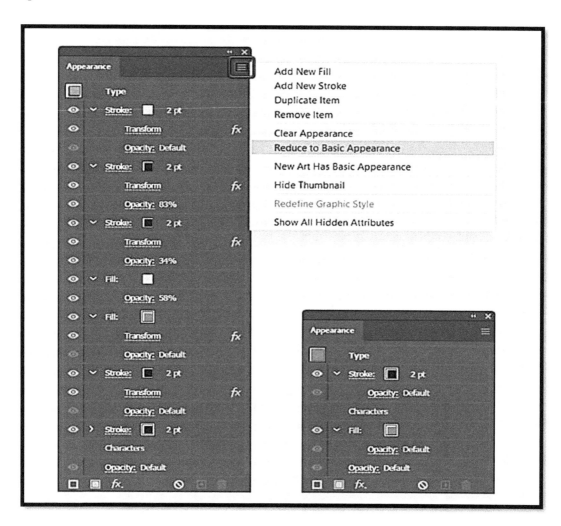

Step 7

To make new objects take the current **Appearance** settings, open the **Appearance** panel's fly-out menu, and deselect the **New Art Has Basic Appearance option**. By utilizing the **New Art Has Basic Appearance option** found in the fly-out menu, you may save one **Fill** and **Stroke** from the current characteristics for your new objects if you so want.

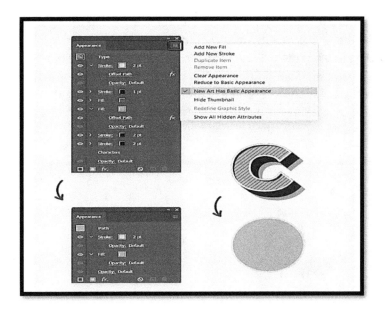

How to Use Graphic Styles in Illustrator

Step 1

You can choose to apply the same **Appearance** settings to another object after you're satisfied with the way a design looks. Whenever you want to mimic the look in Illustrator, you have a few choices. To start, you can place the preview image from the **Appearance** panel over an existing object by dragging and dropping. As a second option, you can access the **Layers** panel by going to **Window > Layers**. From there, you can concentrate on the icons that you want to use. Simply drag the symbol representing the object with the **Appearance** settings onto the icon representing the other object while holding down the **Alt** key.

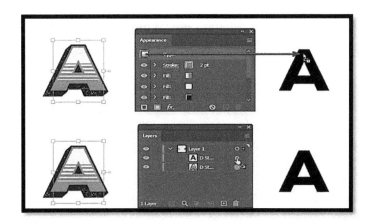

Third, you can save the **Appearance** settings as a graphic style and then use that graphic style to easily apply the same attributes to different objects. To start, you can open the **Graphic Styles** panel by going to **Window > Graphic Styles** or by pressing the **Shift-F5** keyboard shortcut. Just locate the **New Graphic Style** button at the panel's base and click it to save your changes. **Right-click** your new graphic style for a larger preview. After selecting the object, you can easily apply a graphic style by clicking on it. Click the graphic style while holding down the **Alt** key to apply its properties while keeping the current **Appearance** settings.

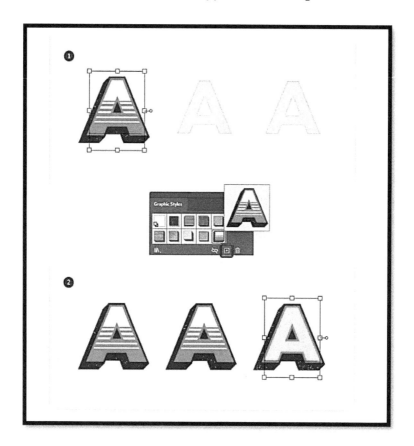

Step 2

Now that we've covered the fundamentals, let's look at the remaining buttons on the bottom panel and how you can use them. You can also access all of these functions via the fly-out menu, just like in the **Appearance** panel. Let me start by telling you that one of your graphic styles can also be duplicated by clicking the **New Graphic Style** button **(1)**. All you have to do is drag a graphic style on top of the button. If you want to delete a graphic style from Illustrator, you can do so by clicking the **Delete Graphic Style button (2).** Keep in mind that you can quickly switch between different visual styles by holding down the **Control** or **Shift** key.

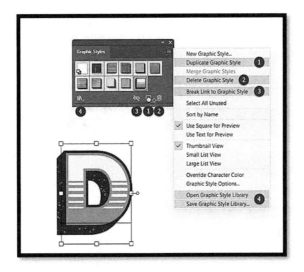

When you use the **Appearance** panel's fly-out menu to **redefine the graphic style**, you'll also see the **Break Link** command **(3).** Assume for a moment that you've been designing using the same graphic style for several objects. A graphic style will be applied to these objects when you choose them, and you can see it in the title bar of the **Appearance** panel. The link between these settings and your stored graphic style will be broken by clicking the **Break Link** button. Once you've made changes to the graphic style on one object and then go to **Redefine Graphic Style**, the style is updated in the **Graphic Styles** panel with the new settings. All instances where your graphic style is used will also be updated. If an object isn't associated with a certain graphic style, then it will retain its original appearance. Keeping both the original and modified visual styles could be useful in some situations. You can use the **Duplicate Graphic Style** command in this situation. Just make a copy of the style first, and then use the **Redefine Graphic Style** command.

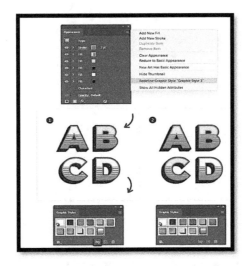

Graphic styles can be shared among Illustrator documents. Using the **Graphic Styles Libraries (4)** button, you can open some panels with built-in graphic styles **(A)**, you can save your own set of graphic styles **(B)** or open other sets of graphic styles **(C)**.

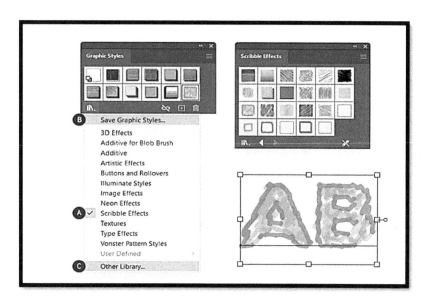

Step 3

To merge the properties of many graphic styles into one, just hold down the **Control** key while selecting them all. Then, open the fly-out menu and choose **Merge Graphic Styles**.

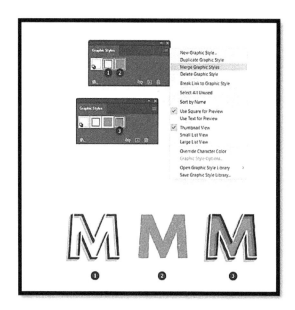

Step 4

To swiftly choose all of the panel's unused graphic styles, utilize the fly-out menu and choose **"Select All Unused" (1).**

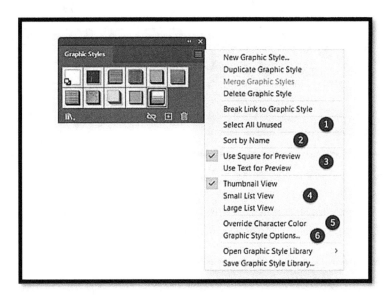

For a more naming-based organization of your graphic designs, use the fly-out menu's **Sort by Name (2)** option. To rename a graphic style, select it and go to **Graphic Style Options** in the fly-out menu.

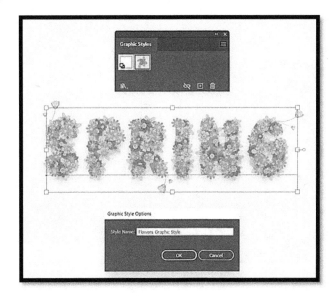

Check one of the two options to preview your graphic styles applied either to a shape or to text **(3)**.

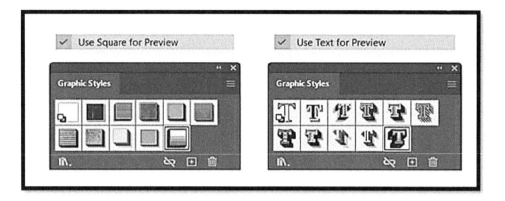

Aside from the usual **Thumbnail view**, two other view options are available **(4).** You can use them if you want to see how your graphic style has changed. Keep in mind that you can still access a bigger preview of your graphic styles by right-clicking on them.

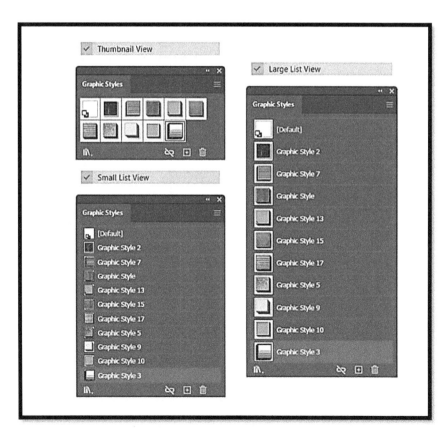

Step 5

Finally, **Override Character Color** will only affect the text in your design. When applying a graphic style, keep it enabled to remove the original font color; disable it to maintain it.

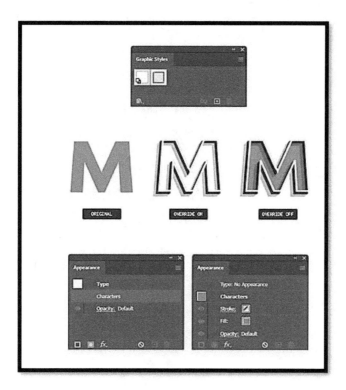

Applying 3D Effects and Extrusions

With the help of 3D effects, you can transform 2D artwork into 3D objects. One can manipulate the look of three-dimensional objects by adjusting their lighting, shading, rotation, and other attributes. On top of that, you can add artwork to each surface of a 3D object individually.

Types of 3D Effects in Illustrator

3D Effects in Illustrator is primarily divided into two processes,
1. EXTRUDE
2. REVOLVE
1. **Extrude**

A 2D feature in the X-Y plane can be made thicker by developing it along the Z-axis, a process known as extrusion. Alternatively, it is the act of raising a two-dimensional drawing to a three-dimensional model. In terms of power and ease of use, it is unparalleled for creating 3D objects.

Using Illustrator's Extrude tool, you may extrude any complicated shape or size. The length and thickness to be extruded can be customized. We will observe an example of extruding text in Adobe Illustrator to learn more about the extrude tool.

Step 1: First, launch Adobe Illustrator and create a new project. Pick a page size from the options. Your program will launch with a white blank page.

Step 2: After that, you need to enter the text that you want to extrude. One can observe a vertical toolbar situated at the far-left side of the illustrator. There are all the tools you need to create different effects in that toolbox. You can see the toolbox in the image below.

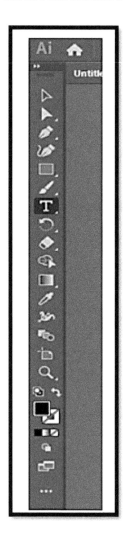

Step 3: The third step is to add texts in Illustrator using the type tool (T). To begin typing, use the "type" tool on the toolbar and then use the mouse to click and drag a text box onto the artboard. Whatever you choose to write, you can write. I extruded the word "**ILLUSTRATOR**" here as an example. See the image given below.

Step 4: You can customize the text by selecting a font that suits your needs. From the character panel, you can adjust the text size. Selecting the window choice will bring up the dialog box where you may adjust the text size. Navigate to the Window menu, and then choose **Type**, and finally, **Character**.

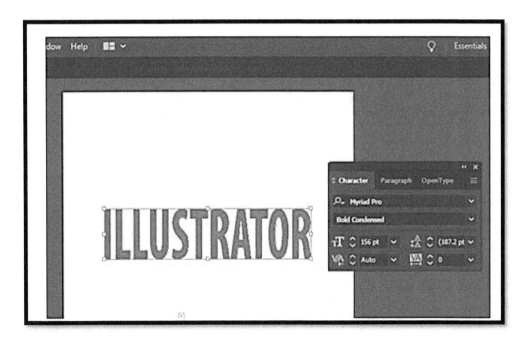

Step 5: To extrude the text, you have to convert the text into shapes so that you can extrude the shape easily. For that, select your text using the selection tool (V), then go to **Type> Create Outlines.**

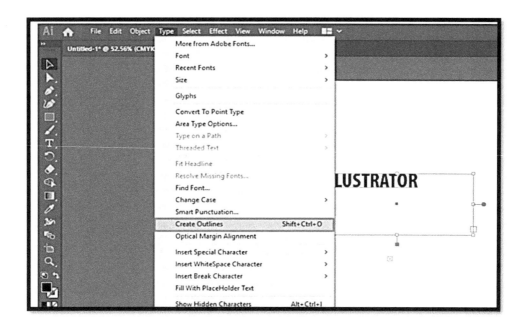

Step 6: Then, an outline will be created around your text. This shows your text is converted to shape. See the image below.

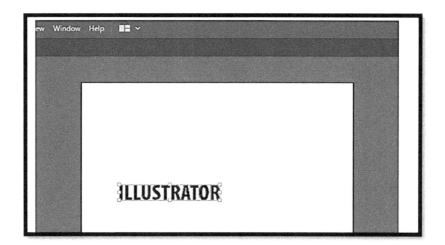

Step 7: Adding color to your text is another effect you can use. Any color in the list can be applied to your text. Click **Window > Color** to bring up the color panel, where you can select a color from the palette.

Step 8: Form a group before you transform the text into 3D. When you group the text using **Object > Group**, the letters will retain their shape regardless of the effects you apply.

Step 9: A dialog box will open; pick your text and then go to **Effect>3D>Extrude and Bevel** to apply the 3D effect. Among its many features is the ability to modify the extrusion's depth, location, perspective, Bevel, and so on. A text field for the extrude depth can be seen in the dialog box. Following the example in the image below, enter the depth value you need.

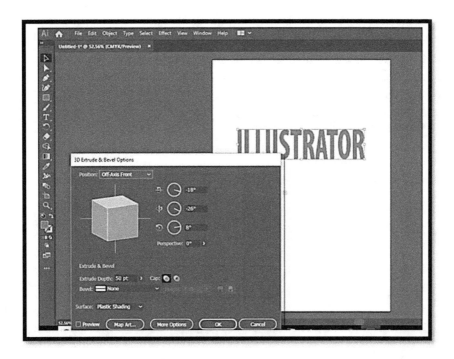

Step 10: If you click the preview button in the 3D dialog box, you can see how your text will look after extrusion. Look at the image I've included below.

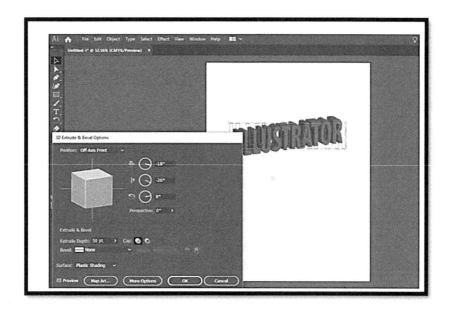

You can see the extruded text is out of perspective since it is so big. By adjusting the value of perspective in the extrude dialogue box, you can resolve this issue.

2. **Revolve**

A revolutionary step in design is making a two-dimensional drawing into a three-dimensional object by angling it along one axis. Another definition is rotating a 2D drawing around its axis to make it seem thicker. Just as crucial as extruding is the revolve tool. The illustrator revolve tool is most commonly used to make circular and hollow objects. Building a bottle is going to be the project to practice with the revolve tool.

Step 1: First, launch Adobe Illustrator and create a blank page. Sketching out the bottle's profile is the starting point for this procedure. That requires you to use a pen tool to depict the bottle's half. To create a half-profile like the one below, use the pen tool.

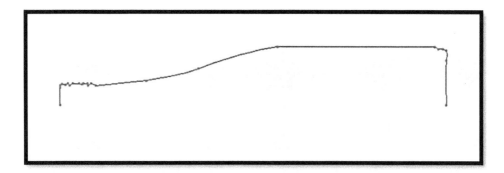

Step 2: After the first step, you have to determine the axis of rotation. The plane and edge that will be revolved must be chosen. Use the selection tool to choose this option.

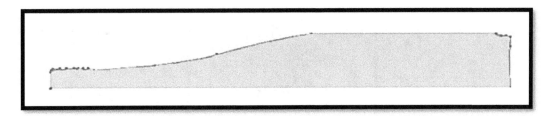

Step 3: When you've finished drawing, pick it, and then, in the effects menu, choose the revolve option. **Effects>3D>Revolve**. Afterward, a dialogue window will appear, offering many choices for revolving the drawing. Here you can find the 3D revolve settings; they allow you to adjust some revolve characteristics. You can watch the revolved bottle on the screen by selecting the preview option, as demonstrated below.

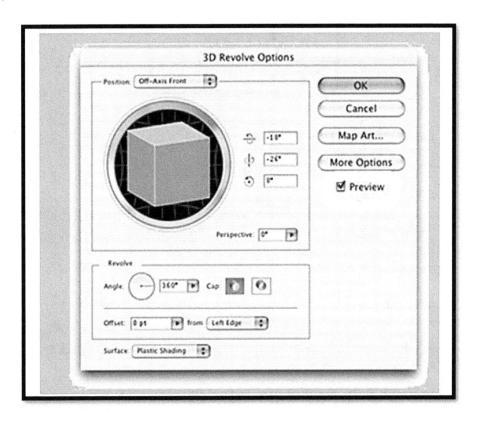

Step 4: Here you can adjust the rotational angle, thickness, offset, and more using these revolve options. Alternate perspectives of your three-dimensional object can be accessed by simply rotating the cube.

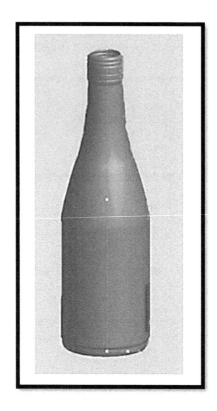

Mockup Creation and Visual Prototyping

Create a mockup with your image

1. Open **Window** > **Mockup**. The **Mockup** panel appears.
2. Next, choose **Create Mockup** from the **Mockup** panel once you've selected the image and vector art together using the **Selection** tool. Mockups are created by applying vector graphics to images.

The free image templates in the **Mockup** panel will also show you a glimpse of your vector art. Simply drag and drop a picture on the canvas to replace your own.

3. Simply drag the vector art to the canvas and drop it where you want it on the image. The artwork will automatically resize itself to fit the object's shape.

4. To move the artwork to its present spot, click outside of the image. Click **Edit Content** ⊙ in the **Properties** panel after selecting the artwork to reposition it.

Save mockup as a template for later use.

By selecting it and then clicking on the **Mockup** panel, you can save your mockup as a template. Under the panel's "**Your Mockups**" submenu, you'll see the newly uploaded template. A placeholder showing the location of the vector graphics is displayed in the template. As with any other well-selected template, you can utilize your template. The number of mockup templates you can upload to **Your Mockups** can be up to 20. On your PC, they are available across all Illustrator documents. Using Illustrator 28.5 or previous versions, you cannot simply import mockups into **Your Mockups**. To start over, you must first make the mockup public.

Create a mockup with a free image template

1. Open **Window** > **Mockup**. The **Mockup** panel appears.
2. Before choosing **Preview Mockup** in the **Mockup** panel, use the **Selection** tool to pick out the vector art. On the free image templates in the panel, you may see a sample of your vector artwork.
3. Choose the appropriate template category for your application by using the panel's drop-down menu.
4. Drag a template you like on the canvas to create a mockup.
5. Simply drag the vector art to the canvas and drop it where you want it on the image. The artwork will automatically resize itself to fit the object's shape.
6. To move the artwork to its present spot, click outside of the image. Once you've chosen the artwork to reposition, go to the **Properties** panel and choose **Edit Content.**

Midway through the **Mockup** workflow, changing your selection to another vector object on the canvas will clear the preview in the **Mockup** panel.

Edit a mockup

You can edit a mockup as a whole, or edit the image or vector art on its own.
1. Select the mockup.
2. Choose **Edit Image**, **Edit Content**, or **Edit Mockup Group** from the **Properties** panel.

Edit vector art as a symbol

The vector art becomes a symbol when you make a mockup, opening up additional editing options. To edit the symbol, double-click the artwork, and then double-click the mockup group to activate isolation mode.

Release a mockup

1. Select the mockup.
2. Select **Release** in the **Mockup** panel.

Current limitations

- Mockup art cannot include elements like graph, raster, placed art, non-native art, raster effects, or gradient mesh. A warning notice stating that **Mockup** will lead to an appearance mismatch will show or **Object > Mockup > Preview Mockup / Create Mockup** will be grayed out for unsupported elements.

- Vector artwork that contains or expands to a clip group, such as a pattern, is not acceptable as mockup art.
- Not even within another mockup can you make a new one.
- Images of the sky, tiny grooves, and reflecting surfaces can all lead to quality problems.
- Vector art that is part of a mockup group cannot have effects applied to it directly from the **Effect** menu. Vector effects may be applied by switching to the symbol editing mode.
- Illustrator files that are linked will not be supported. To utilize the files in mockups, embed them.
- You cannot use numerous pictures to make a mockup.
- With **Mockup**, you need a graphics processing unit (GPU) on your PC.
- Mockups that include several vector objects cannot be added to **Your Mockups.**
- Mockups made with Illustrator 28.5 or before cannot be imported straight into **Your Mockups.**

CHAPTER 10

OUTPUT AND FILE MANAGEMENT

Understanding Illustrator File Formats: AI, PDF, SVG, EPS

Knowing the many file types you can utilize and what makes each one special is crucial while working with Adobe Illustrator. Knowing the differences between AI, PDF, SVG, and EPS can help you choose the correct one if you need to save a project for later, transmit it to a customer, or use it online.

1. **AI (Adobe Illustrator File)**

When you open Adobe Illustrator, the default file type is AI. This file format was developed by Adobe, especially for storing Illustrator vector artwork. **Let me explain the significance of the AI format:**

- **Editable Vector Content**: Keeping your artwork completely editable is best done using an AI file. It is easy to return and make adjustments since you can save all paths, shapes, text, layers, and more.
- **High-Quality Graphics**: AI files save vector graphics, which means they can be scaled without sacrificing quality. For projects that may require artwork to be reproduced in numerous sizes or utilized across many platforms, this is essential.
- **Compatibility**: Although Adobe Illustrator is the primary application for opening AI files, other Adobe products such as Photoshop can also open them (with certain limitations). To be able to use other design tools, you may need to convert them or install certain plug-ins.
- **When to Use AI Files**: If you're working on a project that requires a high level of editability, then you should use AI files. Due to the format's lack of complete support from many other applications, it is not suitable for sharing with those who do not have Illustrator.

2. **PDF (Portable Document Format)**

- PDF, created by Adobe, is a very flexible file format. The ability to transfer files between devices while keeping their formatting and style makes it a popular choice.
- **Universal Format**: PDFs are universally compatible and can be accessed on nearly any device, so they are a fantastic option for customers or coworkers who do not have Illustrator to view your artwork.
- **Preserve Vector Data**: When you export a PDF from Illustrator, the vector components are kept, ensuring that the artwork is always crisp and scalable. When transferring documents that require printing, this feature becomes invaluable.
- **Editable Option**: You can preserve the PDF's editability by choosing the correct export options in Illustrator. What this implies is that you can open the PDF in Illustrator again and all of the components, layers, and paths will be accessible.

- **Security Options**: When sharing critical designs, a layer of security can be added by using PDF files that have security options like password protection and encryption.
- **When to Use PDF Files**: If you need to print or distribute your design but would like to keep the quality and editability, a PDF file is the way to go. It's perfect for proofreading or presentations when the receiver won't be making any changes.

3. **SVG (Scalable Vector Graphics)**
- Web designers created SVG, an XML-based file format. Because it enables browsers to show vector pictures, it is very helpful for web graphics.
- **Scalable without Quality Loss**: Because they are vector-based, SVGs can be resized to any size without sacrificing quality. In responsive web design, this is crucial since images must display properly regardless of the user's device resolution.
- **Lightweight**: SVG files are often tiny, which aids in the loading of web pages. The speed and ease of use of the web will both benefit from this.
- **Editable in Code**: Since SVG is XML-based; it can be opened and edited in a text editor. This makes it editable in code. Because it permits simple adjustments and animations with CSS or JavaScript, developers frequently value this flexibility.
- **Interactive Features**: SVG files are great for complicated online visuals that need user engagement since they can incorporate interactive features like hover effects.
- **When to Use SVG Files**: When making images for applications or websites, SVG is the way to go. If your logo, symbol, or other picture has to look great across a variety of devices, this is the way to go.

4. **EPS (Encapsulated PostScript)**
- Created for high-resolution printing and graphics, EPS is an older vector format. It finds extensive application in prepress and professional printing processes.
- **Cross-Platform Compatibility**: Many other vector-based products, not only Adobe Illustrator, can open and edit EPS files. For clients or printers that don't have Illustrator, this is a great alternative.
- **Preserve Vector Data**: Just like AI and PDF, EPS keeps your artwork's vector components. Banners and billboards, which require designs that can be magnified substantially, benefit from this.
- **Limited Web Use**: Due to its lack of support by the majority of browsers, EPS is not recommended for usage on the web. For creations that will be printed or designed to be transferred to other applications, it is more suitable.
- **When to Use EPS Files**: Use an EPS file when you need to submit a design to a printer or are working on a project with someone else that uses vector software. Additionally, it's a good pick for items that will be printed in bulk.

In summary

The following are some of the best uses for each of these file types:
- **AI** works wonders in Adobe Illustrator when it comes to keeping your project editable and prepared for subsequent tweaking.

- When it comes to sharing and printing, **PDF** excels in preserving layout and quality.
- If you need lightweight, scalable graphics for your website, **SVG** is the way to go.
- **EPS** is perfect for sharing vector graphics with different design tools and for professional printing.

When it comes time to publish, print, or show your work, knowing which format to use can make all the difference. Before settling on a file format, think about your project's requirements and intended purpose.

Packaging a file

Navigate to **File > Package** in Illustrator (AI) to copy the whole document, including any embedded images and fonts. Illustrator will generate a folder in the place you choose in the "**Package**" dialog box; after that, you may copy its contents. As an option, you can rename the folder if required. Make sure you click **OK** after selecting **Package**.

Creating a PDF

Portable Document Format (PDF) files record your project and make it easy to read and share even when you're not using Illustrator. If you follow these instructions to make a PDF, your Illustrator project will look exactly like the PDF, so anybody with a free PDF reader can see it.

- Select **"File" > "Save As"** to save the document as a PDF. Change the name of the file in the **Save As** dialog box, then select Adobe PDF as the file type, and then click the Save button. To produce the PDF, go to the Save Adobe PDF dialog box and click the Save PDF button.

Creating pixel-perfect drawings

Set up pixel-snapping

- Pick **View > Pixel Preview** from the main menu to start. If you zoom in to a setting of 600% or higher, you can see the pixel grid at this point.
- Also, before you rasterize your artwork, you may see how it will look with the Pixel Preview function. This capability is quite useful when you want to customize the size, position, and appearance of objects in a rasterized visual.
- Click the **Snap to Pixel option** located in the **Snap Options** section of the Properties box when there is nothing selected elsewhere on your artboard.

Draw pixel-perfect artwork every time.

Now, as you draw straight-edged paths or vector objects, they will automatically align to the pixel grid. Consider how much time you may save by starting with clean, precise lines.

Art stays pixel-aligned even when moved around.

Because they will always stay aligned to the pixel grid no matter where you drag them, your paths and shapes won't change appearance. If the anti-aliased art appears fuzzy, you may also try moving it around. If the anti-aliased edges are still visible, you can move the impacted anchor point or path segment to the nearest pixel grid using the **Direct Selection tool**. The leftover anti-aliased edges will be removed by this.

Fearlessly scale artwork

The shape segments, path segments, and anchor points in your artwork will all automatically resize to fit the pixel grid.

Make any artwork pixel-perfect with just one click

- **Make Pixel Perfect** is an option that you can get by right-clicking on the region you wish to edit. Artwork or icons with anti-aliased effects and fuzzy edges will be the result.

Please be aware that this method will not improve the appearance of curved or diagonal lines in your artwork, but it will make straight edges look sharper.

Previewing artwork in Pixel Preview mode

By switching to this mode, you may see your image just how it will look when shared online. The **"ctrl +" button** can be used to enlarge the picture. Pressing the right keys on your keyboard will reveal how each pixel contributes to the creation of this artwork. These pixels will stand out more as you enlarge the image. On any given occasion, you can use the **"ctrl -"** keys on your keyboard to zoom out.

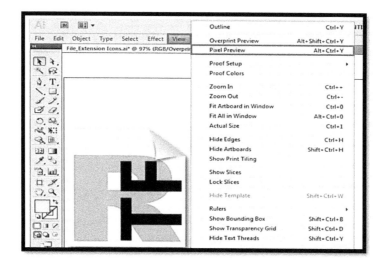

252

Aligning new artwork to the pixel grid

With Illustrator, you can create pixel-perfect art that looks sharp and separate on screens, and you can also experiment with different stroke lengths and alignment options. A new object can be aligned exactly as you are drawing it, or an old object can be aligned to the pixel grid with only one click. Pixel alignment can be preserved even when objects are being edited, ensuring that artwork remains undistorted. Not only can objects be manipulated using pixel alignment, but also their constituent path segments and anchor points.

Aligning existing artwork to the pixel grid

You can utilize the art you currently have to pick out specific objects or parts of objects and line **them up with the grid of pixels. You will discover that this feature is particularly useful when you copy and paste objects from other documents that are not pixel-aligned.**

1. Get the object you want to line up with the pixel grid by using the Selection tool. Pixel alignment can also be applied to specific areas of the object. To achieve this, choose horizontal or vertical sections of the object using the **Direct Selection tool.**
2. If you want a replica of an existing object, you can do one of these things:
   o Find the **"Align Selected Art to Pixel Grid"** icon in the control panel and click on it.
   o Choose **"Object"** then **"Make Pixel Perfect"** from the drop-down menu.
   o Right-click the object, then choose **Make Pixel Perfect** from the in-context menu to get flawless pixels.

Considerations

- Alignment adjustments to bring objects into line with the pixel grid will not be applied to objects without any vertical or horizontal segments.
- If the object you've chosen is already pixel-aligned, Illustrator will let you know with this notice:

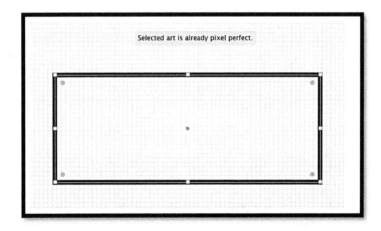

- Illustrator will let you know if the artwork in the selection can't be pixel-aligned. For instance, the chosen work of art in the image below is completely devoid of any horizontal or vertical components.

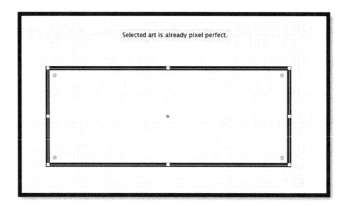

PDF

One of the most popular ways to distribute your final works is in Portable Document Format (PDF) form. To open a PDF, you can download Adobe Acrobat Reader for free. Pro, the more robust sister of Reader, is Adobe Acrobat, which users can use to alter PDFs or add new features to them. If you're not sure whether you have an Acrobat Reader, you can use the built-in PDF reader in most web browsers to open and view PDF files. When compared to Illustrator documents, Acrobat PDFs have the advantage of preserving the layout and text formatting of the original program, even if the recipient doesn't have the same apps or fonts as the creator.

Presets

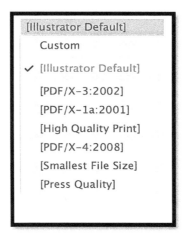

You can immediately save your Illustrator files to a PDF format by going to File > Save > Adobe PDF. When you're asked to name and save the file, you can choose where to store it. You may adjust the rendering quality and color settings in the dialog box that follows. There will be no PDF created if you cancel at either point. In the Save As PDF dialog box, you can find the Adobe PDF Presets dropdown menu, where you may access the presets for saving a file. **The Presets in brackets ("[" and "]")** are built-in and cannot be changed. By selecting Custom from the list of Presets, you can modify the parameters at a later time. And you could wish to alter a lot of items! Many printing companies have their preferred presets and will gladly recommend one or even provide a custom one they've created for their specific workflow. A word of caution against going with what "sounds" correct when selecting a preset. Saving your work with Illustrator Default will be your best bet if you're unsure about the Presets. Even if maintaining a tiny file size is your primary concern, I advise against ever using Smallest File Size.

The receiver will receive a file that does not like the one you originally prepared since **Smallest File Size** deletes much of the information from it, including the typefaces you have used. If you want professional-looking results from your home printer without paying for photo lab prices, **High-Quality Print** is the way to go. If you are getting your file ready to be printed by a print shop with high-end equipment and excellent paper quality, **Press Quality** is a solid choice. The graphics printing business has adopted **PDF/X** as its standard. All of the file's graphics, fonts, and colors are rendered to a professional standard by this preset. All the essential information to edit the file is likewise contained in these files. Most recently updated PDF/X standards include changes to the color rendering in versions 1, 3, and 4.

General Options

When you save a file as an Illustrator PDF, the first set of options are the General options.

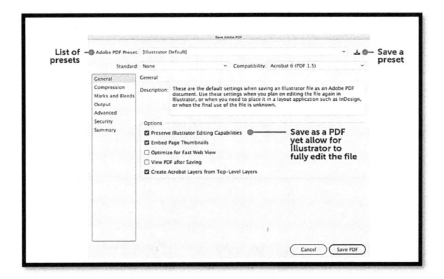

255

If you find that the Illustrator default does not meet your needs, you can select the presets below. With the **Preserve Illustrator Editing Capabilities** option, you can make sure that the complete file can be edited in Illustrator. However, other users who don't have Illustrator or don't need to modify the file will see it as a PDF. If the file is going to be edited, this is a nice option to have checked. With the help of **Embed Page Thumbnails**, you may capture a picture of every artboard in the PDF and use it as a thumbnail for each page when you open the file in Adobe Acrobat or Reader. **Optimize for Fast Web View** speeds up the preview and reading process if the PDF is to be displayed on the web. The **Create Acrobat Layers** tool takes the Illustrator file's top-level layers and preserves their original layout in the PDF.

Compression

Images that are either linked to or integrated into an Illustrator file are the most common targets of compression. The picture quality is drastically reduced by using the Smallest File Size setting, making the final product unsuitable for printing but perfect for viewing on screen. Instead of using JPEG, which discards data and produces compression lines in the photographs, a more print-friendly option would be to use ZIP compression, which is lossless. Any picture whose resolution is greater than the provided value will have its resolution reduced to the lower value using the Downsampling option. Even when the quality drops, the file size will go down. In general, 300 pixels per inch (ppi) is the minimum acceptable picture resolution for professional printing. While 72 ppi is considered low resolution and is best reserved for use on screens or the internet, 150 ppi is fine for home printing.

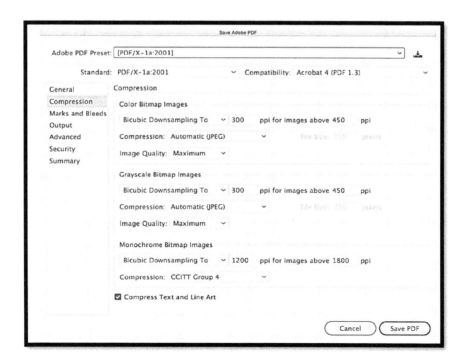

Marks and Bleeds

After the final print run, the paper will be trimmed according to the bleed and crop marks, which extend beyond the artboard's edge. Additional information, such as the filename or the date, may be required by some printers (Page Information). To illustrate the ink density when the file is sent to press, color bars can be included.

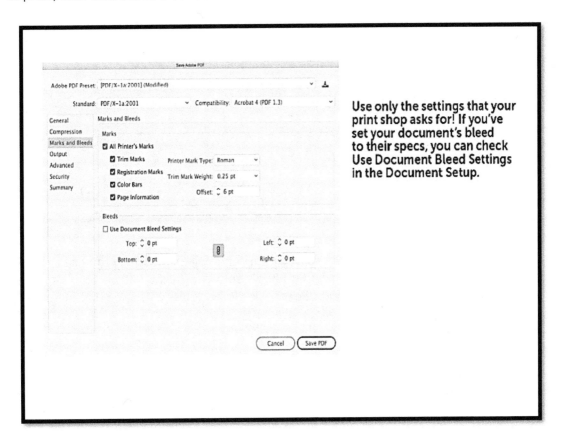

Use only the settings that your print shop asks for! If you've set your document's bleed to their specs, you can check Use Document Bleed Settings in the Document Setup.

Output

To adjust the color output, go to the Output menu. Here, the Destination is the most important option. The sRGB profile stands for standard displays if the PDF is only going to be seen on a screen. When it comes time to print, select the profile that your print shop has recommended. They could even provide you with one to install. Color Conversion: **Convert to Destination (Preserve Numbers)** must be specified once a Destination profile has been chosen. If you've made any CMYK decisions in Illustrator, converting all RGB information to the printer's chosen profile is a breeze using a CMYK Destination.

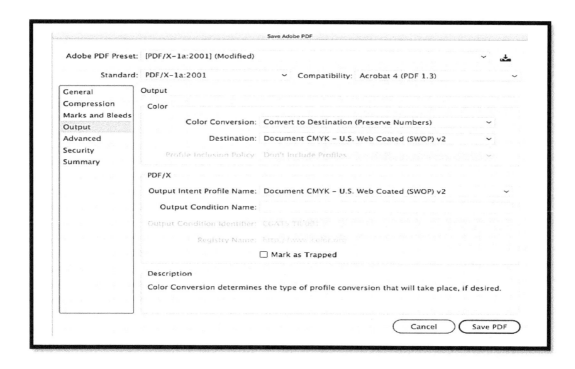

Maybe the printer will want you to skip color conversion altogether so they can use the most recent profile on their own. Since the print shop's software might not be fond of having extraneous data contained in PDFs, the Profile Inclusion Policy is also a decision that they make.

Advanced

Determines the cutoff for embedding full fonts depending on the percentage of characters used by the font in the document with **Subset Fonts When Percent of Characters Used Is Less Than (X%)**. When a font's character count in the document surpasses a certain threshold, it is considered fully embedded. The file size will rise if you incorporate all typefaces, however, if you want to be sure, enter 0%.

Security

To make a PDF secure from unauthorized access, you can use **Document Open Password** to encrypt it. Adobe Acrobat, and not Illustrator, is where you'll find these options. An Open Password or Editing Password may be required to access or modify a PDF file in Illustrator. Even though it's not as safe, the **Permissions portion** tries to restrict some actions (such as printing or extracting material) without a password. But there's software that gets around it.

Summary

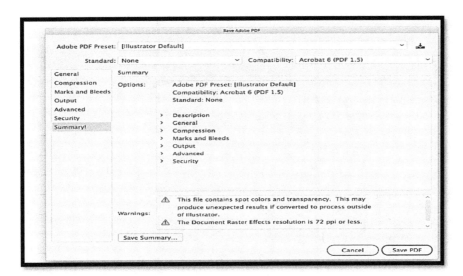

The PDF's configuration choices are included in the **Summary**. Detailed information about the selected options can be viewed by expanding each one in the Summary. If there are any problems with the settings not being compatible with the selected preset and choices, these are displayed in the Warnings section. You can save a digital copy of the summary for future reference by clicking the "Save Summary..." button.

Exporting Artworks

To export whole artboards or specific assets from Illustrator, you can use the **File > Export > Export for Screens command and the Asset Export panel.** This is useful for showing off a work-in-progress or for seeing specific assets. JPEG, SVG, PDF, PNG, OBJ, USDA, USDZ, GLTF, and WebP are just a few of the file types you can export. While most browsers support these formats, their strengths lie in their optimization for various online and mobile environments, as well as in on screen presentations and 3D applications. After being chosen, the artwork is instantly stored as a separate file, separate from the rest of the design.

Asset Export

Creating assets in a variety of sizes and formats has never been easier than with the Export for Screens panel. With the Asset Export panel, you can easily make and export your works to several file types, including PNG-8 and PNG-24, JPG, SVG, and PDF, for use in online and mobile workflows. To make alternative copies of the artwork in various sizes for online usage or for iOS and Android devices, the file sizes can be custom-made.

Adding Assets

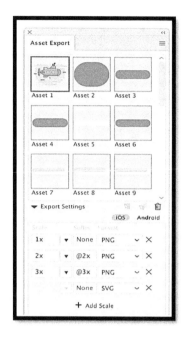

You may easily add your artwork to the **Asset Export** panel (**Window >Asset Export**) by dragging and dropping it into the window. Important: To export artwork to an asset, either combines it into one file before dragging and dropping it into the **Asset Export window** or press **Option (Mac) or Alt (PC)** while dragging. The different shapes of the artwork will all display as independent assets if it is not grouped, which is likely not what you were going for. Feel free to include as many assets from the current document as you need in the export box. Because it is not a library, the Asset Export panel will not display assets from documents other than the current one when you go to a different open document. Having all of your assets in one document could make exporting them easier.

Export Settings

The **Asset Export** panel has a drop-down menu where you may adjust the export settings for each format individually. PNG-8, PNG-24, JPEG quality, SVG, and PDF output parameters can all be modified. You should now export your assets in the sizes and formats required by your target audience or device. To export an object, first pick it. Then, decide on the parameters, file format (es), and file size(s). Depending on the iOS format you choose, the file sizes will appear as 5x, 1x, 2x, etc., of the original artwork's size. Ldpi, mdpi, hdpi, xldpi, and so on are the names of the format sizes available in Android.

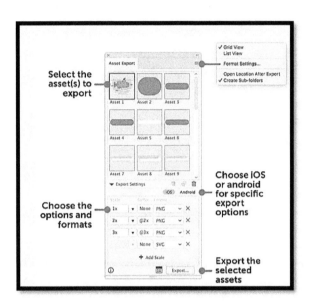

Click the + Add Scale area to add scale and formats to the list. After you select the destination folder and click the export button, a new folder will be generated, with subfolders that correspond to the various scales.

Updating Assets

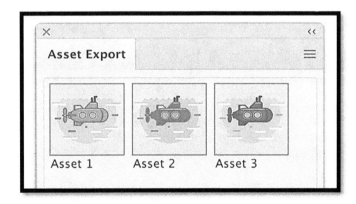

You won't have to reload the assets into the Asset Export panel if you update them in Illustrator. Smarter than that, Illustrator is. The Asset Export panel will reflect any changes made to the artwork instantly. Whether the final artwork is grouped or not, this applies to all artwork, grouped or ungrouped. For example, if you update artwork with several objects and each object is in the Asset Export panel, all pieces will update. To produce a copy of an existing piece of artwork, just make a copy on the artboard, alter it as needed, and then drag and drop it into the Asset Export panel. You will receive a one-of-a-kind rendition of that artwork from this. The Asset Export panel will also remove the version of the Asset when artwork is removed from the file. Only assets that are present in the file will be seen in the panel.

Export for Screens.

- Get the file open.
- Choose **View > Fit All In Window**.
- Choose **File > Export > Export For Screens**.
- One can select to export assets or artboards in the resulting Export For Screens dialog box. You can adjust the export parameters on the dialog box's right side once you've decided what to export.
- Review the artboard thumbnails by clicking the Artboards tab. Remove the checkmarks from the last two artboards but keep the first three selected.

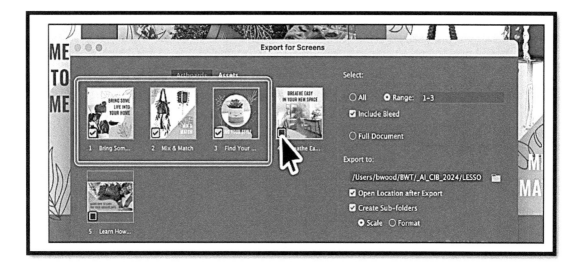

- Either all artboards or a selected range can be exported. In the "**Export to**" area, choose the destination where you wish to export to.
- Choose your favorite option by clicking **Format**.

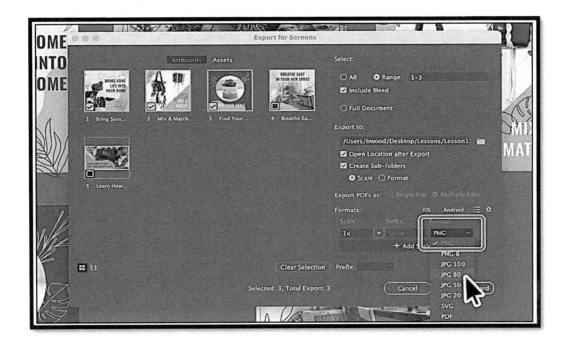

- You can alter the format, add or remove a suffix from the filename, and adjust the scale factor in the Formats section of the Export For Screens dialog box. You can export many versions with different scale factors and formats by selecting the + Add Scale button. To view it under the Formats section, you may have to scroll down.
- Click **Export Artboard**.

Tip: To prevent the creation of subfolders such as "1x," you can uncheck Create Sub-folders in the **Export for Screens** dialog box. This will be active when you export.

Inviting others to edit

Illustrator allows you to invite other users to modify your document once you've produced it, so you can collaborate on projects with others. One must save a document to the cloud to allow others to make edits to it. One contributor at a time can edit a cloud project in Illustrator; this is known as asynchronous editing. I will need the email address of someone with whom I can share the file to follow along with the following phase.

1. Select **File > Invite to Edit** while your file is open.

Before proceeding, ensure that the document has been saved as a cloud document, specifically to your **Creative Cloud account**. A popup labeled "**Share**" will pop up in the app's top right corner. Do not click the **Share button** if it is not open; instead, select **File > Invite To Edit** once again.

2. To save the file as a Creative Cloud document, click **Continue** in the **Invite To Edit** dialog box.

3. Press **Save** when prompted to do so in the dialog window for **Save to Creative Cloud**. **Two new options to invite people will be available in the Invite To Edit dialog box located in the top right corner of the app:**

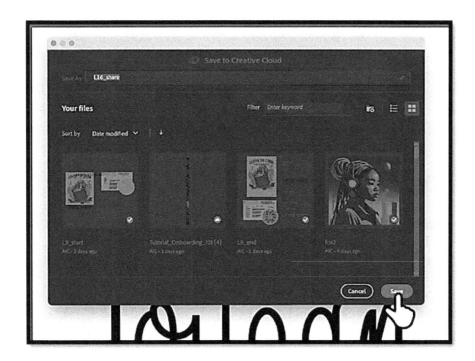

Note: A user will need to have Illustrator installed and be logged into Creative Cloud to modify the Illustrator document.

- Users can be invited to make edits to a document using the Creative Cloud desktop software and an email will be sent to their inbox when you provide their email address. The next figure shows it with a **red** highlight.
- A link can also be shared with users to invite them. When clicked, users will be sent to a web page where they can, if enabled, launch Adobe Illustrator to access the Illustrator file. The next image shows it with a **blue** highlight.

Select **anyone with the Link Can Comment** from the **Who Has Access** option to enable others to open the Illustrator file that you've shared with them.

Tip: In the **Invite to Edit** dialog box, you can see the gear icon. Click on it to determine whether users can comment or download a copy.

4. Fill up the email field located at the top with an email address. Tap the **Return** or **Enter** key.
5. You can then enter a message (optional) and click **Invite To Edit**.

A desktop notice and an email will be sent to the invited user via Creative Cloud.

6. To exit the **Invite to edit** dialogue box, click away from it.

Please be aware that when you send an email invitation, the recipients will be able to access the file directly from the Desktop Illustrator home page 🏠 by selecting **Shared with You.**

Sharing for review

Similar to how you invited someone to edit the Illustrator document before, they may also view it in a browser or the Creative Cloud desktop client and provide comments (as long as the commenting rights are enabled). You can also utilize the **Share for Review** feature to ask someone to examine your document instead of making changes. You can utilize Share for Review to share with someone who doesn't have Illustrator. The review can be done on the web or the **Creative**

Cloud desktop client, so it's convenient for everyone. We may look at the best way to send the prior file for feedback.

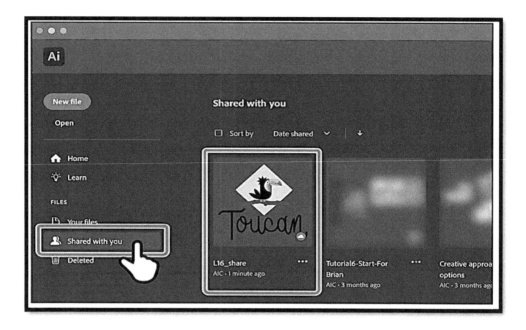

1. While your cloud document is still open, go to the app's top right and select the **Share** button.

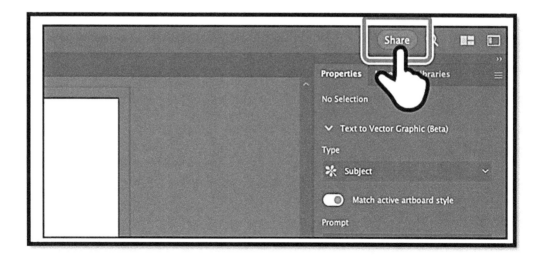

Sharing a file for review does not need saving it to the cloud beforehand, unlike the **Invite to Edit** option. The reason behind this is that when a document is shared, a link is created from it.

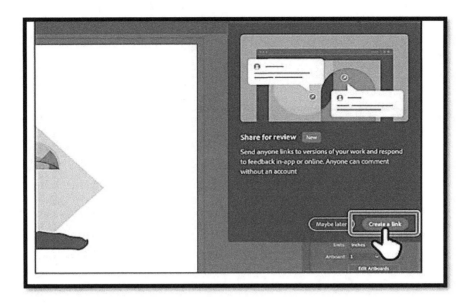

Note: Please be aware that after resetting the application options, you may get a different dialog box if you have utilized the Share for Review function. You should always choose the option to generate a link.

2. **To generate a shared link, just click the "Create Link" button.**

As with the **Invite to edit** feature, you can invite someone to review via email or by sending them the link. The recipients of your email invitations will receive two notifications: one in the Creative Cloud desktop app and another in their inbox. **Only Invited People Can Comment** from the **Who Has Access** option will allow you to restrict access to the link destination to those who have been invited via email. The alternative is to choose "**Anyone with the Link Can Access**" from the **Who Has Access** drop-down box if you're fine with anybody reviewing, whether they were invited via email or emailed a link.

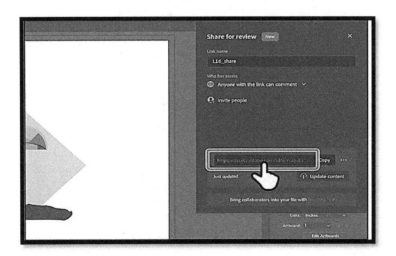

3. To open the document in a web browser, click the blue link that appears in the Share dialog box.

Note: A helpful notice referring to the URL may appear; please take note of it. To skip, you can click **Skip**.

At right is what someone who is reviewing the document in a browser will see.

4. **Return to Illustrator.**

As a concluding point, I should mention something that is, arguably, the finest feature of Share for Review. Imagine you wish to have others go over the document after you've made some edits in Illustrator. The reviewers will then see the most recent version of the document if you click **Update Content.**

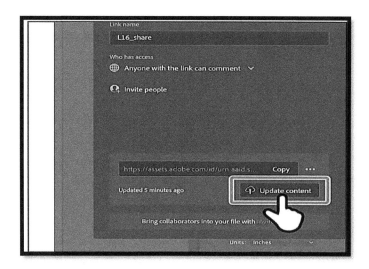

5. The **Share dialog** box can be closed.
6. For all open files without saving, select **File** > **Close**.

Preparing Files for Print

I may now print out the file to check its appearance now that we've finished all the hard work. Open the printer dialog box by selecting **File > Print**. Your device's connected printer will be displayed in the printer information at the top of the dialog box. If more than one printer is available, use the drop-down option to choose the one you need.

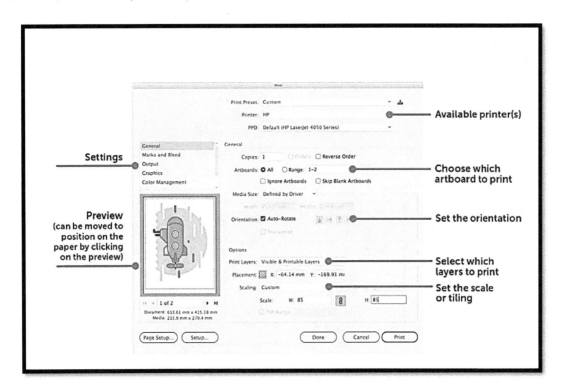

Decide on the number of copies and the artboards to be printed. In cases when you wish to print only one artboard out of several, you can do that by using ranges like 1-4 or 2, 3, or 5. In the Orientation section, you can rotate the paper if your printer's settings allow it. If you have instructions on a layer that doesn't print, you can easily fix this by going to the options and printing either all layers or only the visible ones. ou can adjust the artwork's size and check the results in the Preview box. The Preview's dashed line gives you a good idea of the printing area and where the artwork is on the paper. To reposition the artwork on the paper, simply click on the Preview. Users will also be able to choose the placement of different artboards and artwork on the paper.

CHAPTER 11
WORKING WITH BRUSHES

You can use brushes to add patterns, figures, textures, angled brush strokes, and more to your paths. You can also modify the pre-installed Illustrator brushes or create your own from the ground up. Either use the Paintbrush tool to simultaneously draw a path and apply a brush stroke, or you can add brush strokes to paths that have already been made. After you've applied a brush, you can change its size, color, and any other property (such as adding a fill) as well as modify paths. There are five types of brushes in the **Brushes** panel, which can be reached via **Window > Brushes**: **calligraphic, art, bristle, pattern, and scatter.**

Using Calligraphy brushes

The calligraphic brush will be covered initially. Similar to the way the pointed end of a calligraphic pen creates strokes, calligraphic brushes mimic this technique. If you want your calligraphic strokes to look like they were written by hand with a flat, angled pen tip, you can use a brush with an elliptical shape whose center follows the path.

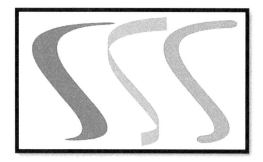

Types of brushes

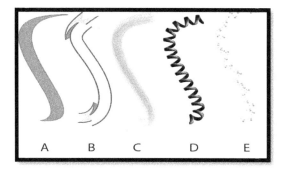

270

A. Calligraphic brush

B. Art brush

C. Bristle brush

D. Pattern brush

E. Scatter brush

Applying a Calligraphic brush to artwork

First things first, under the Brushes panel, you'll want to filter the brushes that are visible to just include the Calligraphic brushes.

Here are the steps:

1. From the main menu, choose **Window > Brushes** to open the Brushes panel. Pick the menu-like icon in the Brushes panel to go to **List View**.

2. Follow these steps to return to the Brushes panel menu: click the icon, then uncheck the following objects while keeping the Calligraphic brushes visible:
    o   Display the Art Brushes
    o   Display the Bristle Brushes
    o   Display the Pattern Brushes

In the Brushes panel menu, a tick next to a brush type indicates that it is now visible in the panel. Since you can't remove them all at once, you'll have to keep clicking the menu symbol (a) to bring up the menu.

3. Click the **Selection tool** in the toolbar. To choose the pink text object at the top of the artboard, click where it says "**Pink Text Object.**" The language had to be changed to create the appearance you see, thus it was transformed into paths.

4. To zoom in, you need to repeatedly click the **Command and + keys (on macOS) or the Ctrl and + keys (on Windows).**

5. From the Brushes panel, select the 5 pt. Flat brush to apply to the pink text shapes, and then click the OK button.

6. In the Properties panel, first set the **Stroke weight to 5 points** to preview the effect of the brush, and then set it to 1 point to make the effect permanent. Using a calligraphic brush, such as the **5 pt.** Flat brush is analogous to sketching with a real calligraphy pen in that the more vertically you draw a line; the narrower the path's stroke seems to be. This is because the brush has a flatter surface.

7. Select the **Stroke color** in the **Properties** panel. Next, click on the **Swatches** option. Finally, choose Black from the drop-down selection. To hide the Swatches panel if necessary, press the **Escape key**.

8. Select the objects you want to deselect, and then go to the **File menu** and select **Save.**

Editing a brush

By double-clicking on a brush in the Brushes panel, you can access its options. Pressing this will open the menu of choices. The artwork that a brush has been applied to can be changed when the brush is edited. You can choose this option whenever you want when editing.

Here are the steps:

1. Just double-click the brush thumbnail in the Brushes panel to the left of the text "**5 pt. Flat**." Or, you can double-click the thumbnail to the right of the name to bring up the Calligraphic Brush Options dialog box.

2. Follow the steps outlined below to make the necessary changes in the dialog box:
    o   **Name:** 8 pt. Angled
    o   **Angle:** 35°
    o   Select **Fixed** from the drop-down option that's located to the right of Angle. (Every time you draw, a unique brush angle will be generated, based on a random selection of possibilities when Random is selected.)
    o   **Roundness:** 15% (Brush strokes will be more or less circular depending on how you modify this option).
    o   **Size:** 8 pt

3. Select "**OK**"

4. When a dialogue box pops up, choose the **Apply to Strokes** option. This will make your brush adjustments visible in the text shapes that are presently using the brush.

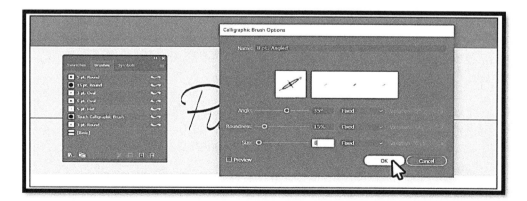

272

5. Click **Select > Deselect** if the preceding step was necessary, and then choose **File > Save** to save the file.

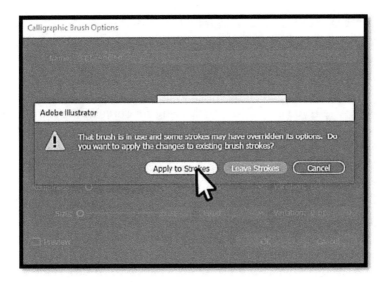

Drawing with the Paintbrush tool

You can choose whatever brush you like when you use the Paintbrush tool. The Paintbrush tool generates vector routes whenever you paint. You can modify these paths using the Paintbrush tool or any of the other drawing tools. You will now use the Paintbrush tool and a Calligraphic brush you found in the brush library to paint a section of the letter "**t**" in the text.

1. Make your selection in the toolbar for the Paintbrush tool.
2. To access the Brush Libraries Menu, click the arrow-labeled button at the bottom of the Brushes panel and choose **Artistic > Artistic Calligraphic**. Illustrator gives you access to several brush libraries, so you can create artwork with ease. For every kind of brush, there are several libraries to pick from, some of which have been discussed before.
3. Click the menu icon in the **Artistic Calligraphic** panel to get the **list view**.
4. Close the **Artistic Calligraphic** font's brush library window. Brushes from libraries like Artistic Calligraphy will only be added to the current document's Brushes panel when you pick a brush from that library.
5. Verify that the fill color is None, the stroke color is Black, and the stroke weight is 1 point in the Properties panel. Note the asterisk next to the Paintbrush cursor in the Document window. The reason for this is that once you have the pointer in the Document window, you will be able to paint a new path.
6. To locate "**Puremental**," simply shift the arrow to the left of the word "**t**" position. Using paint, make a meandering path that moves from left to right.
7. To make the freshly drawn path the active path, click on it using the Selection tool. Edit the stroke weight to 0.5 points in the Properties tab on the right.

8. Pick **File > Save** once you've chosen **Select > Deselect** (if necessary).

Editing paths with the Paintbrush tool

Moving on, the Paintbrush tool will be used for altering paths.

1. To choose text shapes, first click on them after making sure the Selection tool is chosen.
2. Choose the Paintbrush tool from the toolbar. The capital letter "**P**" should be where you put the cursor. The presence of an asterisk will not be indicated whenever the pointer is placed anywhere along a chosen path. To redo the path, simply move the mouse. The location from where you initially began drawing will serve as the starting point for altering the pathway you have chosen. The letter shapes will no longer be available for selection in the Paintbrush tool's menu once you've completed drawing with it. The default selection of paths will not be applied.
3. To pick the curved path you made on the letter "**t**," use the Selection tool (**Command on macOS or Ctrl on Windows)** and then click on the path you wish to pick. The Paintbrush tool will reappear once you release the key after clicking.
4. Hold down the Paintbrush tool and drag the mouse over a specified segment of the path. When the asterisk disappears from its proximity to the cursor, move it to the right to redraw the path. The following step is to modify the Paintbrush tool's settings to alter the tool's painting behavior.
5. Click the **OK button** after bringing up the Paintbrush Tool Options dialog box by double-clicking the tool in the toolbar; then, make the necessary modifications.
   - To adjust the fidelity, move the slider to the smooth position (to the right).
   - **Keep Selected:** Selected.

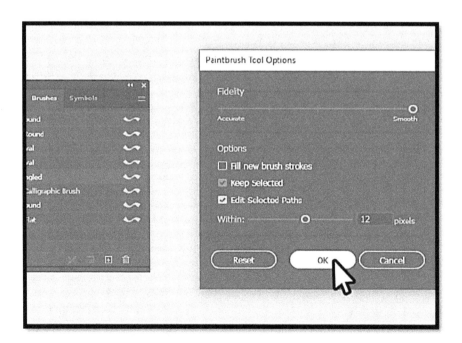

6. To proceed, click **OK**. To modify the way the Paintbrush tool works, open the Paintbrush Tool Options dialog box. If you choose the Fidelity option and drag the slider to Smooth, the path will be smoother and have fewer points overall. Furthermore, the paths will remain chosen even after you finish sketching them, if you choose to **Keep Selected**.

7. To pick the curving path you sketched earlier, press and hold the **Command (macOS) or Ctrl (Windows)** key while still using the Paintbrush tool to switch to the Selection tool. Then, click on the letter "**t**" to select it. Secure it by inserting the key. Perhaps the path might need a fresh coat of paint.

Keep in mind that the path will remain chosen after you've completed painting, so you can always go back and edit it if you need to. To avoid accidentally leaving the Paintbrush tool chosen after you've completed constructing paths, it's best to set it so that it doesn't stay selected. This will allow you to easily create overlapping pathways. It will be feasible to make overlapping routes using this strategy without modifying the existing paths.

8. If required, choose **Deselect** from the **Select** menu before going to **File > Save**.

Removing a brush stroke

The addition of brush strokes to artwork in undesirable places can be easily erased. The brush stroke that had been applied to the path stroke will be removed at this point.
Here are the steps:

1. To see everything, go to the menu and choose **View > Fit Artboard In Window**.
2. To pick the black trail with the chalk scribble-like pattern going down its length, use the Selection tool.
3. You can get rid of it by going to the Brushes panel and clicking the **Remove Brush Stroke** option down there. When you remove a brush stroke, just the brush itself is erased; the stroke's color and weight are preserved.
4. Set the stroke weight to **1** point in the Properties tab.
5. Go to the **File menu** and choose **Save** after selecting the objects you wish to deselect.

Use Art brushes

Brushes can be used to expand artwork or raster images added along a path. Like previous brushes, this one has settings that you can tweak to alter the brush's look and how it applies to paths.

Applying an existing Art brush

Pick an existing paintbrush and paint over the lines on each side of the modified text. **Here are the steps:**

1. Click the **Brushes panel menu icon**, located in the Brushes panel, and then uncheck the option to **Show Calligraphic Brushes**. The Art brushes will become available in the Brushes panel once you select **Show Art Brushes** from the option located inside the same panel.

2. Select **Decorative > Elegant Curl & Floral Brush Set** from the Brush Libraries Menu by clicking the button labeled with an arrow that is located at the bottom of the Brushes panel.
3. Select **List View** by clicking on the symbol that represents the panel menu for the Elegant **Curl & Floral Brush Set**. To add the brush to the Brushes panel for this particular document, go to the list and select the "**Floral Stem 3**" brush by clicking it.
4. Exit the panel group for the **Elegant Curl and Floral Brush** Set.
5. While holding down the Selection tool, click the path that is to the left of the text at the very top of the page.
6. To zoom in, repeatedly click the **Command and + keys (on macOS) or the Ctrl and + keys (on Windows)**.
7. To pick the path to the right of the text as well, click the path with the **Shift key** held down.
8. In the Brushes panel, select the **Floral Stem 3 brush** and click on it.
9. To keep them together, you can do this by clicking the Group option in the Properties window.
10. After that, select **Deselect** from the Select menu, and then go to **File > Save**.

Creating an Art brush

You can make art brushes from vector artwork or raster pictures with a few simple rules: no gradients, blends, other brush strokes, mesh objects, graphs, linked files, masks, or text without outlines. **Here are the steps:**
1. To access the second artboard containing the tea leaf artwork, choose **2** from the Artboard menu in the Properties panel. The screen's center contains this artboard.
2. Click the leaves to select the artwork you wish to work with while the Selection tool is active.

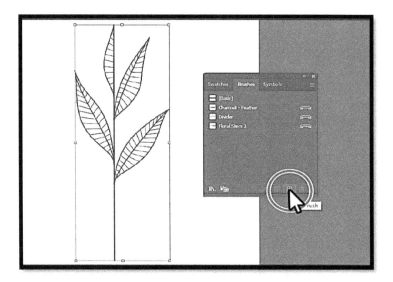

3. Go to the **Brushes panel** and click the **New Brush button** at the bottom of the panel while the artwork is still chosen. Now that the artwork has been chosen, the process of making a new brush to mimic it begins.

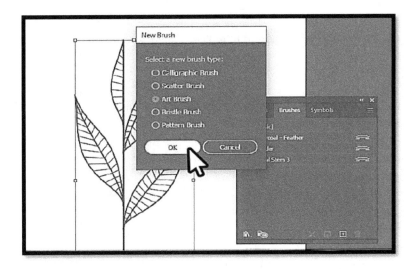

4. In the New Brush dialog box, click the **OK button** after selecting **Art Brush** from the drop-down menu. As an alternative, you can create an Art brush by dragging an artwork into the Brushes panel and then choosing **Art Brush** from the drop-down selection that appears in the **New Brush dialog box**.
5. In the Art Brush Options dialog box that suddenly opens, change the name of the brush to **Taves**. Select the **OK button**.
6. Choose the **Select > Deselect menu option**.
7. In the Properties panel, you can see the Active Artboard option. Select 1 to go back to the initial artboard. This will return you to the very first page of the document.

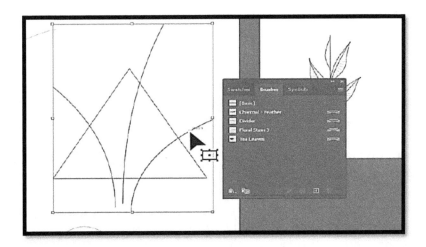

8. Hold down the **Shift key** as you click on the vertical curved lines above the triangle in the center of the artboard to choose them. This will activate the Selection tool.

9. Open the **Brushes panel** and choose the **"Tea Leaves"** tool. Pay attention to how the original tea leaf artwork is distributed along each path before using this brush. In all cases, this is the default behavior of an art brush. Sadly, things are going backward from the way they should be. The next thing you'll do is fix it.

Editing an Art brush

On the artboard, you will be able to change how the path looks.

1. To access the Art **Brush Options** dialog box, hover over the brush thumbnail to the left of "**Tea Leaves**" (or to the right of the name in the Brushes panel) while keeping the paths selected on the artboard. Double-click on the thumbnail to open it. You can also access this feature in the Brushes panel by clicking on the name to the right of it.

2. You can preview your edits in real-time by selecting **Preview** in the Art Brush Options dialog box; to see the line with the applied brush, simply move the dialog box. **Please implement the following changes:**

   ○ **Stretch between guides:** The guidelines do not match up with any real artboard guides. To accommodate the length of the path being painted by the painting brush, they are utilized to identify the area of the artwork that has to be stretched or contracted. Scale can be applied to any part of the artwork that isn't specified in the rules. You can choose where on the original artwork to set the guidelines by modifying the "**Start**" and "**End**" parameters.

   ○ **Start:** 7.375 in

   ○ **End:** 10.8588 in (default setting)

   ○ **Flip Along:** Selected

3. Select "**OK**"

4. You can change the paths that are being painted with the Tea Leaves brush by selecting the **Apply to Strokes option** in the dialogue box that appears. Now that you have a copy of the brush, you will adjust it such that the artwork along the center path continues along the path as it would if the choices weren't chosen.

5. To use the Tea Leaves brush, first choose **Select > Deselect**. Then, with the brush, click the larger, center path.

6. You can make a copy of the Tea Leaves brush by dragging it from the **Brushes** panel to the **New Brush button** at the panel's base.

7. In the Brushes panel, double-click the thumbnail of the **Tea Leaves brush** copy to make adjustments.

8. To ensure that artwork is scaled properly along the path, use the Brush Scale Options section of the Art Brush Options dialog box to choose **Scale Proportionately**. Choose the **OK** option.

9. To make the change to the one path that is now bound to the **Tea Leaves Copy brush**, in the dialogue box that appears, click the **Make to Strokes button.**

10. Remove the checkmark from the path.

11. Pick the other paths surrounding the artboard using Shift-click, and then apply the **Tea Leaves or Tea Leaves Copy** brush to them. An arrow points in the direction of travel.
12. Press the **Select** menu item and then press the **Deselect** menu item.

Using Pattern brushes

Separate pieces or tiles can be painted into a pattern using a pattern brush. Applying a Pattern brush to artwork causes various pattern tiles to be applied to distinct path parts based on their location on the path, whether it's at the end, center, or corner. You can find a wide variety of grass and cityscape patterns among the hundreds of intriguing brushes available. **Here are the steps:**

1. Navigate to the **View** menu, and then choose **Fit Artboard In Window**.
2. While in the Brushes panel, click the icon that looks like a panel menu, pick **Show Pattern Brushes** from the menu, and then uncheck the option that says **Show Art Brushes**.
3. To highlight an ad, first, click the triangle in its center after making sure the Selection tool is selected.
4. To access the Brush Libraries menu, click the button labeled at the bottom of the Brushes panel and choose **Borders > Borders Geometric**.

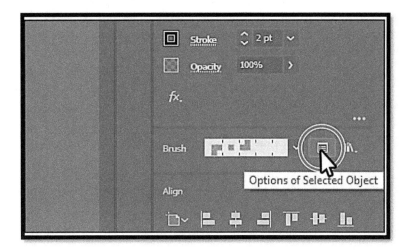

5. To apply the brush to the pathways, click the brush titled **"Geometric 17,"** and then add the brush to the Brushes panel for this particular project by selecting it. Put a stop to the Borders Geometric panel group's activities.
6. In the Properties tab, adjust the stroke weight so that it is 2 points. Additionally, the **Options of Selected Object** button can be found in the Properties panel or at the bottom of the Brushes panel.
7. In the Properties panel, pick the button labeled **Options of Selected Object** to make changes to the brush options that apply just to the selected path on the artboard.

8. Make sure that the **Preview option** is selected in the Stroke Options (Pattern Brush) dialog box. Either by sliding the Scale slider or entering the number, bring the Scale value up to 120% and save the changes. Select the **OK button**.

You are only shown a selection of the possible brush possibilities when you try to modify the brush settings of the currently chosen object. To change the brush's properties without updating the path itself, open the Stroke Options (Pattern Brush) dialog box and click on the path you want to change.

9. Select the objects you want to deselect, and then go to the **File menu** and select **Save**.

Creating a Pattern brush

You can create a Pattern brush in some different ways. For instance, under the Brushes panel, you can find the **New Brush button**; after choosing the content to use as the pattern, click it. This will apply the pattern to a straight line. The straight line will be adorned with the pattern. For a more intricate pattern that can be applied to objects with curves and corners, you can have Illustrator auto-generate the Pattern brush corners. You can also use the Document window to select artwork to be used in a pattern brush, and the Swatches panel to create swatches from that artwork. Doing so will let you design a pattern that can be used on curved and cornered objects. Only the side tile has to be provided in Illustrator. Illustrator automatically generates one of four types of corners based on the picture used for the side tile. The four choices that were generated automatically work well with the corners. Planning the Pattern brush that will encircle the UPLIFT text is the following stage. **Here are the steps:**

1. Launch the **Properties** panel and navigate to the **Artboard menu** to access the second artboard. To go to the second artboard, select **2** from there.
2. To choose the artwork at the top of the artboard, click once on it while the Selection tool is active.
3. Pressing **Command and the plus sign (+)** many times (on macOS) or **Ctrl and the plus sign** (on Windows) will zoom in.
4. Click the panel menu symbol in the Brushes panel to get the **Thumbnail View**. You will see that the Pattern brushes are divided apart when you look at the Brushes panel in the Thumbnail view. A pattern tile stands in for each section.
5. Make a new brush by selecting the **New Brush button** in the Brushes panel. As a consequence, the artwork will be transformed into a pattern.
6. From the New Brush dialog boxes drop-down option, select **Pattern Brush**. Choose the **OK button**. No matter what artwork is presently selected, you always can create a new Pattern brush. When you make a Pattern brush without any artwork chosen, it is expected that you will add it later by dragging it into the Brushes panel or by choosing it from a pattern swatch you make as you work on the brush. Yes, this is true regardless of whether you choose artwork when creating the Pattern brush.
7. After opening the Pattern Brush Options dialog box, rename the brush to Decoration. A pattern brush can hold up to five tiles: the side, start, end, outer-corner, and inner-corner tiles, which are used to paint path corners with sharp edges.

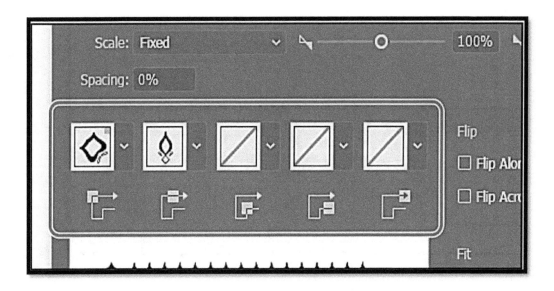

Pressing the tile button next to the desired tile allows you to define it, and then you can choose between an auto-generated selection (if available) or a pattern swatch in the pop-up menu. A tool tip indicating the tile presently being pointed at will display in the Pattern Brush Options dialog box when the pointer is moved across the tile squares.

8. Move the cursor to the second tile from the left in the Spacing menu and click the button. Then, choose the **Side Tile checkbox**. In the menu that appears next to **None** and any pattern swatches in the Swatches panel, you can find the decorative artwork that was chosen initially.

9. Click the box on the outside corner tile to see the options. A double click will occur. Once to close the current menu and once to open this one.

Illustrator has generated an automatic replica of the tile that will go in the exterior corner based on the first piece of decorative artwork. There are four different kinds of automatically generated corners that you can choose from in the menu:

- **Auto-Centered:** With Auto-Centered, the side tile is automatically centered and extended around the corner.
- **Auto-Between:** The auto-between feature involves placing a single copy of the side tile on either side of the corner, with the extra copy covering the whole corner. The next step is to gently stretch them till they reach the final shape.
- **Auto-Sliced:** The Auto-Slice function slices the side tiles at an angle, creating pieces that fit together similarly to the miter joint seen at the corners of a wooden picture frame.
- **Auto-Overlap:** When Auto-Overlap is turned on, the tiles will overlap at the corners.

10. Choose **Auto-Between** from the **Outer Corner Tile** box's menu. If you want to apply the Pattern brush to a certain path in the decorative artwork you've chosen, this will make that corner.

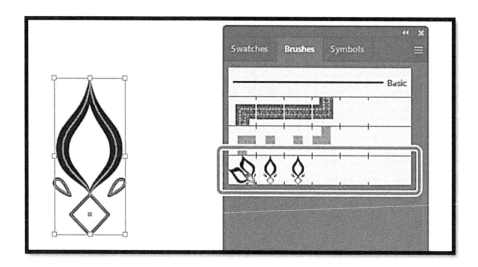

11. Press the **OK button**. The "**Brushes**" panel is where the Decoration brush can be found.
12. Navigate to the **Select > Deselect menu**.

Editing the Pattern brush

The following procedures can be employed to edit the pattern brush:

1. To expand the Swatches panel, either click on its icon or go to **Window > Swatches**.
2. Then, from the right side of the artboard, zoom in on the life preserver by clicking **View > Pattern objects.**
3. Place the life preserver in the Swatches panel by dragging it with the **Selection tool**.

You can see the new pattern swatch in the Swatches panel. If you don't intend to utilize the pattern swatches for any more artwork after creating a pattern brush, you can remove them from the Swatches panel. In this way:

1. Click on **Select > Deselect**.
2. You can double-click the pattern swatch you made in the Swatches panel.
3. From the **Pattern Options** dialog box, name the swatch **Corner** and choose 1 x 1 from the Copies menu.
4. Press **Done** to complete editing the pattern.
5. Tap on **View** and then choose **Fit Artboard In Window**.
6. Border Pattern can be accessed in the Pattern Brush Options dialog box by double-clicking it on the Brushes panel.
7. Select the Corner pattern swatch from the selection that comes after clicking on the **Outer Corner Tile** box.
8. Click **OK** after adjusting the Scale to **70%** in the **Pattern Brush Options** dialog box.
9. To update the artboard border, click **Apply To Strokes** in the **Brush Change Alert** dialog box.

Note: The artwork can be dragged from the artboard onto the tile of the Pattern brush in the Brushes panel. To change the pattern tiles in a Pattern brush, press the Alt key (Windows) or the Option key (Mac OS X) and then choose the desired tile.

10. Select one of the paths with a row of windows using the Selection tool.
11. In the Brushes panel, choose the Border brush to apply it.
12. Choose **Edit > Undo Apply Pattern Brush** to get rid of the brush from a path.
13. Pick **Select**, then Pick **Deselect**.
14. Click on **File**, and then **Save**.

Using Bristle Brushes

Using bristle brushes, you can mimic the look of a genuine brush with bristles to create strokes. Use the Paintbrush tool to apply a bristle brush effect; the resultant vector routes will seem like brushes.

Painting with a Bristle brush

The Mop brush will allow you to add more strokes behind your artwork, creating a textured backdrop for the ad. A more natural and flowing path may be achieved by painting with a bristle brush. **Here are the steps:**

1. Choose **View > Fit Artboard in Window** from the main menu.
2. With the Selection tool open, click and hold the "**UPLIFT**" text with the mouse to select it. By doing so, you may choose which layer contains the text shapes; from then on, any new artwork you create will be placed on that layer. The word "**UPLIFT**" is represented by text shapes on a layer beneath most of the artwork on the artboard.
3. Pick the **Select > Deselect menu option**.

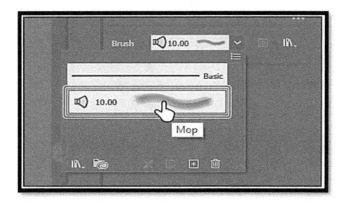

4. To access the paintbrush tool, click on its icon in the toolbar. To add the Mop brush to your selection, go to the Properties panel and look for the Brush choice. If it isn't there, you can find it in the Brushes panel. You can also select the brush from within the Brushes panel if it is open.

5. In the **Properties panel**, verify that the fill color is set to **None** and that the stroke color is the same light green as the Decoration brush. To hide the Swatches panel, press the **Escape key** on your keyboard.
6. Set the stroke weight to 5 points in the Properties window.
7. Reposition the pointing device such that it is on the right side of the page's center triangle. To make an inverted V shape, lower and left-click the cursor once, drag it across the artboard, and then right-click to release. Once you've reached the endpoint of the path you want to draw, release the mouse button.
8. Paint more trails all over the artboard using the Paintbrush tool, using the **Mop brush** as your brush. The ad will have more texture thanks to these paths.

Grouping Bristle brush paths

Here are the steps:
1. Go to **View > Outline** on the menu bar to see all the paths you've just created. After this, you will choose and group all of the Bristle brush trails you have painted.
2. From the menu bar, choose **Select > Object > Bristle Brush Strokes**. Then, using the Mop brush, pick all of the trails created with the Paintbrush tool.
3. To group them, click the **Group option** located in the Properties section.
4. Select **View > Preview** (or **GPU Preview**).
5. After you've chosen which objects to deselect, hit the **File menu** and choose **Save**.

Working with the Blob Brush tool

Expanded brush strokes can be created in Illustrator using the **Blob Brush Tool (Shift-B)** tool. Many designers believe that the blob brush tool is all they will ever need to create line drawings, character drawings, or sketches. The illustrator's blob brush can be activated by either selecting it from the toolbar or the **Shift-B** keyboard shortcut. When it's on, you may make a brushstroke by clicking and dragging. The larger brush will be applied to your design the second you let go of the mouse button.

To open the **Blob Brush Tool Options** window, **double-click** on the toolbar's **Blob Brush Tool (Shift-B)**. These are some of the options available:

- Click the **Keep Selected** box and then **OK** to apply the changes.

- Make a fresh stroke with the **Blob Brush Tool (Shift-B).**
- Please be aware that once a brush stroke has been drawn, it will stay selected.

- The two options that go hand in hand are **Merge Only with Selection** and **Keep Selected.**
- Click on **Merge Only with Selection** box and click **OK** to apply.

You can add a new brushstroke by using the **Blob Brush Tool (Shift-B).** Assuming the objects have an overlapping region, it will merge the chosen shapes.

To make your brushstrokes look smoother, drag the **Fidelity** slider to the right. To make your input more precise, drag it to the left. The size of your Illustrator blob brush is controlled by the **Size** value. You can adjust the size of the blob brush in Illustrator in two different ways.

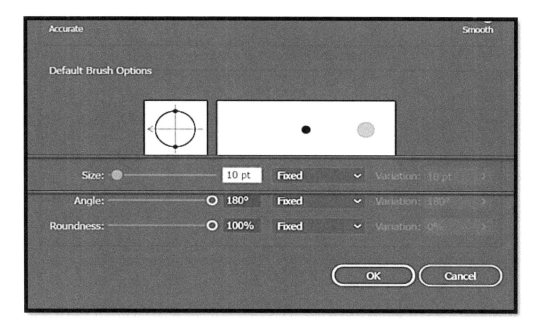

The angle at which Illustrator's blob brush is applied is controlled by the **Angle** value.

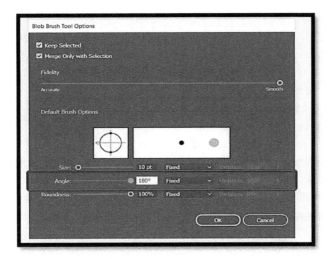

The shape of the blob brush in Illustrator is determined by the setting of **Roundness**. If you want a perfectly round brush, you can turn it up to **100%.** If you enter a value below **100%,** the brush will be flatter. **Angle, Roundness**, and **Size** all have their respective drop-down options where you can select alternative values. When you have a graphics tablet, this function can be really helpful.

- **Fixed**: This establishes a predetermined angle, roundness, or size.
- **Random**: Variable angles, roundness, or size can be set using the random method. The image below shows what happens when you set the **Size** and **Variation** values to **10 points** each: your brush's diameter will randomly range from **0 points to 20 points.**

- **Pressure**: You can set a variable angle, roundness, or size based on the pressure of the drawing stylus. This feature is available only for graphics tablet users. When the **Size** value is set to **10 pt** and the **Variation** value is set to **10 pt**, the thickness of your brush will range between **0 pt** and **20 pt**, depending on the pressure that you apply with the pen tablet.
- **Stylus Wheel**: Using the stylus wheel, you can adjust the angle, roundness, and size of your drawings. A graphics tablet that can identify an airbrush pen with a stylus wheel on its barrel is required to use this function.
- **Tilt**: Based on the angle, roundness, or size that a drawing stylus can be tilted to, you can adjust these parameters. You can't use this function unless your graphics tablet can measure the pen's vertical position.
- **Bearing**: Depending on the pen's bearing, you can adjust the pen's angle, roundness, or size. If your graphics tablet can identify the pen's tilt angle, you'll have access to this capability.
- **Rotation**: The drawing stylus pen tip's rotation can be used to set a varied angle, roundness, or size. But you can't use this function unless your graphics tablet is capable of detecting this kind of rotation.

CHAPTER 12

ADVANCED ILLUSTRATOR TECHNIQUES

Using the Blend Tool for Gradient and Object Blends

Using Adobe Illustrator's Blend Tool, you can give your shapes and letters amazing effects. It improves the realism of your work by adding depth and texture. When working with Illustrator's Blend Tool, you have two options. **Selecting the Blend Tool**, which may be found on the **toolbar**, is one option. The alternative is to go to the **overhead menu** to select **Object > Blend > Blend Options**. After that, return to that menu and select **Object > Blend Options > Make.**

Key Takeaways

- To create a blend, use the following keys on your keyboard: **Alt + Ctrl + B** for Windows, and **Command + Option + B** for Mac.
- Select **Object** > **Blend** > **Blend Options**. Here you can adjust the Blend's parameters, such as the number of stages, the smoothness of color transitions, and the spacing between them.
- By choosing it and then navigating to **Object > Blend > Expand**, you can transform the mix into vector objects that you can alter.

I'll show you two examples using two different ways to blend this image below. The images were captured using the Windows version of Adobe Illustrator CC. The Mac version and others can look different.

Step 1: The first step in creating a blend is choosing the objects. A minimum of two objects must be selected. The sample object below will serve as an example for the sake of this demonstration.

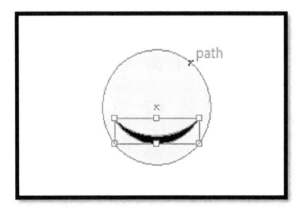

Step 2: Next, go to the toolbar and pick the **Blend Tool**.

Blend tool options will have a little plus symbol (+).
Step 3: You should be able to observe the blended objects once you click on them. This is how our objects will seem now.

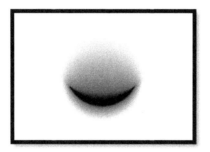

The **Blend Tool** automatically applied the **Smooth Color** effect from the Blend Options, giving our example this appearance. Just double-click the Blend icon and choose specified steps (where you may enter the desired number of steps) to see the exact shape transition. The Blend Tool, accessible from the toolbar, interacts with the characteristics of objects, which can make its use challenging. For example, if you selected the **Specified steps** option earlier, the blend tool will automatically apply those settings when you click it from the toolbar. I recommend using the Blend Options for blending objects if you have clear preferences for the blend settings. Using the blend tool to combine two shapes can provide the illusion of depth.

How to Use the Blend Options

To get the Blend Options window, go to the Blend tool in the main menu and select **Object > Blend > Blend Options.** Make the objects seem to fade into one another by using the various sliders in the blend option windows.

Step 1: Select your objects.

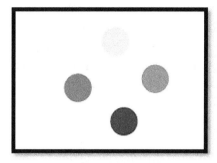

Step 2: Click **Object** > **Blend** > **Blend Options**.

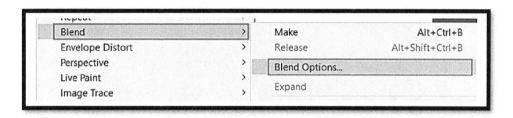

Step 3: Select the **Spacing** option.

An important blend option that changes how your objects seem is **spacing**. You can choose to smooth the colors, set steps, or show the distance between objects in this area. Now we can examine the many options that are located under the spacing field.

- The **Smooth Color** allows you to blend two colors to form gradient effects.

- The **Specified Steps** blend your objects by creating multiples of them, giving them a beautiful touch. (it shows the transition from one object to another following the different steps).
- **Specified Distance** allows you to determine the gap you want between your objects.

However, default values will be displayed in the various fields when you choose the **Specified Steps** and **Distance**. The values you choose can be entered, though. What you want the blended objects to look like is determined by their **orientation**. If the objects are **vertical** (portrait) or **horizontal** (landscape), their positioning is determined by it. Then, let's figure out how to blend our objects the most effectively.

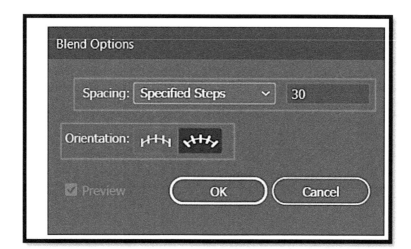

- You can save the settings by clicking **OK**.

Step 6: To apply the blending settings to the objects, go to **Object > Blend > Make**.

- Check out the appearance of our object.

By going to **Object > Blend > Reverse Spine** or **Reverse front to back**, you can alter the object's color or orientation.

The outcome is this:

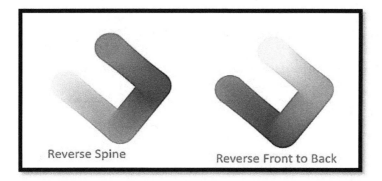

Reverse Spine   Reverse Front to Back

How to Blend Text in Illustrator

In Illustrator, you can blend text by following these easy steps.

Step 1: One must first write the texts they want to blend (you can choose the type option for your fonts in the overhead menu).

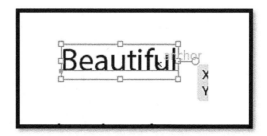

Because you will have to work on more than one text, make a duplicate of the text.
Step 2: Create an outline after selecting the text. Alternatively, you can expand an object by selecting **Object > Expand** from the overhead menu. Or by using the keyboard shortcut **Shift + Ctrl + O.**

Note: *Creating a text outline converts your text to an object and makes it editable.*

Step 3: Organize your text and fill it up with various colors. The blend is more noticeable when using various colors.

I will select colors pink and purple for my text. Before applying the Blend Tool, I will resize them. To get the desired rising effect, I will arrange the smaller text beneath the more significant text and vice versa. To achieve your design goals, you can arrange the text in any way.

Step 4: Pick the text and then go to **Object > Blend > Blend Options**.

To change how your text blends, use the settings in the blend options windows. The number of steps that will be used can be changed using the **Specified Steps**.

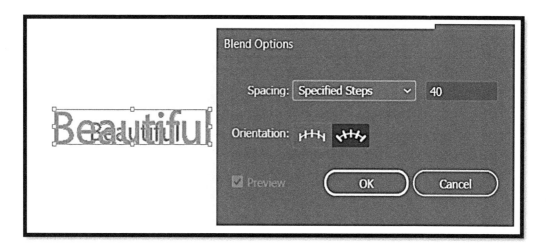

- You can select the number of steps and choose the orientation that best suits you.

Step 5: To apply the blend effect, go to **Object > Blend > Make**. The blend effect is not applied when you go to **Object > Blend > Blend Option**. You only specify your preferred blend settings.

- The blend effect can be applied by going to **Object > Blend > Make**. At that point, you can begin to blend the objects.
- See our blended text.

That concludes everything! Any way you wish, you can touch up your texts.

The Gradient Mesh Tool for Complex Shading

The purpose of Adobe Illustrator's **Gradient Mesh Tool** could be puzzling to those who are unfamiliar with graphic design. To be honest, the same question might be plaguing you regardless of how long you've been working in the field. The reason is: that the **Gradient Mesh Tool** is one of the more recent additions to the software. **But have no fear; I will explain all you require to use this design tool.**

The first is the **Gradient Mesh Tool**, which gives you a lot of leeway when it comes to adding color to your design. In your design, it makes a grid inside an object, and you may color the grid points as you like. The colors between the grid points melt into each other with a feather appearance once applied. Because of its usefulness in creating shading and blending effects, the tool is named with the term "gradient" in it. You will be able to personalize your design even further and transform it into something even more distinctive by utilizing this tool. Your picture will look more three-dimensional and less flat after applying it. It can also help your design seem more polished and professional.

How to Use the Gradient Mesh Tool: The Step-by-Step Ultimate Guide

Step 1: Select the object

I want you to start by picking out the object you'll be using in your design. Making a shape with the shape tool is one option for accomplishing this. Next, go to the top of the screen and click on "**Object**." Then, select "**Create Gradient Mesh**."

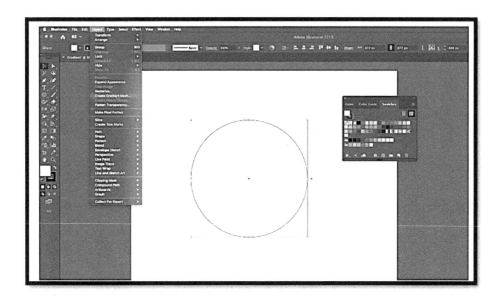

Step 2: Set the number of rows and columns

Step two involves deciding how many rows and columns the object will have. Be careful to tick the "**Preview**" option if you would like to see the grid with the exact numbers you have selected. After that, hit the "**OK**" button.

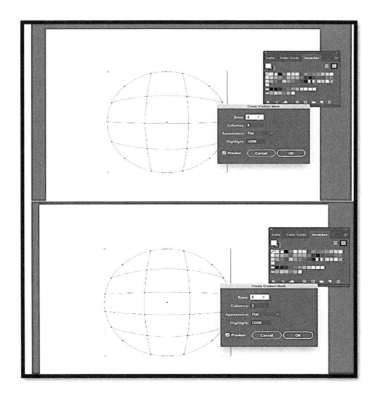

Step 3: Adjust the contour of grid lines

You will notice that the grid contains anchor points at each end and junction of the lines. For any of the anchor points, just click on the "**Direct Selection Tool**."

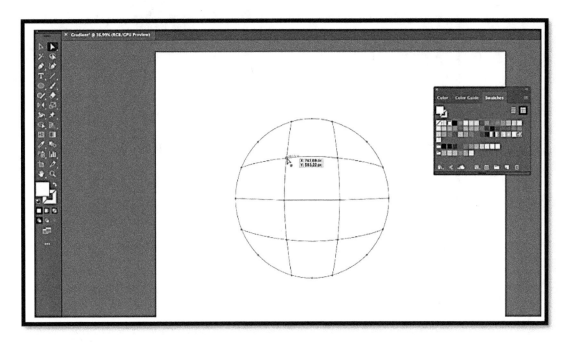

Connector Points with Bezier handles will become visible when you do that. Doing so will give you complete control over the shape of the grid lines.

Step 4: Adding color to the object

You need to choose the "**Gradient Mesh Tool**" to give your object color. The 'Fill' function must be turned on. Once you've verified that, you may access the object's grid by clicking on any of its points. Finally, utilize the **'Swatches Panel'** to choose a color that suits your needs. You can keep picking new grid points and applying new colors to them if you want to give the object additional color. Be wary of clicking on paths without grid points; this is an important detail to keep in mind. This will result in the addition of an additional grid line to your object. Stay away from this if that isn't your goal. Remember that the **Gradient Mesh Tool** restricts you to selecting a single grid point at a time. Hence, the "**Direct Selection Tool**" is the way to go if you wish to colorize several grid points simultaneously.

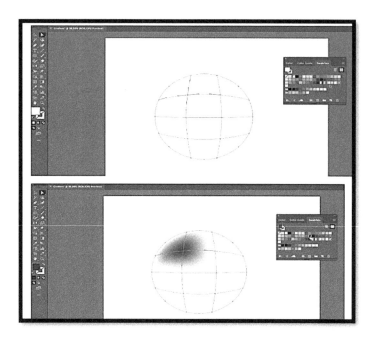

To use this tool, click the first grid point and then press and hold the "**Shift**" key. Doing so will give you the option to choose more grid points to color.

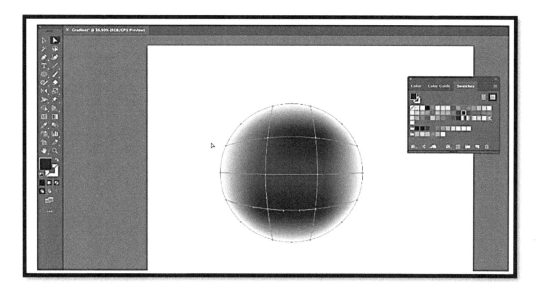

Once you've added the first color, you can add other shades or colors by selecting various grid points. You can observe that the circular shape has deeper indigo hues added to its perimeter in the image below. This makes the object seem more three-dimensional by giving it greater depth.

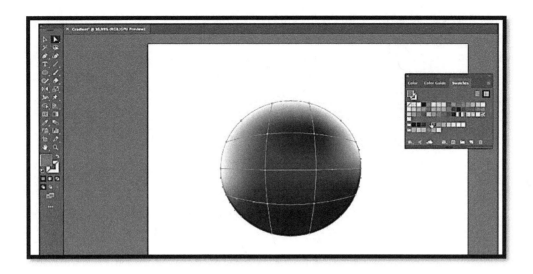

Step 5: Adjusting the shape of your object

Additionally, the shape of the object will start to alter if you click and drag any of the grid points. This means you may play with the grid points to get the exact shape you want for your design.

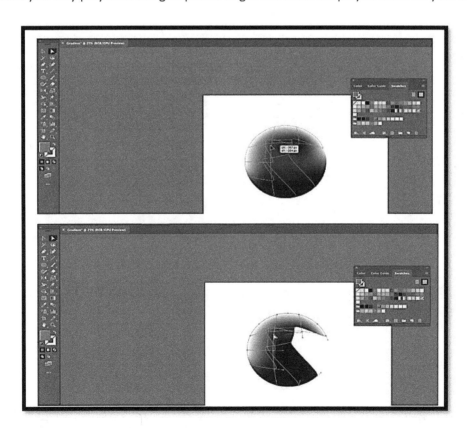

You can use the **Gradient Mesh Tool** on any kind of design. Your design's colors can be customized to your liking with its greatest flexibility. The prior examples of screenshots serve as a straightforward illustration of how the tool can be applied. If you're just starting, you can follow the steps outlined above to get a head start. You will be able to understand it quickly because the processes are straightforward.

Applying the Perspective Grid for 3D Effects

You may make a new file, add some shapes to it, and then use the effects menu or the appearance panel to apply 3D effects. In the appearance panel, you may adjust the effect's parameters by double-clicking on it. To make an effect that you're happy with editable, you can choose Object > Expand appearance. This will divide the effect into smaller shapes, which you can then ungroup and modify individually.

Create shapes in perspective

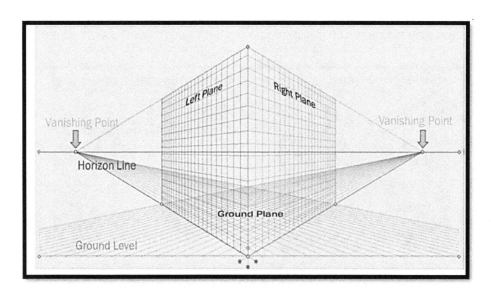

You will need to be familiar with these basic definitions:
- Horizon Line—this is the level of the earth that you see in a far-off distance
- Ground Level—this is where you would be standing
- Left/Right Plane—these are the sides that lead off into the vanishing points
- Vanishing Point—most important point. Is where things head to and disappear off into the horizon

Choose the perspective grid tool and click on it. You will see the grid. (you can also choose between one, two, or three points of view under the view menu, where you can also enable the perspective grid).

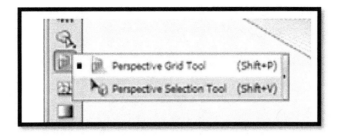

The Perspective Widget is the small cube in the upper left corner. You can easily switch between the two sides of the box by clicking on them; the one with the color indicates which one you are now selecting. Alternatively, you can use the 1, 2, 3, and 4 buttons to cycle between them. Selecting 4 will take you to a standard rectangle that is detached from the Perspective Grid Tool.

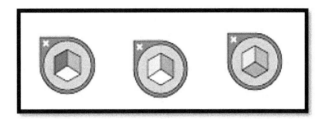

To build a rectangle, align your Perspective Widget so that you're on the blue side of the box, and then click the **Rectangle Tool**. Then, you may observe the result. By default, the rectangle will "fit" or "snap" into the side of the chosen viewpoint. After that, make a slightly darker rectangle of the same shade as the previous one by clicking on the orange side of the box in your Perspective Widget. In little time at all, you will possess an excellent 3D box.

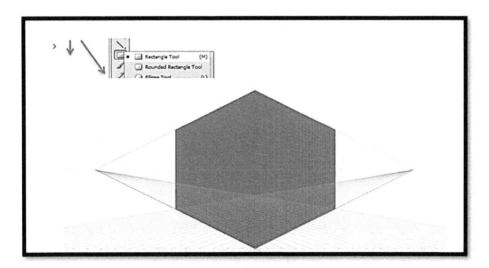

Get more height for your structure by grabbing the handle at the top of the Perspective Grid Tool (with the Selection Tool) and dragging it higher to your liking.

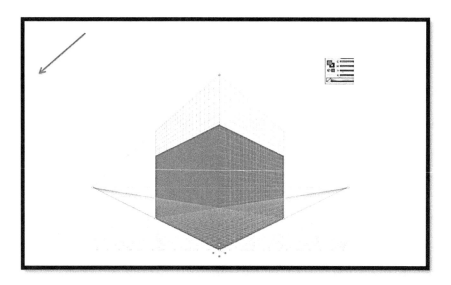

Additional levels can be made and positioned beneath the existing ones if desired.

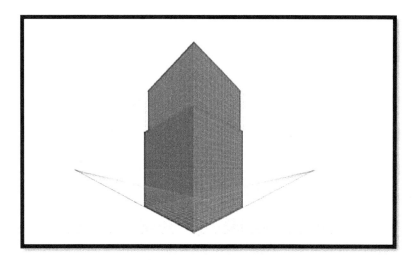

You can draw basic rectangles to go for the side windows, or you can disable the grid or press 4 to draw outside of it for more intricate window designs. Construct a window and set it as a group. Next, choose a side of the perspective grid to reactivate and then move the window to your desired location using the perspective selection tool. It will be given the viewpoint. You can make multiples of it by dragging and dropping while holding the Alt key and you may resize it as needed. To do it again, press Ctrl/Cmd + D or go to Object > Transform > Transform again.

Turn off your perspective tool and admire your cool building!

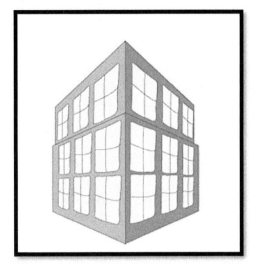

There is nothing tangible about the perspective grid; it serves just as a reference. You can choose from one-, two-, or three-point viewpoints under the Perspective Grid option in the View menu at the top. Another option is Define Grid, which provides far more flexibility over the grid you're using. Remember that after you've begun working on the grid, you can drag it around, but any objects you've drawn in perspective won't follow.

Using Symbols for Efficient Design Workflows

Symbols guarantee **efficiency** and **consistency**. By building a base object and utilizing it again across each artboard and document, we can save time. Every time we make a change to the original object, all instances are updated instantly since these copies are connected to their corresponding Symbol. And we can make **Dynamic Symbols,** too. **Instances made from Dynamic Symbols retain their original shape but have a distinct look** (color fill, stroke, etc.). Astounding method for researching and making different logos and icons. In **Symbol Libraries**, users can save and exchange symbols, making them easily accessible to everyone on the team. However, we will examine **CC Libraries** in more detail shortly. We can also utilize them to store Symbols.

Creating Symbols

A **simple vector shape**, a **stroke path**, and a **text object** will be used to make symbols. It's amazing how Symbols can multitask! In this lesson, we will visit beautiful Granada, Spain, and utilize a map as a background, adding markings and notes to help us navigate the city.

The **Symbols panel** is the first place we should open. A Mac user can utilize the shortcut **Shift + Command + F11,** whereas a PC user can use **Shift + Control + F11**. By going to the **top menu bar,** selecting **Window**, and then **Symbols**, we can get to it. The **Symbols** panel is where we can locate the Illustrator default symbols. These can vary depending on the version you're using, although they usually don't alter much. There is a plethora of more symbols available for exploration in the Symbols panel beyond the ones that are first displayed. Illustrator also provides us with access to some Symbol Libraries, which we may peruse at our leisure. To access these, click on the **Symbol Libraries Menu** button in the bottom right corner. Although I don't frequently employ them, you may be familiar with these symbols; thus, feel free to experiment with them. In this piece, we will ignore other influences and concentrate on our creations. Let's start by making a **location marker** as our first symbol.

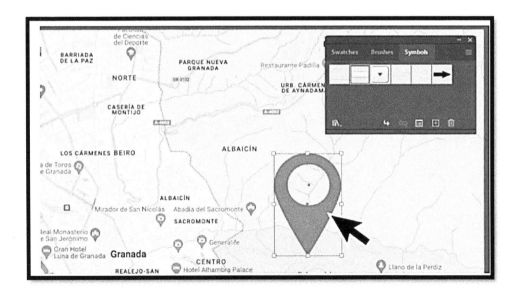

You may have seen this type of shape on maps or GPS interfaces; it's a **simple vector shape.** Now that we have the shape selected using the **Selection tool** (shortcut **V**), we can add our location marker to the Symbols panel by clicking on the **New Symbol button** (the one with a **plus** icon).

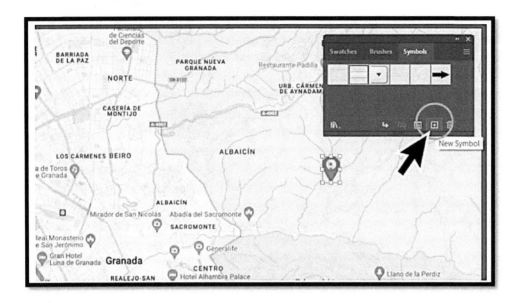

The window for **Symbol Options** will open. Insert the name of our new Symbol, which I'll call Location. After that, we choose **Static Symbol** from the list when we set **Export** to **Graphic**.

The instances of **Static Symbols** are connected to the Symbol itself. Only by modifying the original can their look properties be modified; they can be manipulated, but not scaled, rotated, flipped, etc. Keep in mind that automated updates will be applied to all instances. Because they retain the original Symbols shape, instances of **Dynamic Symbols** can be modified and have their visual properties changed. When you are finished, click **OK**. In the **Symbols panel**, you can now see the new Symbol as a thumbnail. When you put your mouse pointer over it, its name will pop up. You may access the editing window by double-clicking the thumbnail.

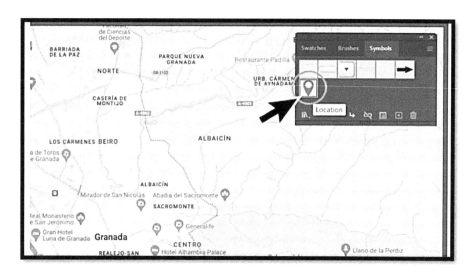

A charming circular swoosh or other Symbol will be created next from a **stroked path**. To enter the **Options window**, we call our path symbol (I'll wow everyone by calling it "Path"). Then, we select the **New Symbol** button. For this instance, let's go with the **Dynamic Symbol**. Lastly, let's make a new Symbol from a **text object**. We simply have to repeat the process.

306

From text objects, we can create symbols.

An important tip for Type Symbols

- Live Type Dynamic Symbol instances cannot be edited. When the original Symbol is edited, all instances will be instantly updated to reflect any changes made to its content or appearance.
- The text can remain live while having numerous look settings thanks to the ability to produce a Symbol version for each style.
- We can modify its look but the content is no longer changeable if we convert the text to outlines before storing it as a Symbol.

As a last point:
We can easily **differentiate Static and Dynamic Symbols** in the Symbols panel. Dynamic Symbols have a small **+** icon at the lower-right corner of their thumbnails.

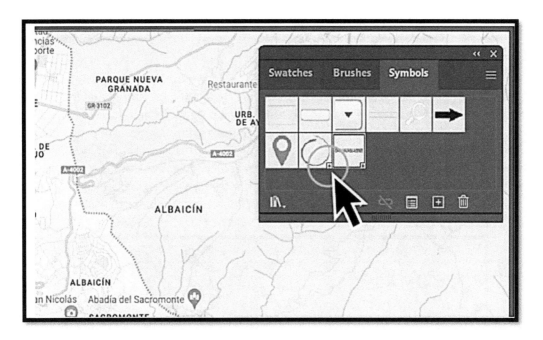

Placing and Editing Instances

The Symbols we've made can be used again and again now. For the sake of argument, let's pretend we need to mark down many spots on the map. Instances of your "**Location**" Symbol will need to be placed over those locations. Sure, we can just **click and drag new instances** from the thumbnails in the **Symbols panel**. However, since I'm your teacher, I feel obligated to show you other ways to accomplish things in Illustrator. So, instead, we can click the **Place Symbol Instance** button, and a new instance of the selected symbol will be copied to the artboard.

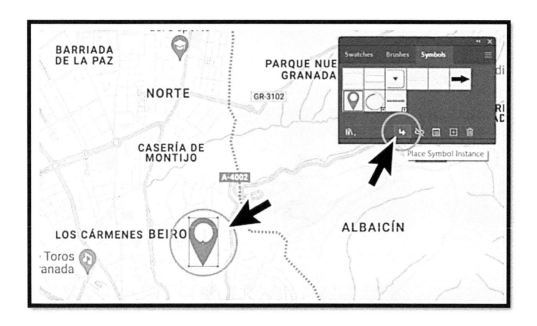

No effort is required! A new instance is created whenever we drag and drop symbols from the Symbols panel or press the Place button. Now, we may change the indicators that indicate where we are. Since these instances are exact replicas of a Static Symbol, their appearance cannot be altered, as we have learned. Modifying the meaning of the original symbol is necessary to alter its look. In the **Properties panel**, we can find the Edit Symbol button or just **double-click the thumbnail** to access it. A warning notice like the one below may appear if this is your first attempt; it states that changing the symbol will impact all connected instances. Before clicking OK, make sure the **Don't Show Again** box is checked if you don't want this reminder to show again.

To make the necessary adjustments, we will now enter Isolation Mode. I'll just increase the stroke size to 6 pixels and switch between Fill and Stroke using the shortcut Shift + X. After we finish editing symbols, we either press the **Escape** button or choose the **Exit Symbol Editing Mode** option.

We can now see that our location marker's new style has been **updated on the preview thumbnail and in all instances**. Efficiency and consistency, all at once! Cool, huh?

How about the **stroke path**, our swoosh symbol? I thought we made it **dynamic**; do you remember? Then you do! We can adjust its instances, let's see how. Without giving an exact address or mentioning any particular points of interest, such as parks, roads, or town areas, I will only circle select map places to serve as reminders to visit particular regions of Granada.

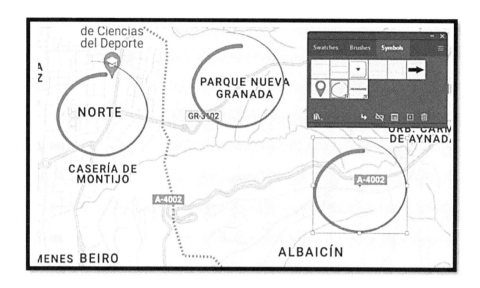

Seems good! Imagine for a second that we need to highlight a single circle to remind ourselves that we can't use any other means of transportation than a bicycle to get there. We modify the stroke color of the middle circle by clicking on it with the **Direct Selection tool** (shortcut **A**) and then using the **Color Picker.** It is as easy as pie!

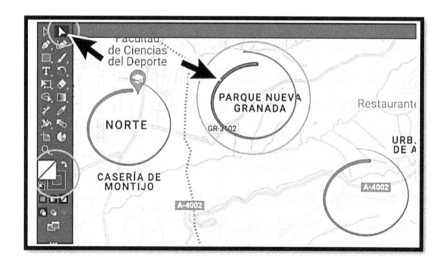

There was a modification to only that one instance. The original Symbol and the other two instances did not receive the upgrade for this new hue. And we intended it to happen just that way! Is it possible to modify the Symbol? **After we have updated a new color to an instance, what will happen to it?** How about we check it out? Just double-click the thumbnail! **Isolation Mode** has returned! We may keep things simple by rotating the screen by 90 degrees and then returning to our workplace by using the **Escape** key.

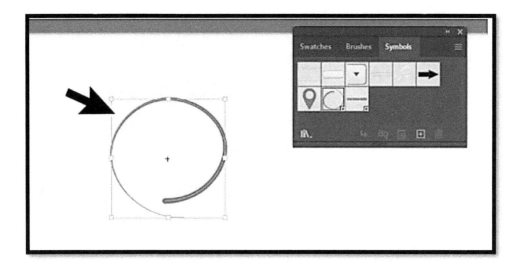

The three instances were all given new Symbol settings, except for the middle one, which retained its original stroke color! How cool is that?

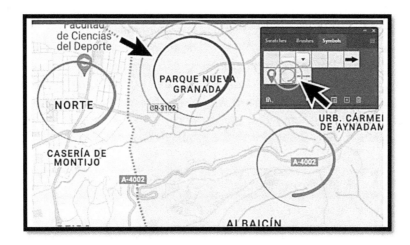

Saving and Loading Symbol Libraries

You could also be wondering, "Are these Symbols exclusive to this document? "I'm pleased to say "**no**" in response to that inquiry. A **Symbol Library** is a place where a collection of symbols can be stored and then used in other publications. See what we can accomplish using CC Libraries to facilitate the sharing of our design materials, and let's save our **Symbols as a Symbol Library**. Choose the option to "**Save Symbol Library**" from the flyout menu that appears when you click the button with **three horizontal lines** inside the **Symbols panel**.

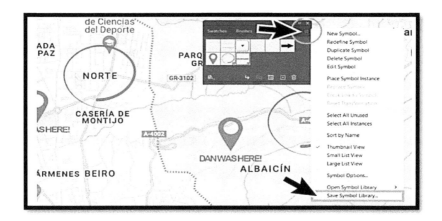

We should move our new symbol set to a separate library now. The next step is to save the **Symbol Library .ai file** to the **Symbols folder** under the Adobe Illustrator Settings path on your computer. After you've given it a memorable name, hit the "**Save**" button. A general one like "Map Symbols" would do, or you can be creative and choose a name that specifically pertains to your project. Let's learn **how to create a new Illustrator document and then load the Symbol Library.** Get to the **Symbols panel by starting a new document.** Navigate to the **user-defined** option in the panel's **Symbol Libraries Menu**, and click on the **file name** of the Library you saved in the previous step. The Symbols we created for our map of Granada are now available inside the new document, inside their **library panel**. We can now **click and drag each symbol to place new instances on the artboard** or **double-click the thumbnails to copy them to that document's Symbols panel.** We can do one more thing. Think of a scenario where we only needed to utilize the text label and location marker once. We can remove any link to the original Symbol by placing an instance on the artboard and then clicking **Break Link** in the **Properties Panel**.

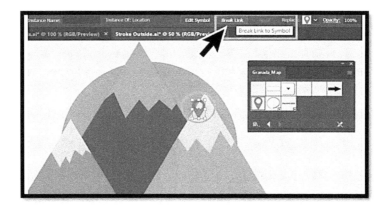

We can now freely alter the objects' shapes and attributes and, if necessary, save them as new symbols.

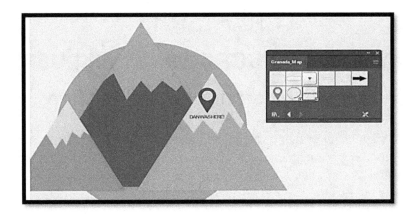

Saving Symbols as Graphics Assets in a CC Library

The "old way" to reuse design graphics across several artworks is using Symbol Libraries. Please don't misunderstand me; they are perfectly practical for a one-man show, freelancing portfolio building, and local storage of designs on any cloud service. This method is still popular among designers, and it's not bad at all. On the other hand, the "new way" **Creative Cloud option** is a productivity godsend if you're on a fast-paced design team and frequently need to share your work with other designers or a project manager. The "old way" is essentially unchanged. Just **open the Libraries panel**, makes a folder named **Symbols**, and then **drags the objects into the panel** to build your Granada Symbols library. One other way to do it is by **selecting each object** we want to save, **clicking on the Add Elements button** at the bottom of the Libraries panel, and picking the **Graphics** category. Done!

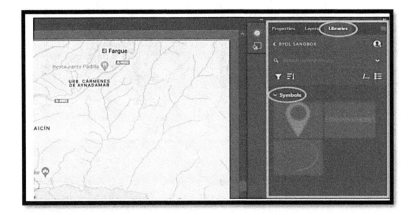

Our staff, management, and stakeholders will be able to access them without any more delay. It's simple! We enter the new user's email address and select whether they can change or only see the assets kept inside the library. Then, we click on the Invite to Library button at the top of the Libraries panel.

CHAPTER 13

AUTOMATION AND SCRIPTING IN ILLUSTRATOR

Creating Actions in Illustrator for Automation

Once recorded, a function or sequence of functions can be "played back" as an Action. This might be anything as basic as scaling an object by 125% or as involved as applying a document-level operation to several files at once, such as exporting to a specified file format. As you can see in the picture below, Illustrator loads a collection of Default Actions whenever you start the program. By expanding the presently chosen Action, we can view its instructions; for instance, the following Action changes the Transparency of any selected object(s) to 60%. Delete, New Set, Play, Record, and Stop are the icons located at the panel's base.

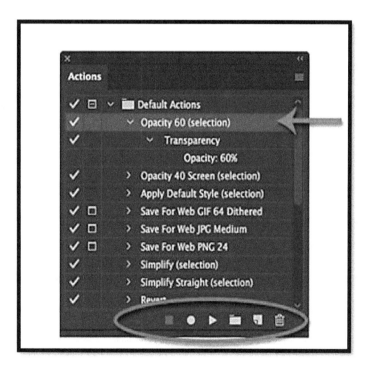

Recording a command that includes a dialogue box will preserve the values we first typed. This is the value that is used when an Action is played back that has a 30° rotation. But we may make these values editable every time we apply the Action if we want to. The modal control is located in the second column to the left of the action panel; toggle its on/off state by clicking here. To adjust the values applied at a specific phase in the Action, turn this on. When we play back the Action, a dialogue box will appear.

You can use the Modal Control on the entire Action or certain instructions inside it. You may utilize the first column to select which instructions to include or omit from an Action or a Set of Actions. Remember, it's as easy as toggling a switch to the on or off position to deactivate a command; no deletion is required. To begin organizing our custom actions into a set, we can use the folder icon located at the bottom of the Actions panel. Next, give the set a name by typing it into the text field.

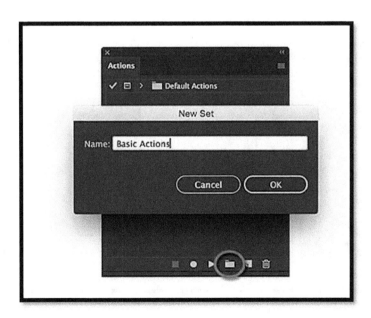

At this point, select the New Action icon. Most usefully, we can now designate a keyboard shortcut based on Function Keys with modifier keys if necessary, in addition to naming the action, selecting the set it is kept in, and assigning a highlight color. After the Action is created, you can additionally assign or update these choices.

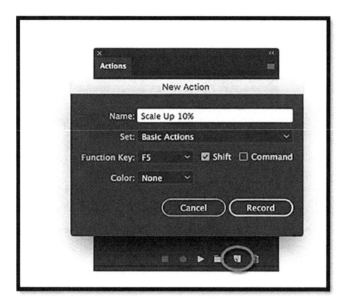

Once we press Record, the Record symbol at the Action Panel's bottom will turn red. The Action will now capture any updates or transformations made to the page's objects.

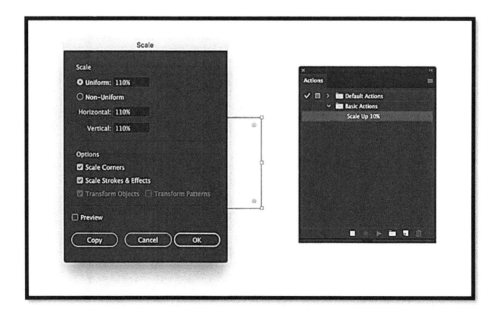

With a Function Key assigned, Copy set to No, Scale Strokes & Effects included, and 110% scale captured, we are good to go. If we are creating a simple Action, we can stop here; if it is more complicated, we can keep modifying it. The Record indicator remains red.

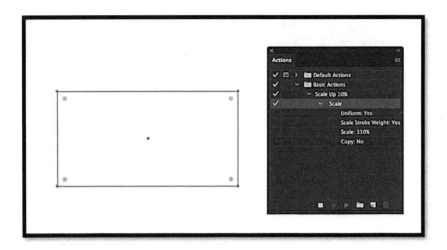

After creating an Action, it is also possible to add more stages to it. With a single click in the Action, you may choose which command to record next; any changes you make will be appended to the selected command. A handy tool that allows you to quickly and easily construct variations of comparable activities is the ability to replicate Actions. Here we have an example of a straightforward Action that raises the scale by 10%. It would be reasonable to combine this with an Action to reduce by 10%. This would also allow us to scale objects easily using shortcut keys, which are not available in Illustrator by default. Go to the Panel Menu icon and choose "**Duplicate**" from the drop-down menu while our Action is chosen.

After that, go to the "Action Options" section of our duplicate Action, where we can rename it and give it a function key, before clicking OK.

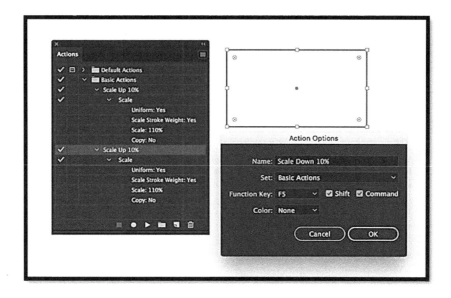

We can adjust the settings by double-clicking on the 'Scale' command in our Action. This will bring up the Scale window, which requires an object to be chosen. Now we can adjust the scale factor to 90% and hit the OK button.

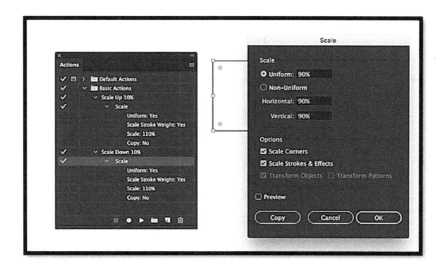

We now have a straightforward scaling tool that can be used using shortcut keys and enables consistent scaling of a single or several objects without the need for menus. Another option is to switch to "**Button Mode**," which removes all but the most essential controls from the Action panel and replaces them with clickable buttons. I have eliminated the other Actions and highlighted our custom Actions in red in the screenshot below for clarity's sake.

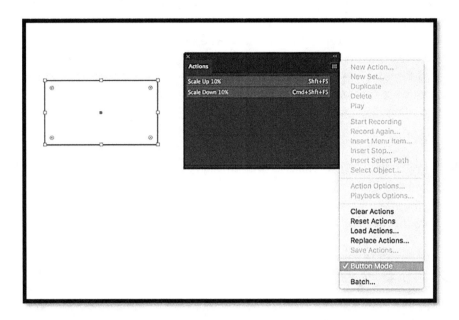

Button mode allows you to quickly access your personalized tool palette once you've created a library of custom Actions. When you're done changing or adding Actions, you can simply return to regular mode. If you're frustrated that Illustrator doesn't provide you with the actions you need to do common activities, it's time to get your hands dirty and create your own set of Actions.

Automation with scripts

Invoking a script causes your computer to carry out a predetermined set of actions. Illustrator or other software like word processors, spreadsheets, and database management systems may be required for these tasks. Illustrator is compatible with a wide variety of scripting languages and frameworks, such as ExtendScript, AppleScript, JavaScript, and Microsoft Visual Basic. Illustrator has both built-in and user-created scripts; the former can be found under the Scripts submenu, while the latter can be added there. Adobe Illustrator <version number>/Scripting is where you may find the scripts that have been installed as samples.

Run a script

To run a script, just follow these instructions.
1. Select a script by going to **File** > **Scripts**.
2. Illustrator supports script execution using the simple drag-and-drop of.jsx files.

But this isn't the safest or most recommended option. To help you avoid unintentional actions, a warning window will be displayed.
Just follow these instructions to run the script and hide the warning message.

1. Create the following content in a JSX file:

app.preferences.setBooleanPreference("ShowExternalJSXWarning", false)

2. Keep the JSX file saved.
3. After you've saved the JSX file, navigate to **File > Scripts > Other Script** and choose it.

Note: Please be aware that for your script edits to be applied when Illustrator is running, you will need to save your modifications.

Install a script

Copy the script to the hard drive of your computer. The script will be accessible through the **File > Scripts** submenu in Adobe Illustrator if you save it to the Scripts folder.
You can access the script from any folder on your hard drive; just open Illustrator and go to **File > Scripts > Other Script.**

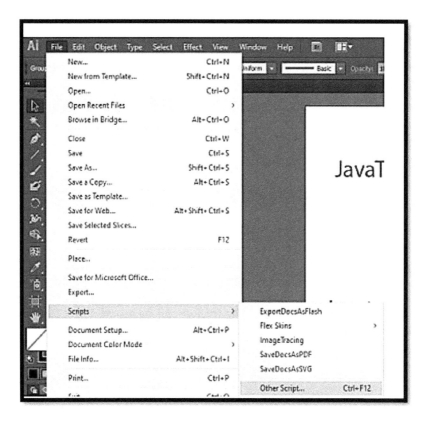

Note: Please be aware that for a script to be visible in the Scripts submenu of Adobe Illustrator, it is necessary to restart Illustrator after placing the script in the Scripts folder while Illustrator is active.

CHAPTER 14
TIPS AND TRICKS

1. How to Stylize Text and Keep It Editable Using the Appearance Panel

We'll begin with text and the powerful **Appearance** panel, which can be accessed through **Window > Appearance**. You can style text while keeping it completely editable by combining the two. The text can be edited according to your preferences once you've added various fills, strokes, and effects.

When you're satisfied with the text's style, you can easily add more text in the same style by **double-clicking** it.

Another fantastic example that demonstrates the extent to which this approach can be extended while preserving the text's complete editability is this one.

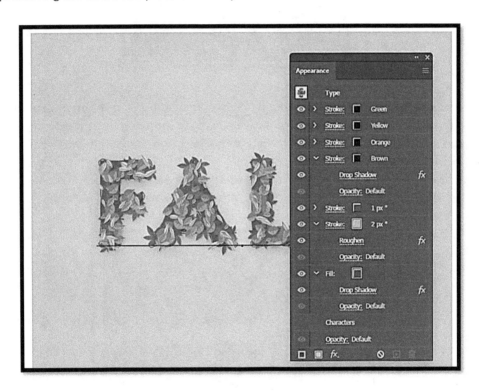

2. How to Copy Appearance Attributes

After applying, you may find it useful to copy the characteristics from the **Appearance** panel. Indeed, you can locate the object with the **Appearance** attributes in the **Layers** panel (**Window > Layers),** then zero in on these specific icons. Press and hold the **Alt** key until you see the icon representing your stylized object; then, click and drag it to the icon representing the other object. Even if this works, there is a more convenient approach to copy and paste **Appearance** attributes.

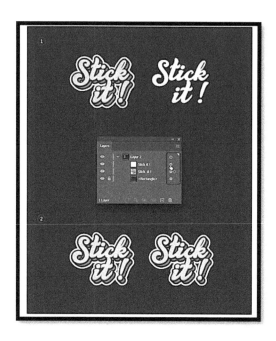

After you **double-click** the **Eyedropper Tool (I)** in your toolbar, make sure the **Appearance** box is checked to ensure that the **Eyedropper Tool** will choose the **Appearance** attributes. Never forget to hit **OK** to save your changes. You can switch to the **Selection Tool** while the **Eyedropper Tool** is active if you hold down the **Control** key. By holding down the **Control** key, you can swiftly choose one object in your design; releasing it will return you to the **Eyedropper Tool**. To quickly apply the same changes to your selection, click the object with the **Appearance** attributes.

3. **How to Scale Appearance Attributes**

The **Scale Strokes & Effects** box can be found under **Edit > Preferences > General**. When you want to scale the **Appearance** attributes proportionally, just tick it.

Tip: You appropriately scale objects with patterns or rounded corners, be sure you tick the boxes for **Transform Pattern Tiles and Scale Corners.**

4. How to Scale Patterns in Illustrator

You can always go back to the original size or make more adjustments to the scaling if you wish to scale a pattern non-destructively. The good news is that a **Transform** effect can solve this problem. Select **Effect,** then **Distort & Transform**, and finally, **Transform**. To begin scaling your pattern, make sure the **Transform Patterns** box is ticked but the **Transform Objects** box is unchecked.

In the **Appearance** panel, you can stop the **Transform** effect or access it at any time to change the scale settings. If you want to go back to the original pattern size, you can do it easily. In addition to moving and rotating your pattern, you can also flip it.

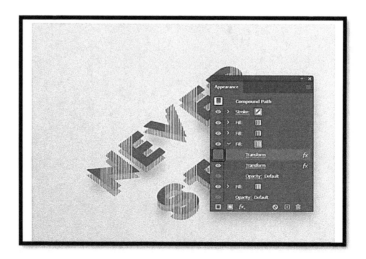

5. **How to Save Complex Patterns**

Moving on, there is a simple method that you can utilize in Illustrator when saving a pattern. Yes, you can easily change the size of your pattern tile by saving it in the **Swatches** panel (**Window > Swatches**), **double-clicking** on it, and then using the **Pattern Tile Tool.**

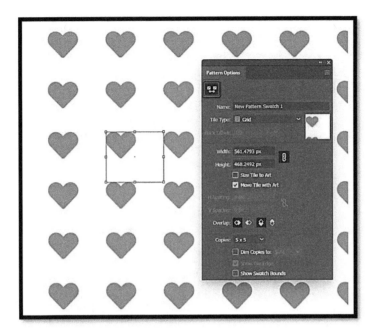

When working with basic patterns, this can work. However, when faced with complicated patterns, Illustrator can become extremely sluggish or even crash, which can be rather annoying.

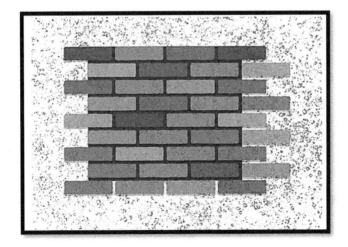

How can this problem be prevented? Measure the size of the pattern tile you were attempting to establish with the **Pattern Tile Tool** and use the **Rectangle Tool (M)** to construct a shape that matches. Use the shortcut **Shift-Control-[** to move this shape to the background, behind all of the other shapes in your pattern. To make it undetectable, remove the fill or stroke color. To create a new pattern, select all of your pattern shapes, including this one, and then drag them into the **Swatches** panel.

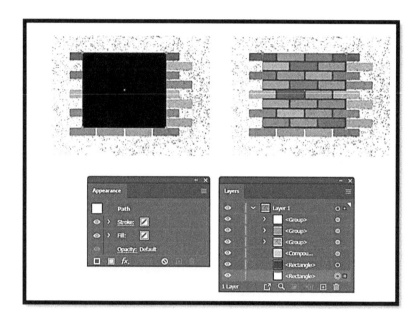

This new pattern has to be **double-clicked**. You can skip using the **Pattern Tile Tool** since the size of the pattern tile is determined by your invisible rectangle.

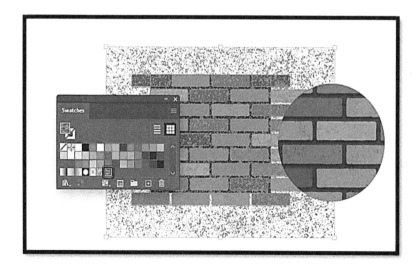

6. **How to Add Custom Toolbars**

The standard toolbar is certainly recognizable to you, but did you know that you can also create custom toolbars? To access the menu containing all of your tools, click the three-dot icon located at the bottom of your toolbar. Navigate to the **New Toolbar** option in the pop-up menu that appears when you click the button in the upper right corner of this panel. After you've given it a name, hit **OK** to add it. Select the tools you require by clicking and dragging them from your new toolbar, which you can access via the three-dot button. If you want to utilize tools without specific keyboard shortcuts, this might be useful.

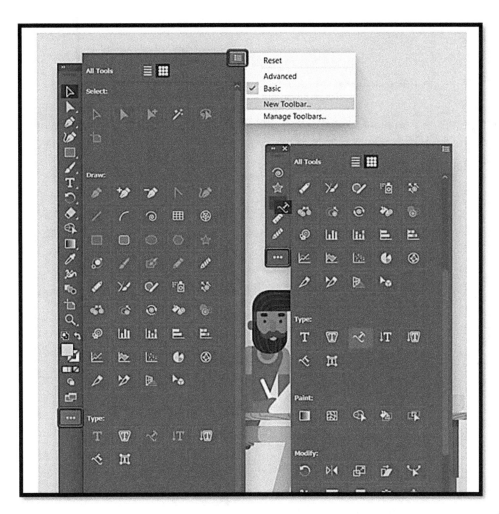

7. **How to Use Drawing Modes**

You can quickly choose between inserting new objects on top of, below, or even inside your current design by using the **Drawing Modes** command. In most cases, new shapes are superimposed over your existing design.

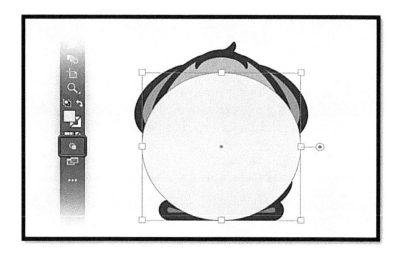

Locate the little button beneath the color options on your toolbar and click on it. When you add a new shape, it will automatically hide behind your current design when you select **Draw Behind.**

Any new object you add will be disguised by your selection as long as you have a shape chosen and choose **Draw Inside.** Never forget to choose **Draw Normal** or press **Shift-D** to go back to the default mode.

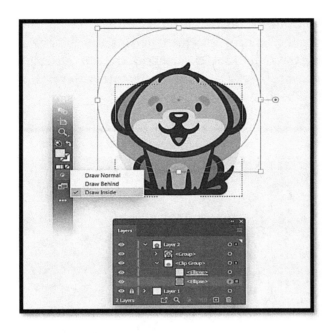

8. How to Quickly Clean Up Asset Panels

Your work efficiency will be much enhanced if your panels are neat and organized. Therefore, you may choose to eliminate assets that aren't being used in some instances. This will be demonstrated in the **Brushes** panel (**Window > Brushes**) but it may also be applied to the **Swatches**, **Graphics Styles**, or Symbols panels. To remove the brushes that you do not need, open the fly-out menu of the **Brushes** panel, and go to **Select All Unused**, which will instantly select all your unused brushes. Once they're selected, you can easily delete them using the trash can button at the bottom of the panel.

9. **How to Zoom in Using the Mouse Wheel**

In Illustrator, you can zoom in and out using the traditional controls as well as the wheel on your mouse. To begin, clicking the **Zoom Tool (Z)** is unnecessary. You can enable the ability to zoom in and out using the mouse wheel by going to **Edit > Preferences > General**, checking the option that says **Zoom with Mouse Wheel**, and then clicking **OK**.

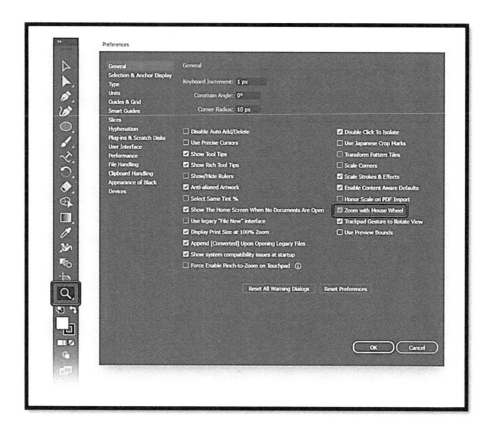

Remember that you can still use the mouse wheel to zoom in and out while holding down the Alt key, even if the **Zoom with Mouse Wheel** option is unchecked.

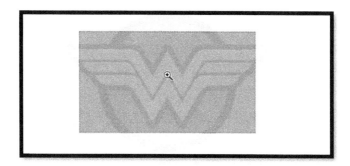

10. **How to Change the Default Font Settings**

You can notice right away that Illustrator always uses the little Myriad font as its starting point whenever you add new text. Press **Window > Type > Character Styles** to bring up the **Character Styles** panel, where you can change the default text settings. To access the **Character Style Options**, open the panel's fly-out menu. To change the default settings to something you want, go to the menu and choose **Basic Character Formats**. If you want to save the changes, click **OK**.

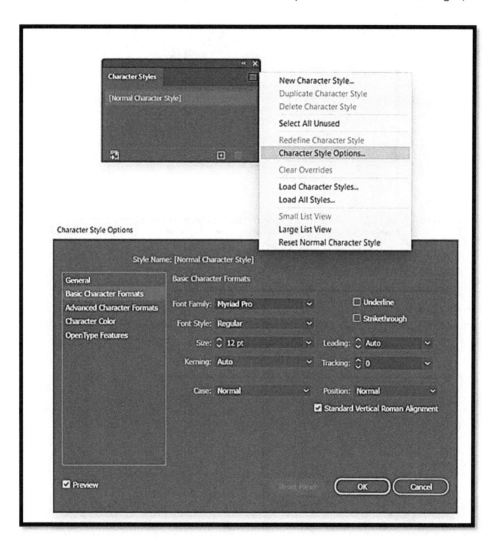

11. **How to Exclude Words From Hyphenation**

Having a list of terms that will never be hyphenated might be helpful when dealing with large blocks of text. By selecting **Edit > Preferences > Hyphenation**, you can simply accomplish this. To add a term to the **Exceptions** list, just write it into the **New Entry** area and click the **Add** button.

12. **Warping Text Using Shapes**

You can distort text in Illustrator in some ways, but this one is among the quickest and most flexible. Text and a shape are all that are required. Choose **Object > Envelope Distort > Make with Top Object** once you've selected both of these items. The text will be distorted to suit the shape's bounds.

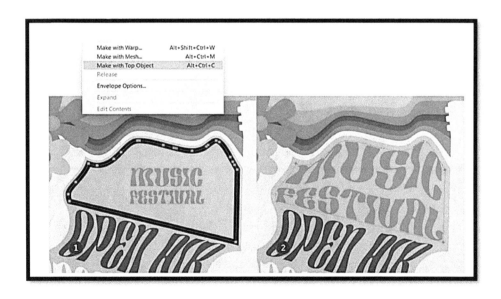

13. **How to Easily Select Objects With the Same Attributes**

Choosing many objects at once can be tedious, particularly when dealing with intricate designs. One of the **Select Same** commands can be used to quickly pick many objects at once if they have some similar **Appearance** attributes. Selecting one of your objects and then selecting "**Select > Same**" will bring up some filters that you can use to narrow down your selection to only those objects in your document that have common qualities.

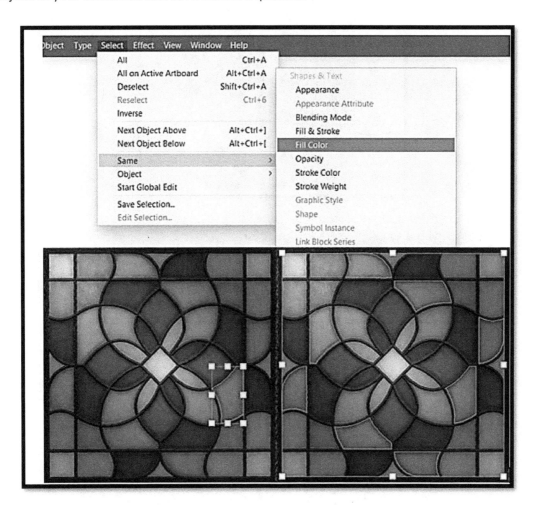

14. **How to Recolor Artwork Using a Photo**

Although you may be acquainted with the **Recolor Artwork** option, you might not be aware that you can also swiftly recolor your design using the colors from a photo. All you have to do is open the **Recolor Artwork** window (click the button from the control panel or go to **Edit > Edit Colors > Recolor Artwork**) and click the **Color Theme Picker** button, and then just click your photo and Illustrator will do the rest.

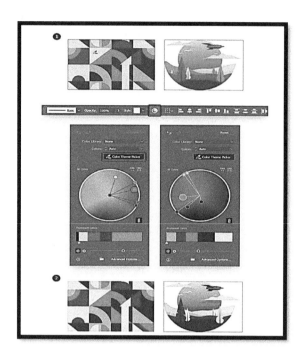

15. 5 Quick Tips to Ease Your Work in Illustrator

Lastly, in the interest of saving you time, here are a few incredibly fast pointers. Go to **Edit > Preferences > General** and uncheck the **Show Rich Tool Tips** box if you're bothered by Illustrator's huge tooltips.

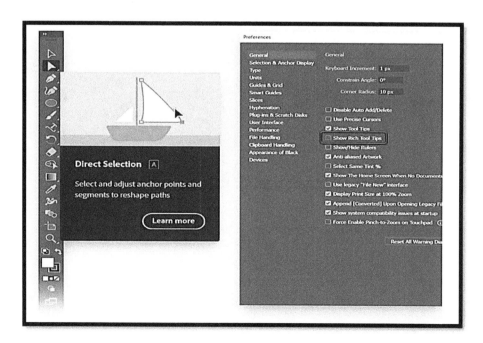

If you're unable to see the outline of a chosen object, you can enable it by going to **View > Show Edges.**

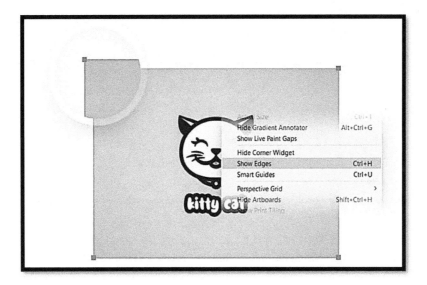

You can view the bounding box of an object when you use the **Selection Tool (V)** by going to **View > Show Bounding Box**. If you don't see it, try again.

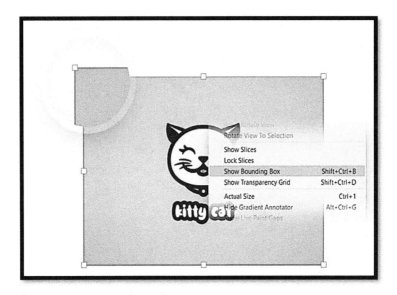

You can enable the corner widgets by going to **View > Show Corner Widget** if they aren't shown when you pick an object.

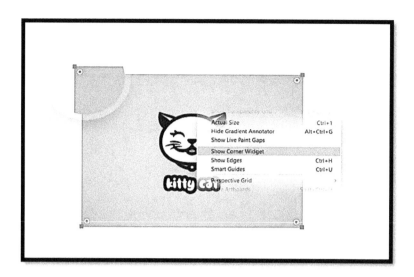

If you're using the **Gradient Tool (G)** and choose an object with a gradient fill but can't see the gradient bar, go to **View > Show Gradient Annotator.**

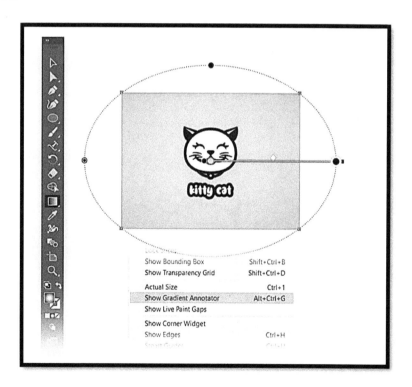

When you inadvertently activate this perspective grid, you can quickly disable it by pressing **Shift-Control-I.**

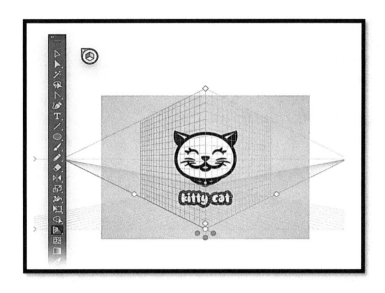

You have achieved a remarkable feat! It's Complete!

Setting Up Keyboard Shortcuts for Faster Navigation

Basic Document Shortcuts

- **Create a New Document**
    - **Windows**: Ctrl + N
    - **Mac**: Cmd + N
- **Create New Document (Skip Dialog)**
    - **Windows**: Alt + Ctrl + N
    - **Mac**: Option + Cmd + N
- **Create Document from Template**
    - **Windows**: Shift + Ctrl + N
    - **Mac**: Shift + Cmd + N
- **Save Document**
    - **Windows**: Ctrl + S
    - **Mac**: Cmd + S

Exporting and Packaging

- **Export for Screens**
    - **Windows**: Alt + Ctrl + E
    - **Mac**: Option + Cmd + E
- **Package Document**
    - **Windows**: Alt + Shift + Ctrl + P

- o **Mac**: Option + Shift + Cmd + P
- **Print Document**
  - o **Windows**: Ctrl + P
  - o **Mac**: Cmd + P

Undo, Redo, and Clipboard

- **Undo Last Action**
  - o **Windows**: Ctrl + Z
  - o **Mac**: Cmd + Z
- **Redo Last Action**
  - o **Windows**: Shift + Ctrl + Z
  - o **Mac**: Shift + Cmd + Z
- **Cut**
  - o **Windows**: Ctrl + X
  - o **Mac**: Cmd + X
- **Copy**
  - o **Windows**: Ctrl + C
  - o **Mac**: Cmd + C
- **Paste**
  - o **Windows**: Ctrl + V
  - o **Mac**: Cmd + V
- **Paste in Place**
  - o **Windows**: Shift + Ctrl + B
  - o **Mac**: Shift + Cmd + B
- **Paste in Front**
  - o **Windows**: Ctrl + F
  - o **Mac**: Cmd + F
- **Paste Behind**
  - o **Windows**: Ctrl + B
  - o **Mac**: Cmd + B

File Placement and Layer Management

- **Place File into Document**
  - o **Windows**: Shift + Ctrl + P
  - o **Mac**: Shift + Cmd + P
- **Add New Layer**
  - o **Windows**: Ctrl + L
  - o **Mac**: Cmd + L
- **Add New Layer (with Dialog)**
  - o **Windows**: Alt + Ctrl + L

- o **Mac:** Option + Cmd + L

Layer and Object Selection

- **Select All Objects on a Layer**
  - o **Windows:** Alt + Click layer name
  - o **Mac:** Option + Click layer name
- **Show/Hide All Other Layers**
  - o **Windows:** Alt + Click Eye icon
  - o **Mac:** Option + Click Eye icon
- **Lock/Unlock All Other Layers**
  - o **Windows:** Alt + Click Lock icon
  - o **Mac:** Option + Click Lock icon

View Shortcuts

Screen Modes and Full-Screen

- **Switch between Screen Modes (Normal, Full Screen, etc.)**
  - o **Windows:** F
  - o **Mac:** F
- **Exit Full-Screen Mode**
  - o **Windows:** Esc
  - o **Mac:** Esc

Artboard and Guides Visibility

- **Show or Hide Artboards**
  - o **Windows:** Shift + Ctrl + H
  - o **Mac:** Shift + Cmd + H
- **Show or Hide Rulers**
  - o **Windows:** Ctrl + R
  - o **Mac:** Cmd + R
- **Show or Hide Smart Guides**
  - o **Windows:** Ctrl + U
  - o **Mac:** Cmd + U
- **Show or Hide Grid**
  - o **Windows:** Ctrl + '
  - o **Mac:** Cmd + '

Snap and Alignment

- **Turn Snap to Grid On or Off**
  - ○ **Windows**: Shift + Ctrl + '
  - ○ **Mac**: Shift + Cmd + '
- **Turn Snap to Point On or Off**
  - ○ **Windows**: Alt + Ctrl + '
  - ○ **Mac**: Option + Cmd + '

Zoom Controls

- **Zoom In**
  - ○ **Windows**: Ctrl + =
  - ○ **Mac**: Cmd + =
- **Zoom Out**
  - ○ **Windows**: Ctrl + -
  - ○ **Mac**: Cmd + -
- **Fit Artboard to Window**
  - ○ **Windows**: Ctrl + 0
  - ○ **Mac**: Cmd + 0
- **View at Actual Size**
  - ○ **Windows**: Ctrl + 1
  - ○ **Mac**: Cmd + 1

Tool and Editing Shortcuts

General Tools

- **View Settings for Selected Tool**: Double click (Win/Mac)
- **Hand Tool**: H (Win/Mac)
- **Hand Tool While Not Entering Text**: Spacebar (Win/Mac)
- **Hand Tool While Entering Text**: Ctrl + Spacebar (Win) / Cmd + Spacebar (Mac)
- **Selection Tool**: V (Win/Mac)
- **Direct Selection Tool**: A (Win/Mac)

Specialized Tools

- **Magic Wand Tool**: Y (Win/Mac)
- **Lasso Tool**: Q (Win/Mac)
- **Pen Tool**: P (Win/Mac)
- **Add Anchor Point**: + (Win/Mac)

- **Delete Anchor Point**: - (Win/Mac)
- **Anchor Point Tool**: Shift + C (Win/Mac)
- **Curvature Tool**: Shift + ~ (Win/Mac)

Drawing and Type Tools

- **Type Tool**: T (Win/Mac)
- **Touch Type Tool**: Shift + T (Win/Mac)
- **Line Segment Tool**: \ (Win/Mac)
- **Rectangle Tool**: M (Win/Mac)
- **Ellipse Tool**: L (Win/Mac)
- **Paintbrush Tool**: B (Win/Mac)
- **Blob Brush Tool**: Shift + B (Win/Mac)
- **Pencil Tool**: N (Win/Mac)
- **Shaper Tool**: Shift + N (Win/Mac)

Editing and Transformation Tools

- **Eraser Tool**: Shift + E (Win/Mac)
- **Scissors Tool**: C (Win/Mac)
- **Rotate Tool**: R (Win/Mac)
- **Reflect Tool**: O (Win/Mac)
- **Scale Tool**: S (Win/Mac)
- **Width Tool**: Shift + W (Win/Mac)
- **Warp Tool**: Shift + R (Win/Mac)
- **Free Transform Tool**: E (Win/Mac)

Advanced Tools

- **Shape Builder Tool**: Shift + M (Win/Mac)
- **Live Paint Bucket**: K (Win/Mac)
- **Live Paint Selection Tool**: Shift + L (Win/Mac)
- **Perspective Grid Tool**: Shift + P (Win/Mac)
- **Perspective Selection Tool**: Shift + V (Win/Mac)
- **Mesh Tool**: U (Win/Mac)
- **Gradient Tool**: G (Win/Mac)
- **Eyedropper Tool**: I (Win/Mac)
- **Blend Tool**: W (Win/Mac)
- **Symbol Sprayer Tool**: Shift + S (Win/Mac)
- **Column Graph Tool**: J (Win/Mac)
- **Artboard Tool**: Shift + O (Win/Mac)

- **Exit Artboard Mode**: Esc (Win/Mac)
- **Slice Tool**: Shift + K (Win/Mac)
- **Zoom Tool**: Z (Win/Mac)
- **Magnify 100%**: Ctrl + 1 (Win) / Cmd + 1 (Mac)

Fill and Stroke Controls

- **Fill**: X (Win/Mac)
- **Swap Fill and Stroke**: Shift + X (Win/Mac)
- **Set Default Fill and Stroke**: D (Win/Mac)
- **No Fill/Stroke**: / (Win/Mac)
- **Add New Fill**: Ctrl + / (Win) / Cmd + / (Mac)
- **Add New Stroke**: Alt + Ctrl + / (Win) / Option + Cmd + / (Mac)

Basic Selection

- **Select Multiple Objects**: Shift + Click (Win/Mac)
- **Select All**: Ctrl + A (Win) / Cmd + A (Mac)
- **Deselect All**: Shift + Ctrl + A (Win) / Shift + Cmd + A (Mac)
- **Reselect**: Ctrl + 6 (Win) / Cmd + 6 (Mac)

Grouping and Object Management

- **Group Objects**: Ctrl + G (Win) / Cmd + G (Mac)
- **Select Object Above**: Alt + Ctrl +] (Win) / Option + Cmd +] (Mac)
- **Select Object Below**: Alt + Ctrl + [(Win) / Option + Cmd + [(Mac)
- **Select Object Behind**: Ctrl + Double Click (Win) / Cmd + Double Click (Mac)

Moving and Duplicating

- **Move Selection**: Arrow keys (Win/Mac)
- **Move Selection by 10 Points**: Shift + Arrow keys (Win/Mac)
- **Duplicate Selection**: Alt + Drag (Win) / Option + Drag (Mac)

Bounding Box and Visibility

- **Hide Bounding Box**: Shift + Ctrl + B (Win) / Shift + Cmd + B (Mac)
- **Hide Unselected Items**: Alt + Shift + Ctrl + 3 (Win) / Option + Shift + Cmd + 3 (Mac)

Creating Outlines

- **Create Outlines from Type:** Shift + Ctrl + O (Win) / Shift + Cmd + O (Mac)

Editing Tools Shortcuts

Drawing and Adjustment

- **Expand/Shrink Proportionally:** Shift + Drag handles (Win/Mac)
- **Move Shape While Drawing:** Spacebar + Drag (Win/Mac)

Brush and Tool Adjustments

- **Increase Brush Size:**] (Win/Mac)
- **Decrease Brush Size:** [(Win/Mac)

Clipping Masks

- **Create Clipping Mask:** Ctrl + 7 (Win) / Cmd + 7 (Mac)
- **Remove Clipping Mask:** Alt + Ctrl + 7 (Win) / Option + Cmd + 7 (Mac)

Sampling and Spelling

- **Sample Color from an Image:** Shift + Eyedropper Tool (Win/Mac)
- **Check Spelling:** Ctrl + I (Win) / Cmd + I (Mac)

Panel Shortcuts

General Panel Management

- **Show or Hide All Panels:**
  - **Windows:** Tab
  - **Mac:** Tab

Specific Panel Shortcuts

- **Align Panel:**
  - **Windows:** Shift + F7
  - **Mac:** Shift + F7
- **Appearance Panel:**
  - **Windows:** Shift + F6

- o **Mac**: Shift + F6
- **Attributes Panel**:
  - o **Windows**: Ctrl + F11
  - o **Mac**: Cmd + F11
- **Brushes Panel**:
  - o **Windows**: F5
  - o **Mac**: F5
- **Color Panel**:
  - o **Windows**: F6
  - o **Mac**: F6
- **Color Guide Panel**:
  - o **Windows**: Shift + F3
  - o **Mac**: Shift + F3
- **Gradient Panel**:
  - o **Windows**: Ctrl + F9
  - o **Mac**: Cmd + F9
- **Graphic Styles Panel**:
  - o **Windows**: Shift + F5
  - o **Mac**: Shift + F5
- **Info Panel**:
  - o **Windows**: Ctrl + F8
  - o **Mac**: Cmd + F8
- **Layers Panel**:
  - o **Windows**: F7
  - o **Mac**: F7

Advanced Panel Shortcuts

- **Pathfinder Panel**:
  - o **Windows**: Shift + Ctrl + F9
  - o **Mac**: Shift + Cmd + F9
- **Stroke Panel**:
  - o **Windows**: Ctrl + F10
  - o **Mac**: Cmd + F10
- **Symbols Panel**:
  - o **Windows**: Shift + Ctrl + F11
  - o **Mac**: Shift + Cmd + F11
- **Transform Panel**:
  - o **Windows**: Shift + F8
  - o **Mac**: Shift + F8
- **Transparency Panel**:
  - o **Windows**: Shift + Ctrl + F10
  - o **Mac**: Shift + Cmd + F10

CHAPTER 15

TROUBLESHOOTING AND ILLUSTRATOR RESOURCES

Adobe Illustrator Performance Issues

- To make more room in the RAM, close some unused open files.
- Go into Illustrator's preferences and raise the amount of RAM it has.
- Turn off GPU performance if it's generating problems.
- Remove unused apps, update drivers, and clear caches to optimize your system.
- To enhance performance, go to low-resolution preview mode.

Adobe Illustrator File Corruption Issues

- Do your best to get the file back into Illustrator by using the recovery option.
- If a backup is available, restore from it.
- To test whether it opens, try saving it in an alternate format, such as EPS or PDF.
- Verify that the problem is not caused by corrupt fonts.
- See if you can get the file back by using file repair software.

Adobe Illustrator Crashing Issue

Method 1: Update Adobe Illustrator

Make sure your software is up-to-date first. In that case, you need to update to the most recent version of the program.

How to update Adobe Illustrator

- **Step 1:** Start by launching Adobe Illustrator.
- **Step 2:** Click the icon of **three dots** on the upper right side of the app.
- **Step 3:** Check **App updates**
- **Step 4:** After checking the updates, look if the app shows an **update button** next to Illustrator CC.
- **Step 5:** Press the button to update the software.
- **Step 6:** Open Adobe Illustrator again to see whether the crash problems persist.

Method 2: Restart and Recover

The next most usual thing to do when this happens is to restart Adobe Illustrator.
- **Step 1:** Close Adobe Illustrator CC and launch it again.
- **Step 2:** Click the Ok button on the pop-up window. Click it to import unsaved Illustrator files.
- **Step 3:** Then, save all the files to your computer.

How do you recover unsaved files on Adobe Illustrator?

Adobe Illustrator crash problems can potentially impact the files that are saved within the program. So, Adobe Illustrator includes a data recovery tool to ensure the security of your Illustrator files. You have to enable this feature to automatically back up your Illustrator files.

Data Recovery Feature

- **Step 1:** Open the application
- **Step 2:** Press **Ctrl + K**, which will launch Adobe Illustrator's **preferences**.
- **Step 3:** Move to **File Handling & Clipboard**.
- **Step 4:** Select the checkbox of Automatically **Save Recovery Data Every** in Data Recovery.
- **Step 5:** You can see an **interval drop-down list** and should select the duration.
- **Step 6:** After this, select the **Choose** button. Through this, it allows you to save the backup files.
- **Step 7:** Turn off Data Recovery for complex documents.
- **Step 8:** To save the changes, click **Ok**.

What to Keep in Mind When Making Use of the Data Recovery Feature

You should choose a long duration period since working on complicated or huge files can be hindered by a short duration. While working with Illustrator, it can be annoying to have the program save your files automatically every time. Overuse, especially with large files, can also cause crashes. Backups of big files will be affected by Adobe Illustrator if data recovery is enabled. A workaround for complicated data is to disable Data Recovery.

Method 3: Run Adobe Illustrator in Safe Mode

Using the safe mode to start Adobe Illustrator is highly recommended. Elements like typefaces, plug-ins, drivers, etc., can work accurately because of this. Altering the system to safe mode and then clicking "Run Diagnostics" will also aid in software repair.

To start Illustrator in safe mode, follow these instructions.

- **Step 1:** Restart your computer
- **Step 2:** Open Adobe Illustrator and select **Run Diagnostics**
- **Step 3:** Select Run Illustrator in **Safe Mode**

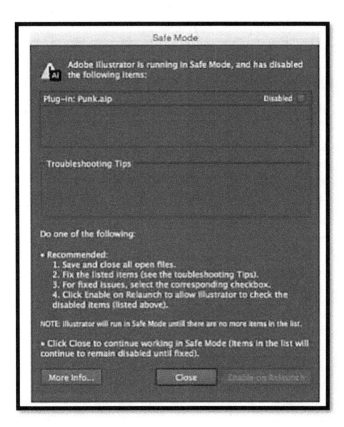

- **Step 4:** A list of choices will then be shown. Each one of those choices must be made by you. (It describes what went wrong with Illustrator and why it crashed.)
- **Step 5:** After that, you should address each problem by implementing the **troubleshooting tips** provided. To fix it, you must adhere to the on-screen instructions.
- **Step 6:** You'll see the option to **enable on Re-launch**. When we've fixed everything, you may start Illustrator again, and it will run smoothly.

Method 4: Fix or Remove Third-Party Plug-ins

There are two methods to fix it.

Through Programs and Features

I may be using an out-of-date plugin with the most recent version of Illustrator. An Illustrator crash can result from this. You can try deleting these third-party plugins to see if it helps fix the issue. Following these procedures will fix the crashing issues caused by these plugins. A new entry will appear in Programs and Features when you install software. Consequently, you need to remove the program that is listed there.

- **Step 1:** Visit the list of **Programs and Features.**
- **Step 2:** Search for Illustrator Plug-ins from the list.
- **Step 3:** Select Illustrator and uninstall it.

Through System Restore

To get back on track after a system crash, you can utilize System Restore, an option in Microsoft Windows. Reverting the computer's status to an earlier point in time is possible with this feature. **This includes the apps installed, system directories, and more.**

- **Step 1:** You can uninstall plug-ins through this System Restore.
- **Step 2:** To enable this feature, you have to create a restore point before installing programs.
- **Step 3:** Close all the opened files and programs
- **Step 4** Then, on the Desktop, you have to right-click **Computer**
- **Step 5:** Click on the **Properties** which will display the system window.
- **Step 6:** Select **System Protection** and it will show the system properties window.
- **Step 7:** Select the **System Restore**
- **Step 8:** Click to **Choose a different restore point** and click **Next**
- **Step 9:** Choose a time and date from the list and click **Next**.
- **Step 10:** Click Finish and **Yes** to save the changes.

Note: Installed apps will not function correctly after the specified date and time. Therefore, you will need to reinstall those applications.

Method 5: Reset App Preferences

It is one of the simplest ways to get rid of the crash issue.
- **Step 1:** Move to the **Edit** option of the Adobe Illustrator
- **Step 2:** Select **Reset Preferences** and click **Ok**.
- **Step 3:** Then, **Restart** the Illustrator.
- **Step 4:** Click **Alt + Ctrl + Shift**

Adobe Illustrator crashes can be fixed using these approaches. Is the cause of these crashes anything you've considered? Software freezing can be caused by several different factors. We've already made a short list of potential items to investigate.

Other Reasons Illustrator Might be crashing

1. Insufficient Memory
An issue with Illustrator's memory is the most typical cause of the program's freezing. Inadequate RAM overloading with apps isn't immediately apparent. Crashing Adobe Illustrator can therefore be attributed to memory depletion. Therefore, increasing your system's RAM is a simple option. Alternatively, you may try to find hardware that can manage the software's demands better. There are alternative approaches you might take if you are confident in your system's memory capabilities. As an example, you can launch your software after closing any unused applications. Check out the other problems that crop up down below if this doesn't fix it.

2. DLL and Driver Issues
The inability to launch or correctly install drivers is another typical problem. To make sure all of your system's parts work together properly when running software, you need drivers. Your software may not launch at all or crash if a driver (the program that enables this) isn't functioning properly. Verifying that your drivers are current and correctly installed is a simple solution to this problem. An error message will be displayed when dynamic link libraries (DLLs) are either missing or not functioning properly. The VCRUNTIMExx.dll or MSVCP110.dll errors are the most typical ones with Illustrator.

3. A New Update
Even though it may sound strange, new users frequently report problems immediately following an upgrade to Illustrator. However, a common complaint from these consumers is that the program freezes or crashes frequently when they are making design changes. The new software update or the necessary configuration modifications can be the source of the issues. Doing a system restore will roll back your program to a previous version, which should cure the issue.

Adobe Illustrator Not Responding Issues

Quit Illustrator or update your drivers if it's not loading properly. Adobe Illustrator's responsiveness is a major problem while using the product. The moment you open a file, this will occur. Unfortunately, you've reached the end of your options because Illustrator is not responding. Adobe Illustrator version, font database, or preference file corruption are the most likely causes. To be honest, I don't find these scary. Action must be taken since the problem persists. Here are a few fixes that will get Adobe Illustrator back on track if you're currently having trouble fixing this specific issue.

Why is my Adobe Illustrator not responding?

While there are a lot of potential causes for an app to stop responding, the most typical ones, when it comes to Adobe Illustrator in particular, are:

- Corrupt or outdated GPU drivers may interfere with Illustrator and cause it to crash.
- Outdated versions of the Adobe Illustrator software
- Bad preference files
- Your device does not meet the minimum system requirements

What can I do if Adobe Illustrator is not responding?

- **Uninstall and reinstall Adobe Illustrator**

There could be issues with the files you're currently working on within Adobe Illustrator that are making them unresponsive. Reinstalling the application with the latest updates is the easiest approach to fix this.

Uninstall Adobe Illustrator

1. To launch the **Creative Cloud Desktop App**, in the taskbar, type **Creative Cloud**.
2. Under the **All Apps** tab, select **Adobe Illustrator** and choose **Uninstall**.
3. If needed, click the **More options icon** to get to **Adobe Illustrator** and choose **Uninstall**.
4. A popup will appear asking if you would like to Keep or Remove your preferences; choose the option that best suits you.

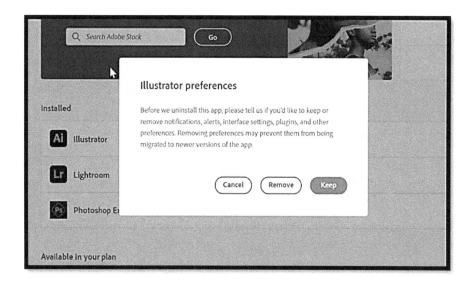

You can begin the reinstallation process when the procedure is finished. Although it is not required, removing the settings and preferences is recommended for a clean reinstallation. Now is the time to wipe your computer clean of any Illustrator files. The uninstaller process could save registry entries and other files that aren't needed, which is a waste of space and doesn't help with uninstalling the program. If the installer procedure mistakenly detects that the software is already on your PC, it will stop the installation and prohibit you from reinstalling the app. Use an uninstaller program to stop this from occurring. You can free up valuable disk space and start over with a clean installation by using these safe tools to scan your whole PC for remaining files and registry entries and securely erase them.

Reinstall Adobe Illustrator

From the same panel in the Creative Cloud Desktop app, you can reinstall the application:
1. Launch the **Creative Cloud Desktop App**.
2. On the **Apps to try** page, choose **Adobe Illustrator**. Press **Install** if Illustrator is part of your Creative Cloud subscription. Choose **Buy** to buy the product, or **Try** to try it out for free.

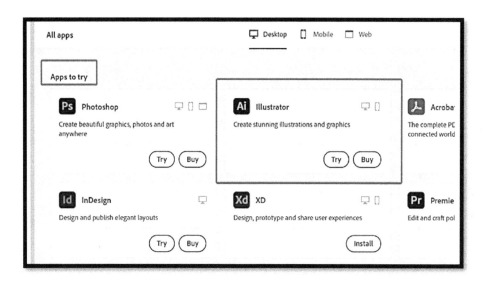

3. Do not attempt to **relaunch the app** until the procedure has finished.
The Adobe Illustrator application should now function properly.
Additionally, you can be assured that you will not encounter any such issues soon by installing the latest version of Adobe Illustrator.
- **Update your GPU device drivers.**
Users who have updated their GPU drivers have reported some issues that were fixed.
1. Launch **Device Manager** by typing Device Manager into the Taskbar.
2. Choose the **Display Adapters** group.

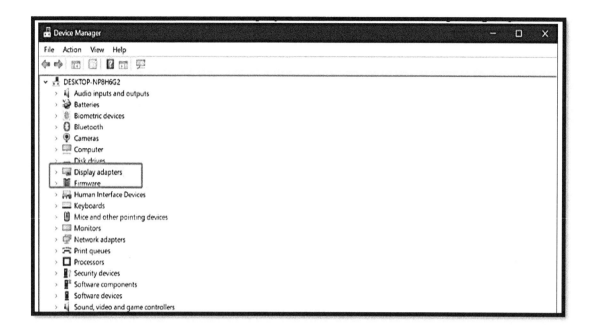

3. Right-click on your GPU device and select **Update driver**.

New driver versions will now be installed automatically by Windows if they become available. After it finishes, you may try launching Illustrator again. Keep in mind that Windows won't necessarily be able to identify updated drivers, even when they're made accessible; in such a situation, you may always search for them manually:

1. Identify your **GPU card manufacturer and version**.
2. Head to the official website of the manufacturer and **download the latest driver version**.
3. Open the file and **follow the installation wizard**.

Because a mismatched driver may cause even more difficulties, such as frequent program failures and BSODs, I suggest you double-check the version of the driver you install. An automatic driver installer, like Outbyte Driver Updater, can scan your computer and tell you which driver version is necessary to install. This is a great help if you aren't sure which driver to use.

- **Try forcing Adobe Illustrator to end.**

Using the Task Manager, you can quickly force Adobe Illustrator to quit if it is unresponsive.

1. To begin, press the keyboard shortcut **CTRL + SHIFT + ESC** to bring up your Task Manager, and then exit any programs that are associated with Adobe.
2. Next, select **Adobe Illustrator**, choose **End Task,** and close **Task Manager**.
3. Please don't be concerned if the software takes a few seconds to close; it should have done so promptly.

The application will be allowed to reconfigure upon selecting this option. If you can, try restarting it to see if it solves the problem. In the event of an application crash, Adobe products will often attempt to preserve your work. Relaunching the program should bring up the Auto-recovery dialog box, which will inquire as to whether you wish to access the data that was autosaved.

Choose "**OK**." Additionally, the **ALT + F4** keyboard shortcut may be more convenient for some of you to achieve the same goals.

- **Turn your computer off and on again.**

If the prior solution did not work, you may want to think about doing a hard reset. You may try again in a few seconds and see if Adobe Illustrator starts responding; there's no risk. On the contrary, if you want to lessen the likelihood of seeing errors like this one, you should turn off your computer once a week.

- **Reset your app preferences.**

If you're experiencing issues with Illustrator not responding or crashing, resetting your options to default should fix it. You should make a backup of your existing settings before you begin.

1. Go to the **Edit** menu, and then choose **Preferences**, and finally **General**.
2. Press **OK** after selecting **Reset Preferences**.
3. Launch Illustrator again.

Tips for Learning Illustrator

- **Practice Regularly**: The best way to learn Illustrator is by applying what you learn through small projects.
- **Follow Challenges**: Participate in design challenges or create your projects to build your skills.
- **Stay Updated**: Keep track of Adobe updates to learn new features that could speed up your workflow.

Conclusion

Wrapping up this guide, remember that getting good at Adobe Illustrator is more than just learning the basics—it's about staying updated with new tools and features and practicing regularly. Keep exploring what the software can do, and don't be afraid to look for extra help through courses, tutorials, or online communities. Illustrator is powerful and lets you create anything from simple drawings to detailed vector graphics. With what you've learned in this guide, you can use the tools, apply useful techniques, and bring your ideas to life with confidence. Keep practicing, trying new things, and growing your skills. This will help you stand out and create amazing work in the world of digital design.

INDEX

B

C

D

E

F

I

M

V

W

X

Y

Z

www.ingramcontent.com/pod-product-compliance
Lightning Source LLC
LaVergne TN
LVHW081330050326
832903LV00024B/1102